WAR ALONG THE NIAGARA

Essays on the War of 1812 and its Legacy

By
Carl Benn, R. Arthur Bowler, John C. Fredriksen,
Donald E. Graves, John D. Morris,
J.C.A. Stagg, Joseph M. Thatcher, Sydney F. Wise

Edited by
R. Arthur Bowler

OLD FORT NIAGARA

OLD FORT NIAGARA ASSOCIATION, INC.
YOUNGSTOWN, NY

ISBN: 0-941967-11-5

This publication is made possible, in part, by support from the Ontario Heritage Foundation, Ontario Ministry of Culture and Communications and the Canadian-American Studies Committee of the State University of New York at Buffalo.

PREFACE

All but one of the essays printed in this volume were originally presented at a conference on the War of 1812 entitled "War Along the Niagara" held in Buffalo, New York in September 1989. The occasion was the 175th anniversary of the last year of the War of 1812, and the papers focused, appropriately, on the center of fighting that year along the Niagara frontier, the peacemaking process and the way the war has been perceived in both Canada and the United States since its end. The essays, which do so much to widen and deepen our understanding of the War of 1812, captured the interest of the conference, and it is with great pleasure that we present them to a wider audience.

The conference and this volume were sponsored jointly by the Buffalo and Erie County Historical Society, the Old Fort Niagara Association, the Toronto Historical Board, and Niagara National Historic Sites, Canadian Parks Service. It was supported by the generous assistance, financial and otherwise, of George H. Musgrove Esq., Canadian Head of Mission and Consul at Buffalo, President Terry White of Brock University (St. Catharines, Ontario), the History Departments of the State University of New York at Buffalo and Brock University, the Niagara Parks Commission (Niagara Falls, Ontario), the Canadian Guild of Antique Arms Collectors (Toronto), Battlefield House (Stoney Creek, Ontario), The Friends of Fort George (Niagara-on-the-Lake, Ontario), and the Military History Chapter of the Buffalo and Erie County Historical Society. The unsung heroes of the conference were the people, too numerous to mention individually, who did everything from stuff envelopes to guide tours of the splendid historic sites on both sides of the Niagara Frontier.

The extensive and skillful work of transcribing the conference papers, inventing the layout and generally preparing things for publication was done by David J. Bertuca of the University Libraries, State University of New York at Buffalo, Harry M. DeBan, chairman of the Old Fort Niagara Association Publications Committee and Brian Leigh Dunnigan, Executive Director of Old Fort Niagara.

Finally, it must be acknowledged that neither the conference nor this volume would have been possible without generous grants from the Ontario Heritage Foundation of the Ontario Ministry of Culture and Communications and from the Canadian-American Studies Committee of the State University of New York at Buffalo.

British contol of Fort Niagara, seen here from the Canadian shore, denied the mouth of the Niagara River to U.S. vessels during the 1814 Niagara campaign. Watercolor drawn in that year by John Henry Slade. *Courtesy, National Archives of Canada, C42570.*

TABLE OF CONTENTS

INTRODUCTION

by
R. Arthur Bowler

The War of 1812 came to an end more than 175 years ago. As the papers in this collection demonstrate, however, we still have much to learn about it. Indeed, it takes only a short while in a good library to come to the conclusion that, compared to most other important events in North American history, our knowledge of the War of 1812 is remarkably thin. There are a number of reasons for this. One is the relative paucity of thorough and extensive research, and that, in turn, is because the war has never drawn the interest of large numbers of serious historians. In Britain the war was and remains a rather unimpressive sideshow of the great clash with Napoleonic France while in the United States it has often been viewed as a pointless war and, because America achieved none of the aims with which she justified its beginning, rather an embarrassment. It is thus difficult to find a study of the war by a Briton and one of the most recent books on it by an American historian is subtitled *A Forgotten Conflict.*[1] Only in Canada, and there primarily in Ontario, has even the memory of the war been kept strong. Even there, however, little serious research was done until Ernest Cruikshank began his work in the late nineteenth century.

A second reason why there is so much still to learn of the War of 1812 is indicated in at least four of the essays in this collection. S.F. Wise, R. Arthur Bowler, Donald Graves, and John Fredriksen all show in their papers how ignorance, propaganda, and patriotic fervor rather than research and disinterested analysis lay at the basis of much of the writing about the war through the nineteenth century and well into the twentieth. It was that situation that led C.P. Stacey to his famous analysis of the historiography of the war. "The War of 1812," he wrote in 1958,

> *... is one of those episodes in history that make everyone happy, because everybody interprets it in his own way.*
>
> *The Americans think of it primarily as a naval war in which the pride of the Mistress of the Seas was humbled by what an imprudent Englishman called "a few fir-built frigates, manned by a handful of bastards and outlaws." Canadians think of it equally pridefully as a war of defence in which their brave fathers, side by side, turned back the massed might of the United States and saved the country from conquest. And the English are the happiest of all, because they don't even know that it happened.*[2]

But, for whatever reasons, it is clear that our knowledge of the War of 1812 in all its aspects, diplomatic, military, social, economic, and political, is far from complete. The essays which follow help to overcome that deficiency by shedding new light on a number of facets of a war which was of immense significance in the development of both Canada and the United States. The war was fought on many fronts. At sea, the tiny American frigate navy embarrassed the Royal Navy by winning a few victories over British ships of the same class before being overwhelmed by sheer size and numbers, and American privateers chased British merchantmen on whatever seas they sailed. On land, battles were fought at New Orleans, the Chesapeake and deep in the American midwest. But the cockpit of the war was the lower Great Lakes. Here - and on one occasion at the northern end of Lake Champlain - occurred all the important land and naval battles of the war, and it is on this area that the papers in this collection primarily focus.

Three of the essays are of general relevance to the whole period of the war. Carl Benn's is important if for no other reason than that it focuses attention on Native American participation in the war and explains how Indians thought battles should be fought. One of the great failures of North American historians has been their unwillingness or inability to bring the native people of the continent into the mainstream of their narratives as real people. Too often Indians are assumed to have ceased to exist once white settlement was established in an area, and when it comes to war, the tendency is to see them as motiveless pawns of white interests who were, at the same time, both cowardly and mindlessly savage in battle. Benn's paper does much to bring into focus a human picture of the Iroquois as members of a distinct society, inheritors of a strong tradition, and important allies of Britain in the War of 1812.

Joseph Thatcher's focus is on the vital but often ignored naval armaments race on Lake Ontario. In 1812 the Great Lakes area was still largely a wilderness, and while road travel was possible in a few places, it was slow and difficult. The lakes themselves were the best highways, and both sides realized very early their importance. For the British, who relied on a supply line stretching back to Quebec and to Britain itself, the ability to use the lakes was vital. As the Battle of Put-in-Bay demonstrated, loss of the command of a lake forced a withdrawal eastward along the supply line. The ability to control the lakes was equally important to the American forces who sought to conquer Upper Canada. Perry's victory led directly to the Battle of the Thames and Harrison's defeat of Proctor, and the American army which crossed the Niagara River in the summer of 1813 moved easily up the Niagara peninsula as long as it had the support of naval forces. The army met a setback at Stoney Creek, but its retreat to Niagara was due more to the withdrawal of its naval support. The United States won control of Lake Erie, but on Lake Ontario there was no decisive battle. Instead, there was an arms race which gave each side command of the lake for short periods but overall resulted in stalemate. It is the story of the American side of this arms race, the building of "a fleet in the wilderness" to which Thatcher introduces the reader.

The third general paper deals with the rather esoteric topic of propaganda. Propaganda is not a technique which we associate with the pre-industrial world, the world without rapid and cheap mass communications. But while the use of the word "propaganda" to describe the deliberate manipulation of information in order to influence people's actions did not evolve until the late nineteenth century, the deed itself is probably as old as man's ability to scheme. Certainly the population of the Canadas, wavering as many were in their loyalty, was a target ripe for propagandists. The Americans had been enormously successful as propagandists during the American Revolution,[3] but in this war it was the British and Canadians who were the most effective in the use of this technique. Indeed, as Bowler points out, they were so successful that some of their concocted versions of events persisted for a century and more.

The last significant American campaign of the War of 1812 took place on the Niagara frontier in the summer of 1814. It involved some of the most vicious and bloody fighting of the war and it is rightly seen as the time when the American army redeemed itself from the ignominious failures of the previous two years. Two of the papers here focus on aspects of the American effort which brought victories at Chippewa and Fort Erie and at least a draw in the desperately fought Battle of Lundy's Lane. The combined effect of the two papers is to shift some of credit for the success of American arms that summer away from General Winfield Scott, where it has traditionally rested and onto General Jacob Brown.

Donald Graves looks with a careful eye at the longstanding belief that the American victories of 1814 were the product of the stern, imaginative and innovative training given the Left Division by General Scott at his camp in Buffalo in the spring of the year. It was the credit given him for this campaign which launched Scott on a long and successful career which stretched through the Mexican War to the Civil War. Graves, by dint of prodigious research in a host of little-used sources, is able to cast doubt on many of the claims to the credit for creating a battle-ready army made by Scott himself and by his hagiographers. While prepared to give Scott his due, Graves concludes that "The Left Division was not so much the creation of one man as it was the culmination of two years of schooling in the hard lessons of war." John Morris looks at the campaign from the point of view of General Brown, the commander of the Left Division. Brown was one of a large group of generals newly commissioned in the spring of 1814 to bring new life to the war effort, and Morris finds the appointment to have been a good one despite Brown's lack of military experience. His disciplined aggressiveness and his ability to control a group of high-spirited and sometimes factious subordinates made him, in Morris's view, "the best field commander in the army." That the campaign achieved nothing strategically, Morris blames not on Brown but on the "poor strategic thinking and lack of communication" which had created American command problems throughout the war.

J.C.A. Stagg takes on quite a different aspect of the war, the process of bringing it to an end. Most accounts of the War of 1812 spend little time on this aspect of it: they assume that the peace came logically when the end of the Napoleonic wars brought a halt to the British practices which led the United States to originate hostilities and when both sides realized that a decisive military victory was impossible. Stagg reveals a far more complex process. Any good history of the war recounts the three occasions on which peace negotiations were proposed, but here we are introduced to the complex and always changing political and military situations on both sides which made coming to agreement on the terms of peace a slow and difficult process. He finds no event which suddenly made peace possible but rather discerns "a process of attrition to expose the hard core of mutual self interest."

The last two papers in the collection deal with an aspect of the legacy of the war, its image as presented to the public by artists and writers. John Fredriksen's paper is a close examination of artists' renditions of moments in the battles of the 1814 Niagara campaign. What the examination reveals is the enormous extent of artistic license or artistic ignorance, as the case may be, for most of the illustrations he presents reveal not merely the minor errors of detail which might be expected but gross errors in the uniforms of combatants and the sequence of events in battles.

Few such errors were, of course, recognized by the public nor, probably, were they important, for the purpose of the prints and paintings was not to depict moments in reality but to recognize heroism and inspire patriotism. Most of the illustrations included here are by American artists, and Fredriksen points out that few could resist equipping columns of American soldiers with proudly flying national flags even though such flags were never carried into battle. Only in one painting, and that by a twentieth century Canadian artist, is battle depicted as the scene of terror and confusion which it usually is.

In his paper, S.F. Wise examines the visions of the war presented to Americans and Canadians in popular histories written in the century after its end, and what he tells us about them is very important. Such histories, he finds, are almost never full or accurate accounts of events. The strong tendency of both American and Canadian popular historians was to focus on victories and create heroes while at the same time exposing all the various shortcomings of the enemy, moral, philosophical and political. "Almost all this literature," he writes, "is patriotic in character; that is it treats history as a means of glorifying the national past, and seeks to maintain or enhance pride of country." But these histories are not to be discarded because of these failings. Indeed, they make them uniquely useful because the patriotic purpose of the authors led them to interpret the war and give it meaning in terms of "national character, national traditions and national institutions." These histories, then, are are an important insight into how these societies wanted to see themselves.

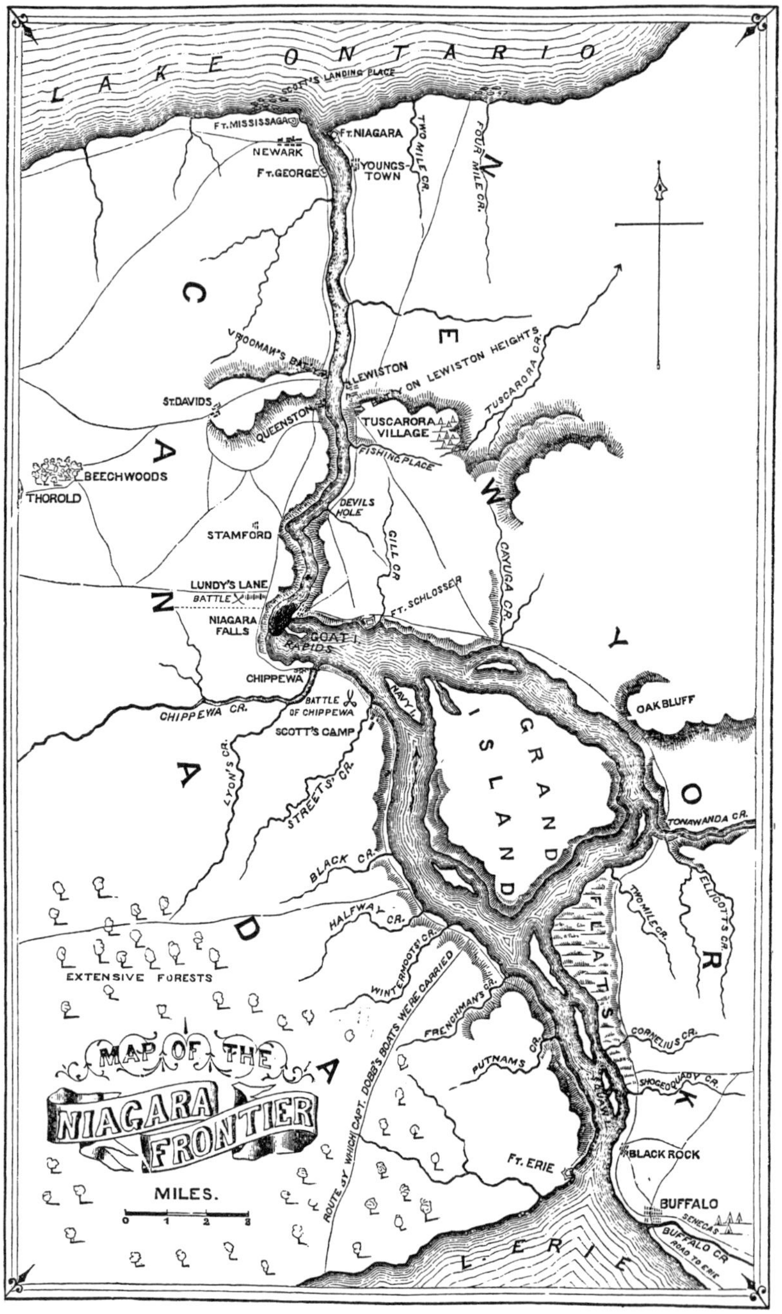

Benson J. Lossing's map showing the primary features of the Niagara Frontier at the time of the War of 1812.

Notes

[1] Donald R. Hickey, *The War of 1812: A Forgotten Conflict* (Urbana, IL, 1989).

[2] C.P. Stacey, "The War of 1812 in Canadian History", in Morris Zaslow (ed.), *The Defended Border: Upper Canada and the War of 1812* (Toronto, 1964), p. 331. The essay was originally published in *Ontario History* in 1958.

[3] Phillip Davidson, *Propaganda and the American Revolution* (Chapel Hill, 1941).

THE ICONOGRAPHY OF THE 1814 NIAGARA CAMPAIGN
The Visual Nuances of Nationalism

by
John C. Fredriksen

Of all the military actions of the War of 1812, none made as indelible an impression upon nascent United States military policy as the 1814 Niagara campaign. The victories of Chippewa, Lundy's Lane and Fort Erie, coming as they did after months of defeat and humiliation, did much to improve morale in both civilian and military sectors. "Few incidents," wrote Russell Weigley, "contributed as much to the prestige of the regular army and its acceptance as the necessary axis of national defense."[1] The principle formation of this endeavor, the Left Division, was a small force consisting of two brigades of regular infantry and a brigade of specially trained volunteers. But under the inspired leadership of generals like Jacob Brown and Winfield Scott, the Left Division's tactical proclivities were famous, and became the locus of reform in the post-war period. "So famous did Brown's little army become," observed Henry Adams, "that details of its force and organization retain an interest equalled only by that which was attached to the frigates and sloops of war."[2] And because the Left Division was the most famous corporate entity to emerge from the War of 1812, its achievements were commemorated in the public mind by a long series of plates and prints, many by America's most distinguished artists. Because art is perhaps the least known or appreciated facet of the Left Division's legacy, this article will examine all known depictions of the 1814 Niagara campaign. My purpose here is to evaluate them as art, comment upon their historical veracity and contextualize the majority of them as stirring examples of nineteenth-century American nationalism. In said manner I hope to lend credence to Peter Paret's cogent assertion that pictures with contemporary themes become potent historical sources whether or not the artist intended them as such.[3]

In order to understand the impact of art on the course of American nationalism, it becomes necessary to assess the cultural and intellectual factors accompanying its rise. During the first half of the the nineteenth century, Americans expended a great deal of energy in writing their history. The young nation was bent on establishing its identity and the surge of nationalism engendered by the War of 1812 made studying American history a vital concern.[4] As a discipline, history was experiencing an intellectual transformation which made it conducive towards nationalistic ends. Prior to 1820, most American schools taught little beyond Greek and Roman history. Where American history did exist, it was invariably regional or antiquarian in nature. But as the post-revolutionary generation matured, new intellectuals became intrigued by the opportunity to test fresh ideas in the building of a new society. They embraced education as a natural means of sustaining and affirming the benefits bequeathed them by the Revolution.[5] Once they believed that the key to understanding the nation's future lay squarely in appreciation of its past, history was elevated to the forefront of cultural indoctrination.

This new awareness of history also represents a profound ideological readjustment since the 1790s. Previously, the founding fathers believed they were conducting a perilous political experiment whose ultimate vindication rested with the passage of time. After 1815 intellectuals felt secure in the knowledge that these national principles, by dint of recent military experience, had attained full validity.[6] They exuded positive affirmation of nationhood and called upon history to glorify and inculcate these same principles in the average citizen. Since awareness of one's national past served as a patriotic cement binding the nation together, Americans should study their history "to awaken their mutual sympathies and promote their general union and general welfare."[7]

A major beneficiary of this nationalistic impulse was military history. Compared to present day curricula, warfare was commonly taught and seems rather over-represented. Textbooks of all grades were inundated with information on armies, leaders, battles, and national consequences. But this emphasis was a manifestation of the expectations held for military history. It was viewed as entertaining and dramatic, capable of instilling virtue and emulation of noble deeds, and would also enhance student minds and memory.[8] As the century progressed, critics railed that American history was far too preoccupied with military affairs, and wished to supplant this didactic approach with greater synthesis. But martial themes were as endearing as they were popular.[9] Most Americans were enraptured by their patriotic past and preferred an intimate biographical approach to history, the drama of military clashes, and the excitement missing in social and intellectual history.[10] Given this receptive cultural mind set, it is easy to appreciate how events like the 1814 Niagara campaign were studied and glorified far out of proportion to their actual achievement.

Abetting this movement for institutional propagation was a concurrent rise of the American publishing industry. During the first quarter of the nineteenth century, the American book trade consisted of little more than importing the latest English works. As late as 1860 almost half of the titles available on the publishing lists were penned by foreign authors. But by 1830, the United States had begun to emerge from under the cultural shadow of England. Nativist currents, combined with the Anglophobic cliches of Jacksonian democracy, spurred development of national literature and publishing.[11] Advances in bookmaking technology, development of sophisticated transportation networks, and a drive for universal literacy all happily coincided to give the nascent publishing trade an impetus it never before possessed.[12] And because this period was punctuated by intense nationalism, books on America's brief but colorful past were assured best sellers from any publisher's list.[13] The book trade was thus eager and well situated to help disseminate these popular mores.

An important component of publishing is illustration. With an increase in the country's economic well being and the rise of a prosperous middle class came demand for books to fulfill both educational and recreational needs. Publishers competing for this mass market discerned that by illustrating titles they could greatly enhance product appeal among discriminating consumers. Subsequently, many types of books, including poetry and novels, were embellished by artists who were more celebrated than the authors.[14] As artistic quality became a marketable commodity, the attitude toward books as material objects also evolved. Once artists were encouraged to do more and better artwork, middle class Americans began to view books in a way previously reserved for the elite; as something to treasure, like works of art.[15]

Like history, American illustration also became caught up in the mania for national definition. For the first few decades of the century, American art was little more than copies of contemporary British forms. This imitative approach was then standard procedure in artistic circles, and it was no disgrace to be regarded as an "American Cruikshank." Eventually American artists began to impart a native flavor to their work which made it especially suitable for domestic literature and themes.[16] This deliberate effort to promulgate an "American" school of art also had its origins in the need visually to distill national principles, and reinforce a common sense of identity. It was hoped historic art, drawn by native talent, could help forestall the "want of national feeling among Americans."[17]

With respect to artistic technique, the early to mid-nineteenth century witnessed considerable innovation. These occurred in response to publishers' needs to keep pace with mass production and quality artwork. Most American books were illustrated through wood engraving which was practical, versatile, and relatively inexpensive. A more involved process was lithography whereby a sheet of porous limestone was etched with a detailed drawing, bathed in numerous wax and acid washes and pressed to high quality paper. But the most admired format was the various forms of metallic engraving, mostly on copper plate, which allowed new heights of creative achievement. In contrast to wood and stone processes, copper engraving allowed minute, almost microscopic details in any given scene. Depending on the skill of the engraver, the finished plate was often as highly prized as the artwork it reproduced.[18] But the introduction of steel plates initiated further artistic and economic advantages. Unlike copper plates, which which were fragile and wore out quickly, steel was virtually indestructible and could be reproduced thousands of times without deterioration. This combination of greater detail in artistic renditions and growing emphasis on mass production ushered in a new age of economic prosperity for art and publishing alike.

Despite the growing popularity of illustrated books, there existed a long-standing dichotomy regarding the pay and prestige of creative talent. Throughout the heyday of American illustration, the engravers dominated the field and received up to ten times the money the artists did.[19] But with the introduction of refined engraving techniques, publishing began to attract a higher grade of professional artist and they eventually supplanted engravers in both pay and reputation.[20] Once mass production became a practical necessity, artists were well positioned to make prints for general sale, book illustration or for straight fees and royalties.[21] By mid-century, several individuals were publicly esteemed for their talent and accrued considerable wealth as a result.

Art's relationship to this renewed emphasis on historical instruction was a direct one. The task of the illustrator is to create images which enhance stories and recreate events in ways intelligible to mass audiences.[22] The breadth of subject matter covered by nineteenth century artists is immense and, collectively, represents a valuable pictorial record of the country's social and cultural development.[23] American artists have dealt with historical subjects since the founding of the republic, and even earlier. Even outside the context of book publishing, history has been one of the most important popular themes of

American artists. Many gifted individuals built their reputations on a deep knowledge of, and abiding interest in, past events.[24] But historical art does not exist in a vacuum; rather, it is a reflection of the social milieu and popular attitudes which help define it. Works of art commissioned by publishers from around 1830 to 1860 shed valuable light on the political and national values that gave Americans identity as a nation.[25] Illustrated history books were a tool of considerable social utility, and a useful conduit for transmitting desirable social values.

The popularity of military history in American education is paralleled by similar demands for military art. Engravings of the 1814 Niagara campaign were a popular motif throughout this period, but constitute a miniscule part of subjects rendered. In fact, battle portrayals have one of the oldest, most continuous descents in American artistic tradition. Like genre, landscape painting and portraiture, the battle scene is a topic which has attracted generations of talented artists.[26] And, like military history, battle scenes incorporate values which societies found most useful. Boldness and heroism were traits that Americans considered desirable, and believed they possessed in abundance by virtue of a free society.[27] The depiction of heroic, selfless sacrifice and victory in battle are reoccurring themes throughout this period.

Another purpose of military art is to reconstruct vicariously an armed engagement for the erudition - and enjoyment - of posterity. Unfortunately, most interpretations of military events are notoriously subject to "artistic license." Even the casual observer should realize that the farther in time a picture is removed from an actual event, the greater cause here is to question its historical veracity. In art as in war, truth is usually the first casualty. Unfortunately, there exists a long tradition of visual inaccuracy associated with American battle art of the nineteenth century. Part of this may stem from the unquestioning belief in one's country, but it could reach ridiculous extremes. Upon onset of war with Mexico in 1846, publishers rushed numerous, inaccurate accounts into print to satiate public demand. In their haste to produce, illustrators usually failed to ascertain exactly what type of military attire American soldiers wore at that time and the result is a bizarre array of European-style outfits. More ambitious publishers sent to France and purchased wood cuts previously used to illustrate histories of the Napoleonic wars. Thus, many American book illustrations which purportedly depict scenes in the War of 1812 and Mexican war display gaudily-attired French and Continental troops. The individual artwork could be stirring, and the American public avidly devoured these books, but from the standpoint of military reality they had been egregiously duped.[28]

In conducting this survey of Niagara campaign

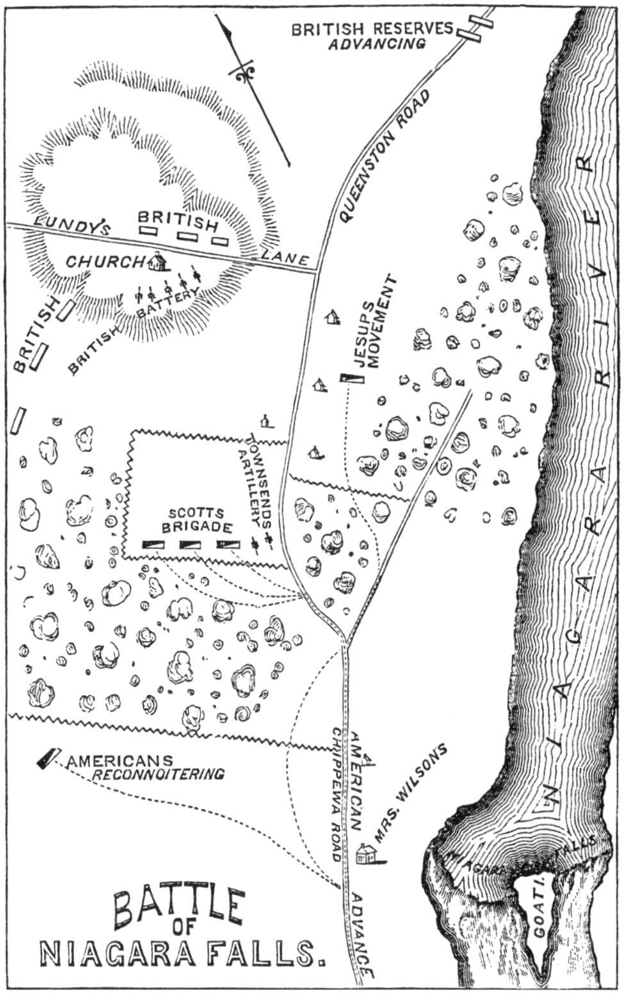

The violent encounter at Lundy's Lane was fought on July 25, 1814. It is also known in various Canadian and American sources as the Battle of "Niagara", "Niagara Falls" or "Bridgewater". Lundy's Lane was a popular subject in the iconography of the 1814 campaign. This simplified plan, from Benson J. Lossing's 1868 *Pictorial Field Book of the War of 1812*, shows the advance of Gen. Jacob Brown's American army. Lossing's sketches provide many of the illustrations which follow in *War Along the Niagara*.

artwork, I must stress from the outset that this is American history viewed through the prism of romantic nationalism. Whatever artistic merits an individual plate or print may possess, most events depicted frequently bear little relationship to actual occurrences. I shall comment upon these transgressions wherever they manifest, and I have thrown in some Canadian and modern renditions for comparative purposes. It is hoped readers will acquire a sense for the heady nationalism evinced in these pictures, and insight into the nexus between historical fact and national mythology. America had become a nation before she had a sense of history, and there was a genuine emotional need for national definition and a sense of continuity. Printed pictures, the triumphs they portrayed and the legends they perpetuated, helped to satisfy that need.[29]

FIGURE 1. A distinguishing characteristic of the 1814 Niagara campaign was the high level of training and discipline exhibited by American soldiers. This was the work of Winfield Scott, the dashing twenty-eight year old brigadier general who instituted the army's first camp of uniform military instruction. As a result, for the first time in the War of 1812, the hitherto untrained American soldiers could stand up to their professional British adversaries in the field.

In this relatively crude woodcut by David Hunter Strother,[30] Scott is depicted personally instructing a young subaltern and his squad. Similar formations are also being drilled in the immediate background. This print also show's Scott's great height to advantage for, at six feet six inches, the young general literally towered over his contemporaries. The soldiers' uniforms are incorrect for this period and date to the period prior to the Mexican war. The officer directly to Scott's right is also of interest; beyond striking a proper Napoleonic pose, he is shown attired in the curious civilian style top-hat, a non-regulation undress covering. This was apparently a popular form of headgear, judging from its numerous depictions in War of 1812 artwork.

From *Illustrated Life of Winfield Scott* (1847).

FIGURE 2. After months of careful preparation, the Left Division was deemed ready for combat operations. On the morning of July 3, 1814, Scott's brigade was ferried across the Niagara river in boats. They formed on the Canadian shore, surrounded weakly garrisoned Fort Erie, and readily induced its surrender. Shortly after, Scott was joined by the remaining two brigades of the Left Division and the American invasion commenced in earnest.

This woodcut by Strother highlights activity on the American shore prior to embarkation. Here a company of soldiers and, to the left, an artillery caisson, are boarding vessels under the watchful eye of Scott and his aide. The mode of transportation is not clearly revealed, but judging from the two masts, it is probably a large, flat-bottomed scow. The striped national flags carried by the soldiers on the extreme right are incorrect; these were never unfurled and shown in battle. Strother's composition of this print is clever and deliberative; Scott is framed between the masts to his right and the Canadian shore to his left, which places him directly at center stage.

From *Illustrated Life of Winfield Scott* (1847).

FIGURE 3. Fort Erie secured, the Left Division pushed north along the Niagara river with Scott's brigade in the van. By the night of July 4 they had advanced as far as Chippewa creek, about half-way up the Niagara Peninsula. The Americans encamped below the creek unaware that a British force commanded by General Phineas Riall was marching upon them from the north. The following afternoon, July 5, Scott's brigade collided with Riall's force on Chippewa plain and after a stiff fight drove them from the field. This was the first victory gained over British forces in the open, and a great source of national pride and celebration.

This Strother woodcut recounts a celebrated incident during the battle of Chippewa. As the British and American lines drew closed and fired muskets, the battlefield became obscured with dense clouds of smoke. Scott, eager to make every shot count, dashed over to the battery commanded by Captain Nathan Towson and helped the gunners adjust their aim. The ensuing salvo staggered the British line, halted them, and enabled the Americans to turn both flanks. Scott is depicted in the act of conveying instructions to the hatless Towson, whose battery had suffered severely from counter-battery fire. The print accurately shows the billowing smoke produced by black-powder ammunition, for the rear-most gunners are almost completely obscured.

From *Illustrated Life of General Scott* (1847).

FIGURE 4. Having assisted Towson's battery, Scott galloped back to his line. There he observed the enemy faltering, and ordered both wings forward to envelop them. The British were unable to withstand such murderous cross fire and fell back in semi-disorder to the safety of Chippewa Creek. The Americans pursued vigorously, but were unable to cut them off. Nonetheless, this victory, brought about by Scott's rigorous training and leadership, underscored the growing tactical maturity of the fledgling U.S. Army.

This exciting Strother woodcut shows the climax of Chippewa, with the Americans charging and breaking the British line, In fact, no such event occurred for the British retreated long before conclusions could be tried with cold steel. Other common mistakes abound. The Americans are consistently shown with their national flag to the fore; a patriotic motif, perhaps, but incorrect as only regimental flags were allowed. The uniforms are also wrong, with the British sporting Victorian age shakos and shoulder wings. The American officer in the left foreground is a curiosity, indeed. Despite this hot July day, he is shown charging in a heavy winter long-coat, and wears the civilian-style top hat more frequently encountered in militia formations. Despite these flaws, Strother's work is vivacious, and captures the excitement of close combat. He is also correct in showing the great quantities of smoke produced by musket fire.

From *Illustrated Life of General Scott* (1847).

FIGURE 5. This steel engraving of a painting by Alonzo Chappel[31] displays the historical sweep and detail for which he was justly celebrated. Here General Scott is ordering Major John McNeil's 11th Infantry to advance upon the British line. In contrast to Strother's print, the opposing forces are displayed some distance apart and not engaged in hand-to-hand combat. Chappel's penchant for realistic touches are quite apparent. The American advance is disorderly, with some soldiers cheering, some marching, others running, but all animated by the martial presence of General Scott. The smoky background, lively poses and detailed engraving make this one of the best renditions of Chippewa from artistic standpoints.

Despite Chappel's well-deserved reputation for accuracy some relatively common mistakes are present in the print. There is the usual misplaced national flag, and the uniforms, while an improvement over earlier prints, still date from the 1830s. The British uniforms are even more sadly mistaken. During the battle Scott's principle adversary was the British 1st Regiment of Foot, the redoubtable Royal Scots. But this was a line unit and is incorrectly portrayed in Highland garb. Another curiosity is the slain figure, center left. Being attired in heavy boots, armored cuirass and tall bearskin hat, he is apparently meant to represent a trooper of the Life Guards, another famous British unit which acted as the King's body guard. Not only was this unit absent from Chippewa, but it never saw service in North America throughout its two hundred-year history.

From Henry B. Dawson, *Battles of the United States* (1858). *Courtesy, the Library of Congress.*

FIGURE 6. This is a modern composition by H. Charles McBarron, long considered the dean of American military art. His treatment of Chippewa is subdued, business-like, and devoid of the romantic notions of warfare so endearing to nineteenth century readers. Here a portion of Scott's line, a detachment of the 22nd Infantry, advances with shouldered arms across Chippewa plain while receiving the fire of the enemy. The unit proudly flies its yellow regimental color and blue national standard, and not the "stars and stripes" so prominent in earlier drawings. As Scott parades himself theatrically before his troops, the 22nd receives enemy fire but continues to advance with grim determination.

This is perhaps the only painting of Chippewa to show the correct War of 1812 uniform. By 1814 the Americans were faced with a shortage of blue dye for their tunics, and Scott was forced to clad his brigade in simple, militia-gray outfits. During the battle British General Riall initially thought he was in fact facing Buffalo militia, but upon seeing Scott's men perform complex evolutions under fire, he exclaimed, "Those are regulars, by God!" In recognition of Scott's victory, the west Point cadets continue to wear the same simple grey tunics first adopted out of necessity in 1814.

Courtesy, U.S. Army Center of Military History.

FIGURE 7. After Chippewa, the Left Division resumed its advance northward. It reached the ramparts of British-controlled Fort George, near Lake Ontario, and lingered nearly three weeks awaiting the arrival of the American fleet. When naval support failed to materialize as promised, the disillusioned Americans fell back to Chippewa Creek, followed closely by the British. Once word was received of a British attack on the American side of the Niagara river, Scott's Brigade was dispatched north again as a diversionary tactic. However, the Americans advanced only as far as Lundy's Lane, beside Niagara Falls, where they encountered a British force commanded by General Gordon Drummond. Both sides brought up reinforcements and suffered heavy losses in the ensuing struggle. The battle of Lundy's Lane was tactically a draw, but the outnumbered and exhausted Americans prudently withdrew to Fort Erie.

This copper engraving by William Strickland[32] depicts the most famous incident of Lundy's Lane; the storming of the British cannon by Colonel James Miller. Published in 1815, it was the first popular reconstruction of that battle, and in terms of topography the most accurate. Strickland, a noted landscape artist, correctly shows the battle field as a low-lying hill crowned by a white church and with a rail fence on its southern slope. Because the battle was largely fought at night, the artist chose shadowy outlines rather than detailed figures. As the conflict is joined, startled gunners fight the Americans while staff officers gallop off to bring up support troops. Strickland does commit small errors by rendering Miller's men in such a precise, straight line, and by placing the national flag in their hands.

From the *Port Folio Magazine,* 1815. *Courtesy, the Library of Congress.*

FIGURE 8. This Strother woodcut caters to a long-standing myth regarding Lundy's Lane; that General Scott personally guided Colonel Miller to the British battery. No such event transpired; during Miller's attack, Scott was in the rear assembling the battered remnants of his troops. This falsehood was probably perpetrated by Scott's political allies to enhance his presidential aspirations. Circulated thirty years after the battle, nobody seems to have seriously challenged this assertion, although in his memoirs, Scott never claims to have performed the deed. The entire issue is disreputable to Scott and a disservice to the brave Miller and his men.

Strother's treatment of this otherwise dramatic event is surprisingly conventional. The American approach Lundy's Lane in close column, led by Scott and Miller, while British cannon blaze away from the heights. In fact, Miller found the battery himself, and stealthily crept to within a few yards of it before charging. Consistent with other prints, Strother places an officer with a civilian-style top hat in the action. Considering the latent abilities of this artist, this is not one of his better prints.

From *Illustrated Life of General Scott* (1847).

FIGURE 9. This is a steel engraving of a painting by Chappel. A visually compelling work, it again demonstrates this artist's grasp of drama and detail. However, as history, it suffers from time compression and simultaneously depicts several unrelated events. The officer in the center is General Jacob Brown, who was wounded and is being assisted by his aides. The mounted figure on the extreme left is General Scott, shown recoiling from a shoulder wound. Both incidents occurred some time after Miller's capture of the battery, which forms the backdrop of the picture. Chappel also makes the mistake of depicting the British troops as Highlanders when no such unit was present in the battle. But in a purely visual sense, this is perhaps the most rousing recreation of Lundy's Lane, and one of Chappel's best.

From Henry B. Dawson, *Battles of the United States* (1858). *Courtesy, The Library of Congress.*

FIGURE 10. Yet another version of Miller's charge, this time by the popular illustrator Felix O.C. Darley.[33] Like Chappel, Darley was an expert in combining action with dramatic composition. His is an exciting print, and successfully conveys the intensity of close combat, but, from the standpoint of uniforms, it is patently absurd. The central figure, Colonel Miller, is attired in what can only be described as the blue and buff coat of a Revolutionary war general. Darley's source of uniform information for the American soldiers is not known, but it is a greater departure from reality than either Strother or Chappel. Certainly, no such costume was ever worn by the U.S. Army. Furthermore, the figure on the extreme left is apparently a buckskin-clad Kentucky rifleman, none of whom ever served with the Left Division. Finally, these men are struggling for possession of the British cannon with Revolutionary war vintage British grenadiers, resplendent in their tall bearskin hats. But despite these transgressions, the print is well-drawn, highly dramatic, and sustains Darley's reputation as the leading book illustrator if his day.

From Robert Tomes, *Battles of the United States on Land and Sea* (1878). *Courtesy, The Library of Congress.*

FIGURE 11. With the British artillery park secure, the Americans took up position along the crest on Lundy's Lane. The British retreated briefly, then launched a series of bitter counterattacks to regain the guns. It was during such an attack that General Scott was hit in the shoulder and disabled. This wound precluded his further participation in the War of 1812 but he recovered, commanded the armies which conquered Mexico in 1848, and remained on active duty until the advent of the Civil War in 1861. Vain, pompous and brilliant, it is little wonder Scott was the object of so many biographies in the nineteenth century.

This Strother woodcut gives sympathetic treatment to the badly wounded Scott. He is shown surrounded by a cadre of concerned officers and friends, but the close proximity of the enemy, as indicated by the firing soldiers on the right, certainly prohibited such sentimental gestures. In fact, Scott was unceremoniously trundled off to the rear, one of 853 casualties the Left Division suffered that day.

From *Illustrated Life of General Scott* (1847).

FIGURE 12. This drawing of Lundy's Lane, probably engraved on copper, is by an anonymous British artist. It is unique in correctly showing British infantry in their proper Napoleonic outfit. However, the artist apparently had little or no information regarding American uniforms; those depicted seem to be a cross between the Revolutionary War and Civil War Confederates. Like their American counterparts, British audiences liked their war steeped in romanticism. This is reflected in the picture; the contestants' ferocious determination, their close proximity, and the use of leveled bayonets. But it has never been determined if either army resorted to cold steel. This is a common misconception. Another problem is that the British, not the Americans, did most of the attacking after dark; here the reverse is shown. But this is still a well-composed, vivacious print, one which imparts to the viewer a sense of the confusion of night combat. It also demonstrates that, from point of technique, British artistic and publishing technology was quite comparable to American.

From *Battles of the Nineteenth Century* (1897).

FIGURE 13. This early twentieth century version of Lundy's Lane is by the noted Canadian artist Charles W. Jefferys.[34] It shows a ragged line of British infantry defending a cannon, while the silhouettes of American soldiers loom menacingly in the distance. Though impressionistic, Jefferys' treatment exudes atmospheric realism missing in others. One or two stalwart individuals are prominently displayed, but fear, confusion and apprehension is apparent on many other faces. The men are shown loading, firing - and even cringing - as one would expect during battle. A major error is that after nightfall the British did most of the attacking. By placing a cannon in the center of the line the artist might be indicating that this is Colonel Miller's charge, but if so, the supporting troops are much too close to the battery and would interfere with its operation. But Jefferys has achieved a splendid print, evocative in its moodiness, and one that captures the range of human emotions soldiers on both sides must have evinced that terrible July night.

Courtesy, The Corporation of the City of Toronto.

FIGURE 14. The Americans fell back in good order from Lundy's Lane and entrenched themselves in and around Fort Erie, their original landing site. After two weeks General Drummond, having been greatly reinforced, settled his forces around the fort in preparation for a formal siege. The American position, however, was well defended, and Drummond judged it prudent to first eliminate three enemy schooners in the adjacent Niagara river which enfiladed his position. On the night of August 12, 1814, a hand-picked British naval force did exactly that. They managed to capture the sleeping crews of both the *Ohio* and the *Somers* while the third vessel, the *Porcupine* escaped into Lake Erie. The threat to his flank removed, Drummond escalated plans for a direct assault on Fort Erie.

This early twentieth century watercolor by Welsh artist Irwin J. Bevan shows the British night attack in its initial phases. The lead vessel being stormed is *Somers,* although *Ohio* succumbed shortly after. The noise of the fight apparently alerted the crew of the *Porcupine,* for she cut her cables and drifted to safety.

Courtesy, The Mariner's Museum, Newport News, Virginia.

FIGURE 15. This is a twentieth century watercolor by noted Canadian writer Henry Snider and it portrays events immediately following the battle. The British, in boats, are towing the captured *Somers* and *Ohio* down-river while *Porcupine,* using long sweeps, is rowing herself out of harm's way. Note how the British naval ensigns are hoisted over the American flags in recognition of their surrender.

Courtesy, the Metropolitan Toronto Reference Library.

FIGURE 16. On the night of August 13, General Drummond launched a three-pronged attack on Fort Erie. Unfortunately, the Americans were prepared for such a move and beat off two assault columns with heavy slaughter. But the third party, led by Colonel William Drummond, the general's nephew, stormed and captured the bastion manned by Captain Alexander Williams. Both men died in the ensuing battle, but just as the British seemed on the verge of success, the ammunition stored in the bastion exploded with great violence, killing most of the attackers. The British recoiled in confusion and returned to their camp, having sustained one thousand casualties to an American loss of eighty-four.

This painting by Philadelphia artist E.C. Watmough was subsequently engraved for the *United States Military Magazine* in 1841. It depicts the British in the act of capturing Williams' battery amidst heavy smoke and fire. At center stage are the battle's two martyrs; Captain Williams is shown bayonetting an enemy, while Colonel Drummond waves his hat, urging the troops on. This is a colorful, exciting scene, but the headgear of the British troops, shown here as a cylindrical shako, is entirely fabricated. An interesting touch, though, are the numerous casualties at the foot of the bastion, lying with numb indifference to the chaos around them.

Courtesy, Chicago Historical Society.

FIGURE 17. Though heavily defeated, the British refused to relinquish the siege of Fort Erie. General Drummond ordered construction of a fourth heavy battery that, once completed, would enfilade the American camp. The American situation, though tenuous, was greatly improved by the arrival of General Brown, who had been recovering from wounds received at Lundy's Lane. Brown determined to destroy the new battery before it was completed, and on September 17 he led a sortie which surprised the British in their trenches. British reinforcements eventually drove the Americans back to Fort Erie, but not before they inflicted substantial damage on three out of four siege batteries. Drummond had apparently had enough and two days after the sortie withdrew his battered army behind Chippewa creek to await further developments. Thus ended the 1814 Niagara campaign. Though essentially a stalemate, the Americans could, and did, look back upon the bloody work of the summer with much satisfaction.

This print, entitled "Defending the Blockhouse," is something of a mystery. It was drawn and engraved by Philadelphia artists Cephas G. Childs and Edward W. Clay around 1820, but little else is known. It might represent one of the British blockhouses stormed during the sortie and circumstantial evidence points that way. The central figures appear to be British, but details of their uniforms are unmistakably American. The standing figure is clad, however, in a red coat with blue cuffs and might well represent a soldier of the Royal Scots, who were present in the battle. On the extreme right what appear to be muskets are poking out of windows and this coincides with one aspect of the battle. But despite these coincidental features, the real intention of this drawing has never been determined.

Courtesy, Royal Ontario Museum.

NOTES

[1] Henry Adams, *History of the United States* (9 vols.; New York: 1889-91), VIII, p. 34.

[2] Russell Weigley, *History of the United States Army* (New York, 1967), p. 131.

[3] Peter Paret, *Art as History: Episodes in the Culture and Politics of Nineteenth Century Germany* (Princeton, 1988), p. 5. He continues: "Works of art and literature, whether they address the past or not, reflect facts of the times in which they originate. Their references to the present may be central or marginal, deliberate or unconscious and indirect. In time, these works are transformed into historical sources. If they are not merely reflective, but influence people's thought and behavior, they become documents and historical force in one."

[4] Russell B. Nye, *Society and Culture in America, 1830-1866* (New York, 1974), p. 115.

[5] David Van Tassel, *Recording America's Past* (Chicago, 1960), p. 88.

[6] Rush Welter, *The Mind of America, 1820-1860* (New York, 1975), p. 23.

[7] Nye, p. 101.

[8] George H. Calcott, *History of the United States, 1800-1860* (Baltimore, 1970), p. 103.

[9] Van Tassel, p. 94.

[10] Calcott, p. 107.

[11] John W. Trebbel, *A History of Book Publishing* (4 vols.; New York, 1972), I, p. 209.

[12] *Ibid.,* p. 209.

[13] Bud L. Gambee, "American Book and Magazine Illustration of the Latter Nineteenth Century", in Frances J. Brewer (ed.), *Book Illustration* (Berlin, 1963), p. 48.

[14] *Ibid.,* p. 45.

[15] Tebbel, p. 234.

[16] Gambee, p. 49.

[17] Lillian B. Miller, "Painting, Sculpture and the National Character", *Journal of American History,* 56 (1966-67), 699.

[18] Gambee, p. 46. For detailed discussion of various artistic techniques, consult John D. Moore (ed.), *Prints in and of America Before 1850* (Charlottesville, VA, 1970) and Gillette G. Griffin, "The Development of Woodcut Printing in America", *Princeton University Library Chronicle,* 20 (1958), 7-17.

[19] Gambee, p. 46.

[20] Sinclair Hamilton, *Early American Book Illustrations* (2 vols.; Princeton, 1968), I, xxxv.

[21] Nye, p. 187.

[22] James J. Best, *Popular Illustration* (Westport, CT, 1984), p. 10.

[23] Gambee, p. 45.

[24] Henry C. Pitz, *200 Years of American Illustration* (New York, 1977), p. 66.

[25] Miller, 704.

[26] Lincoln Kerstein, "American Battle Art, 1588-1944", *Magazine of Art,* 37 (1944), 184. Another brief overview of this much-neglected field is Frank Weiterkampf, "American Military Prints", *Print Connoisseur,* 2 (1922), 284-303.

[27] Miller, 704.

[28] Alexander C. Craighead, "Military Art in America, 1750-1914", *Military Collector & Historian,* 15 (1963), 272. See also Winfred P. Truesdell, "The Mexican War and its Prints", *Print Connoisseur,* 10 (1930), 329-42 and 11 (1931), 55-115 and Ronnie C. Tyler, "The Mexican War: A Lithographic Record", *Southwestern Historical Quarterly,* 77 (1973), 1-84.

[29] Judith Goldman, *American Prints: Process and Proofs* (New York, 1981), p. 22.

[30] David Hunter Strother, 1816-1888. Strother was best known as an illustrator for *Harper's Monthly Magazine* wherein he provided artwork of his numerous travels in the Old South. During the Civil War he joined the Union army as a staff topographer, partook in thirty battles and was discharged brevet brigadier general. See Cecil D. Eby, *Porte Crayon: The Life of David Hunter Strother* (Chapel Hill, 1960).

[31] Alonzo Chappel, 1828-1887. Chappel began his artistic career at the age of twelve and, without any formal art instruction, rose to be one of the greatest illustrators in American history. It is unfortunate that a biography has yet to emerge on this significant figure. For some cursory treatments see Charles L. Lewis, "Alonzo Chappel and His Naval Paintings", *United States Naval Institute Proceedings,* 3 (1937), 359-70, 443-50; Paul M. Angle, "History on Canvas", *Chicago History,* 1 (1947), 185-87; Herman H. Diers, "The Strange Case of Alonzo Chappel", *Hobbies,* 49 (1944), 18-20, 28; and Oliver Ramsay, "Alonzo Chappel", *Essay-Proof Journal,* 18 (1961), 49-53, 109-14.

[32] William Strickland, 1789-1854. During the War of 1812, Strickland did many naval engravings for David Porter's *Journal of a Cruise to the Pacific Ocean* (1815) and dabbled only briefly with land engagements. An accomplished landscape artist, he is best remembered as a famous Philadelphia architect who reshaped the face of that city for four decades. See Agnes E. Gilchrist, *William Strickland, Architect and Engineer* (Philadelphia, 1950).

[33] Felix Octavius Carr Darley, 1822-1888. Like his great contemporary Chappel, Darley received no formal art instruction. Yet, at the age of twenty-one, he had established himself as one of the best American illustrators of the century. His work appeared in magazines, books, prints, novels, and poetry collections. See Theodore Bolton, "The Book Illustrations of Felix Octavius Carr Darley", *American Antiquarian Society Proceedings,* 61 (1951), 136-82 and R.H. Stoddard, "Felix O.C. Darley", *National Magazine,* 9 (1856), 193-97.

[34] Charles William Jefferys, 1869-1951. Despite a long association with Canadian historical illustration, Jefferys is best known as the dean of Canadian landscape painting. See his *Picture Gallery of Canadian History* (3 vols.; Toronto, 1942-50) and Robert Stacey, *C.W. Jefferys* (Ottawa, 1985).

Maj. Gen. Jacob Brown as depicted in an engraving published in 1862.

GENERAL JACOB BROWN AND THE PROBLEMS OF COMMAND IN 1814

by
John D. Morris

The War of 1812 has often been seen as a low point in American generalship. Sometimes it appears as a minor war with more than its share of comic opera quality.[1] Some officers and achievements do stand out, in particular, Major General Andrew Jackson's victory at New Orleans and the spectacular ship-to-ship duels on the high seas by the navy's frigates. The performance of Jackson at New Orleans and of the frigates, however, had no impact on the war. The battle at New Orleans was fought after the peace treaty was already signed, and most of the ocean navy was blockaded in port by the middle of 1813 and of little use afterward. The most important military efforts of the belligerents were concentrated along the Canadian border, particularly in the Niagara area.

Prior to 1814, the Americans attacking Canada at various points met more failure in battle than success. William Hull's ignominious surrender at Detroit, Solomon Van Rensselaer's defeat at Queenston Heights, Alexander Smyth's bombastic behavior on the Niagara frontier, and Henry Dearborn's "invasion" two miles into Canada in the Champlain valley only serve to heighten the almost comedic nature of early American efforts in the war.[2]

In 1813 the Americans did a bit better by successfully defending the important Lake Ontario naval base at Sackets Harbor, raiding York, and capturing Fort George. Farther west, the United States did obtain the security of its Michigan-Ohio frontier because of the victories of Oliver Perry on Lake Erie and William Harrison's campaign in the Thames valley of Upper Canada, but those achievements did little to affect the outcome of the war.[3] Late in the year the Americans abandoned Fort George and lost Fort Niagara across the river when its guards were literally caught napping. The American side of the Niagara was ravaged in December in retaliation for the burning of Newark (Niagara-on-the-Lake). In the St. Lawrence valley the year ended with another disastrous attempt to subdue Canada when James Wilkinson and Wade Hampton failed to link forces and descend the river to attack Montreal. Wilkinson was defeated at Chrysler's Farm and Hampton at Chateaugay, both by inferior numbers of British and Canadian troops. The American forces limped into winter quarters, and the two commanders filled the air with recriminations against each other. When General Dearborn wrote the secretary of war in December 1812 remarking, "It would appear that something like fatality has pervaded the military operations through the course of the campaign,"[4] Dearborn's views might apply just as well to 1813 as to the previous year.

The major reasons for the American military failures early in the war, according to the most recent general work on it, were poor leadership, incompetent senior officers, ill-advised strategy, and the lack of proper directions to field commanders by the War Department.[5] The United States army got much better leadership in 1814 when the most incompetent generals were replaced by experienced younger officers such as Jacob Brown, Winfield Scott, Eleazer Ripley, Alexander Macomb, and Edmund Gaines. Poor strategic thinking and the lack of communication would continue to create command problems throughout the war.

Although American military success in 1814 was limited, the earlier misadventures serve to make the Niagara campaign of 1814 all the more notable. The successes achieved by Major General Jacob Brown's Left Division were all the more laudable because of his continued communication problems with the secretary of war, his troubled relationships with some of the subordinate officers in his division, and the interservice rivalry with the naval commander on Lake Ontario, Commodore Isaac Chauncey.

The over-all strategy of the campaign of 1814 was flawed. Practically everyone knew that Kingston should be the object of American attack. If Kingston fell everything west of it would wither on the vine, but Secretary of War John Armstrong ended up changing the objective of the campaign to the Niagara Peninsula because of continuing communication problems between the secretary and the generals in the field that plagued the American command structure.[6]

In early March 1814, Major General Jacob Brown, at Sackets Harbor with the two thousand troops he had recently marched from the winter quarters on the Salmon River where General James Wilkinson's abortive campaign of 1813 had ended, received two

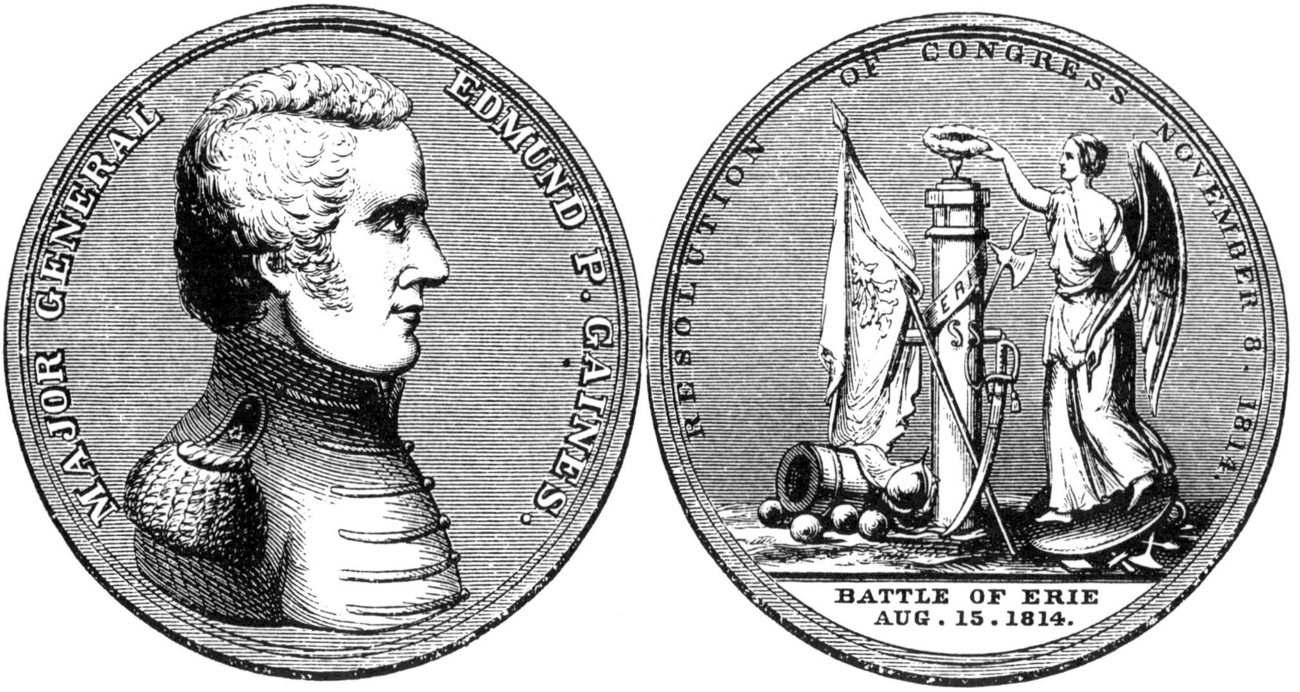

Edmund P. Gaines, who received a medal and promotion to major general for his defeat of British assaults at Fort Erie on August 15, 1814, was one of the group of younger American officers who gained prominence in 1814.

letters from the Secretary of War written February 28. These two letters marked the beginning of General Brown's first problem of command, that of communication with his superiors in the War Department. In the first letter, Armstrong ordered Brown to attack Kingston if certain conditions could be met. Armstrong required that if large detachments had been made from Kingston, if the roads and weather were good, and if the hearty cooperation of Commodore Isaac Chauncey could be obtained, then Brown should cross the St. Lawrence and take Kingston by surprise attack. If an attack on Kingston was viable, Brown was to use the second letter as a mask.[7] The second letter ordered Brown and his troops to Batavia to join Brigadier General Winfield Scott and await orders to drive the British out of Fort Niagara.[8]

The conditions laid down by the secretary for the move on Kingston could not be met. After conferring with Commodore Isaac Chauncey, and Majors Samuel Brown, W.W. Crane and J.B. Crane, Brown concluded the second letter was an alternative order and put his troops on the road for Batavia. At Geneva, Brown met Brigadier General Edmund Gaines who persuaded him he was mistaken about Armstrong's letters. Brown wrote the secretary from Geneva, March 21, that his troops would countermarch to Onondaga and that he would return to Sackets Harbor.[9] Upon his arrival at Sackets Harbor, Brown had another conference with Chauncey who in turn convinced him that their original interpretation of the letters was correct. Back at Sackets Harbor, Brown wrote the secretary to summarize his dilemma. He said that after he had consulted with General Gaines at Geneva, he realized that he had perhaps misunderstood Armstrong's intentions, and that until he had conferred with Chauncey again he was, as he put it, "the most unhappy man alive." Chauncey and others had reconvinced Brown, he wrote, "that my first understanding of your intentions was correct and I am happy again."[10] Upon his subsequent arrival at Batavia, on March 31, Brown still found no relief from his anxiety because of a lack of instructions.[11]

Finally, on April 8 Brown received a letter from Armstrong dated March 20 which "perfectly satisfied" him that his action had been a "fortunate mistake", and he awaited further instructions.[12] In this letter the secretary of war informed Brown that he had, in fact, mistaken the purpose of the two letters of February 28. The letter ordering Brown westward had been intended as a mask for the operations against Kingston. Now Armstrong stated that if Brown had left a sufficient force at Sackets Harbor to defend that important naval base then he should, as Armstrong put it, "go on & prosper. Good consequences are sometimes the result of mistakes."[13]

All this confusion should not have occurred. Brown could not meet the original conditions set by Armstrong for an attack upon Kingston because the British had not made detachments from that post, the weather had been mild, the roads were in poor shape, and the ice not thick enough to cross the St. Lawrence. Brown had sent this information to Armstrong on

Brig. Gen. Edmund P. Gaines convinced Brown that he had misunderstood Secretary Armstrong's instructions.

February 24; his letter had crossed in the mail the letters from Armstrong telling him to attack Kingston.[14]

As a newly commissioned major general, Jacob Brown was anxious to make his mark, and, therefore, he tried his best to obey even these most confusing orders from the Secretary of War. A modern biography of Armstrong by C. Edward Skeen is quite critical of the secretary's lack of explicitness in giving directions to General Brown. Although the biography is an overall attempt to resurrect the reputation of Armstrong, Skeen views the situation as one where the secretary tried to be too clever. The tactic backfired. It ended up changing the entire focus of American operations on the northern frontier in 1814. Armstrong had again, as in 1813, exhibited his failure to pursue a consistent policy.[15] Brown, for his part, could have written for clearer instructions once the impossibility of an attack on Kingston was apparent, but that would have meant even more delay. What Jeffrey Kimball has called the "fog of war" created an implausible situation and entirely shifted the emphasis of the campaign.[16] General Brown's command problems had already begun before the campaign opened.

Despite the initial confusion at the beginning of the campaign season, preparations for operations in the Niagara area went forward in the spring and early summer of 1814. Because of the fears of the war department and the naval authorities concerning the safety of Sackets Harbor from British attack, Brown had to return there on April 20. He left Brigadier General Winfield Scott in charge of the forces in western New York with orders to pay particular attention to the infantry and their training. Scott was also instructed to open all public letters to Brown and take copies if they concerned Scott's command and then send the originals to Brown.[17] A month later Scott became upset because Brown's aide, Lieutenant Ambrose Spencer, was involved in what Scott called "the erroneous practice" of opening Brown's mail. Scott thought he could not relinquish that right without "depriving me of my sword." This is an early

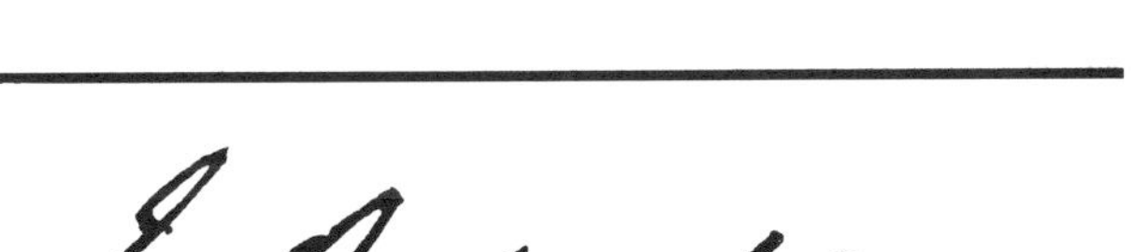

Secretary of War John Armstrong's signature, as reproduced by Benson J. Lossing.

Concern for the safety of Sackets Harbor caused Gen. Brown to return there on April 20 leaving the training of the Left Division in the hands of Winfield Scott. Drawing by Benson J. Lossing after an 1815 print published in *Portfolio*.

indication of Scott's touchiness on what he considered questions of military protocol - a touchiness that would cause Brown problems later in the campaign.[18]

Brown, for his part, inferred from Scott's letters that Scott did not expect Brown to assume command of the forces that would enter Canada. Brown felt that Scott held this "eroneous opinion" because of his correspondence with Armstrong. Brown insisted to the Secretary of War that if he did not command his own forces in Canada, as he wrote, "I should certainly despise myself."[19] Armstrong had, in fact, written Scott on May 25 and Brown on May 26, strongly implying that Scott would command any expedition to Canada.[20] To forestall the possibility that Scott would command on the Niagara frontier, Brown returned to Buffalo in late May to assume command at that place.[21]

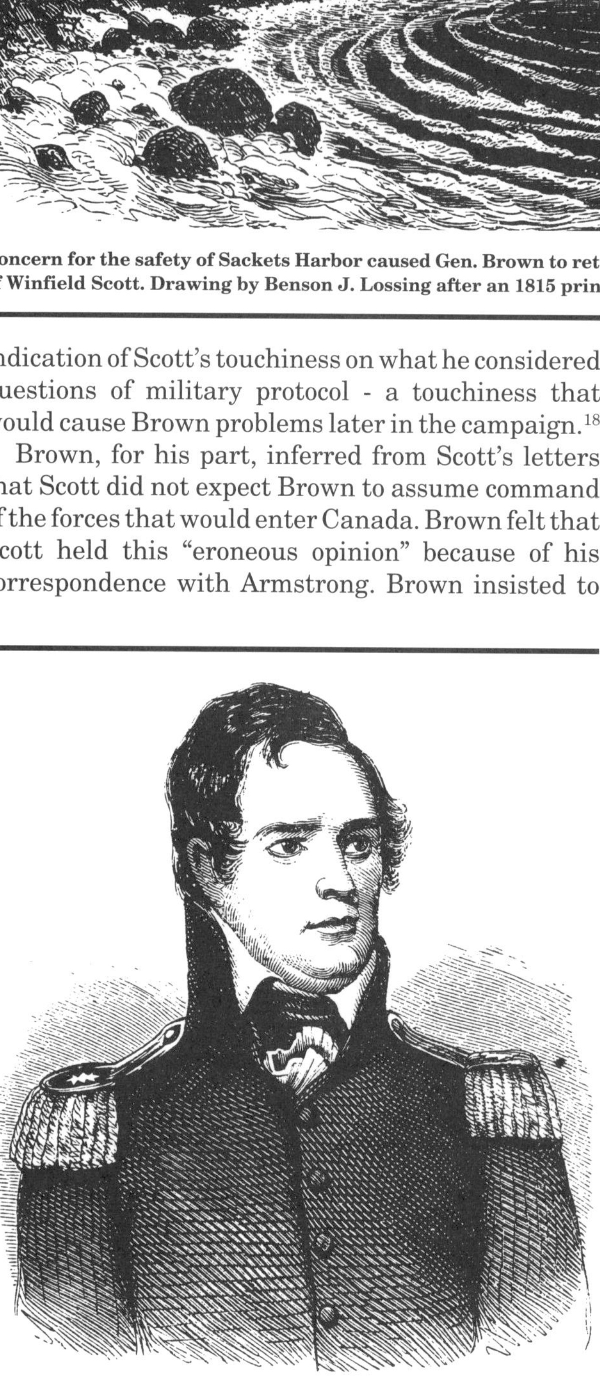

Former War Hawk Congressman Peter B. Porter commanded a brigade of New York and Pennsylvania Militia during the Niagara campaign.

In mid-June 1814, Brown finally received the long awaited War Department instructions for the summer campaign. The plan was to use the Lake Erie fleet to transport Brown's forces to Point Abino on the northern shore of lake, and the army would march from there to Burlington where Brown would meet Chauncey's Lake Ontario squadron carrying supplies and further reinforcements. In the same letter Armstrong, however, raised the problem of logistics because all military operations, as the secretary put it, "begin with the belly." There were not enough ships, horses or wagons to carry the immense amount of stores Brown would need to supply his army. Furthermore, Armstrong then deprived Brown of enough ships to cross Lake Erie by sending most of the Lake Erie squadron to Detroit to carry a force under Colonel George Croghan in what eventually turned out to be an abortive attack on Michilimackinac.

Armstrong concluded his lengthy instructions by saying the operation was approved but "its execution must be suspended, 'til Chauncey shall have gained control of the lake." This delay, he assured Brown, would allow time for him to receive the recruits for the four regiments of Scott's brigade, and also make it possible for another brigade under Brigadier General Eleazer W. Ripley to join him, as well as give Brigadier General Peter B. Porter time to gather his militia forces.

"To give however immediate occupation to your troops," Armstrong concluded, "& to prevent their blood from stagnating - Why not take Fort Erie & its garrison ... push forward a corps to seize the bridge at Chippway, & be governed by circumstances in either stopping there, or going further." If Brown could invest Fort George then he could avail himself of Chauncey's aid in the "*most direct way*."[22]

Thus, the whole Niagara campaign of 1814 resulted as a kind of afterthought by the Secretary of War following his having deprived the Left Division of the transportation it needed to cross Lake Erie, and after he had concluded that the necessary logistical support for Brown did not exist anyway. The secretary's conclusion was that, since all these troops had been gathered, something ought to be done with them to keep them from getting stagnant or bored. The confusion in communication in the spring had resulted in the whole campaign being shifted westward where it would do the least for the American war effort. As a result, Brown would have to invade Canada with only a tenuous supply line and have to face the inability to penetrate Canada to any great distance because of it.

Once the invasion of the Niagara Peninsula began, Brown would be faced by other command problems. In particular, he would have to deal with the personalities of his subordinates, and their over-inflated sense of honor.

Brown himself was considered by some of his contemporaries, Wilkinson and Scott, to be a rank amateur.[23] Wilkinson claimed Brown was ignorant of military matters and in his *Memoirs* made him out to be the duped creature of Scott during the Niagara campaign. Yet consider that, in 1813, Wilkinson had made Brown a brigade commander and relied on his knowledge of the northern frontier and had also put him in charge of the advance of the army down the St. Lawrence and of the winter quarters at French Mills. If one also considers that, at the Battle of Chippewa, Brown saw the distinct possibility of Ripley's brigade enveloping Riall's force while it was engaged with Scott.[24] Perhaps one might conclude that Brown was not quite the military ignoramus Wilkinson and Scott thought he was.

Brown is generally considered to be one of the more aggressive American generals of the War of 1812.[25] He appears to have had the ability to grasp a situation and visualize it quite well, as evidenced by his actions at Chippewa. His pre-war experience as a surveyor had given him an eye for terrain that was often lacking in other generals. Brown also had enough intelligence to rely on subordinates for advice, particularly his two engineer officers, Eleazer Wood and William McRee. His views regarding the contents of the British forts and the destruction of enemy forces as being more important than the mere capture of geographic objectives would seem to indicate that he held a more modern view of warfare than was prevalent at the time.[26] But Brown was also a strict disciplinarian.[27] Whenever his eye caught some infraction which he felt reflected upon the honor of the army, or himself, he acted quickly. As a case in point, Captain Joseph Treat's company was doing picket duty at Chippewa when it ran into trouble, broke and left a wounded man behind. Brown dismissed Treat from the army on the spot, and it took Treat a year to get a court martial which eventually cleared his name.[28] When troops under the command of Lieutenant Colonel Isaac Stone of the New York Militia burned the village of St. Davids, Stone too was dismissed. Actually the destruction of St. Davids was more likely to have been the work of Joseph Willcocks and his renegade Canadian Volunteers, but the onus fell on Colonel Stone.[29]

Of Brown's three subordinates, Winfield Scott, Eleazer Ripley, and Peter B. Porter, Scott and Ripley posed special problems within his command. Scott was aggressive to the point of rashness. At Lundy's Lane Scott's brigade attacked British positions for two hours without accomplishing anything except to increase the American casualty list. Later on in that battle Scott organized a charge of the remnants of his brigade which passed in front of the American lines from one end to the other. Such a maneuver, especially when it is done in darkness, might be considered a folly, particularly since both British troops and Ripley's Second Brigade fired into Scott's men.[30] There is not much doubt, however, that Brown trusted and respected Scott and relied heavily on his brigade to carry much of the brunt of the fighting in the campaign. When the Left Division was before Fort George in mid-July, a question arose as to whether the army should invest the fort or move west to engage the British forces under General Phineas Riall. Brown took Scott's advice to invest the fort rather than that of all his other advisers who argued in favor of attacking Riall.[31]

Eleazer Ripley, lawyer and former speaker of the New Hampshire legislature, became a cross for Brown to bear. Ripley had extensive military experience having been a regimental commander at York, Fort George and Chrysler's Field in 1813. There is no doubt of Ripley's personal bravery, but throughout the Niagara campaign he seems to have been reluctant to move as fast as he should have. Ripley objected to the original plan of even crossing the Niagara, and then was slow to get over the river to invest Fort Erie. At Chippewa he managed to take a roundabout route through the woods and did not get into action in time enough to turn the British flank. One might grant upon that occasion that Scott's infantry and artillery had acted so quickly to repel Riall that Ripley would

Eleazer Ripley, commander of the Left Division's 2nd Brigade, was one of several general officers to receive medals for their heroic service in 1814.

not have been able to cut off the British from their works at Chippewa anyway. But three days later, when the Left Division crossed the Chippewa River, the slowness of Ripley's movements exasperated Brown to the point where he took over direct command of the crossing.[32]

From Brown's point of view, the final straw came the morning after the Battle of Lundy's Lane when Ripley did not get back to the battlefield in time to take possession of the British guns the Americans had captured the night before. It must be admitted, however, that Ripley's decision not to re-open the battle on the morning of July 26 was correct, since the American army had been badly cut up the previous night at Lundy's Lane, especially in terms of losing a great many officers, and was in no shape to renew combat immediately. When Ripley retreated to Fort Erie on July 26 and requested permission to cross over to Buffalo, Brown refused to let him. Fed up with what he considered Ripley's reluctance to take on responsibility and not trusting Ripley to command while he (Brown) recovered from his wounds, Brown sent for Brigadier General Edmund Gaines to come from Sackets Harbor to take command at Fort Erie. In the interval, Ripley did yeoman service in strengthening the defenses of Fort Erie. Colonel Thomas Jesup, in his memoir of the Niagara campaign, was quite critical of Ripley's tardy movements, and states that most officers in the Left Division had little confidence in Ripley after the Battle of Lundy's Lane.[33]

During the sortie from Fort Erie on September 17, Brown assigned Ripley to command the reserve, and relied upon Colonel James Miller and Brigadier Peter Porter to lead the two wings of the actual assault. Shortly after this action Ripley, who had been slightly wounded in the neck, went on leave.[34]

The bad feelings between Brown and Ripley resulted in a post-war controversy that was fueled by Ripley's demand for a court of inquiry and the subsequent publication of his "Facts Relating to the Campaign on the Niagara in 1814." In that publication, in August 1815, Ripley included "from memory" a confidential letter written by Brown under pressure from President Madison and Secretary of War A.J. Dallas absolving Ripley of any misconduct in the Niagara campaign. Brown became incensed by what he considered a breach of confidentiality and his honor. In late 1815, Brown considered filing court martial charges against Ripley for neglect of duty, disobedience of orders, and cowardice.[35] By 1816 the "baneful effects" of the controversy between the two resulted in Ripley being transferred to New Orleans to be under the command of General Andrew Jackson in order to prevent "further collision" between him and Brown. Ripley eventually left the army in 1819.[36] Ripley's inability to move as fast as Brown thought he should, and what Brown saw as Ripley's reluctance to take responsibility drove a wedge deeper and deeper between the two officers.

Peter B. Porter, the New York militia general and

former War Hawk congressman from Buffalo, presented much less of a problem to Brown. Porter definitely did not like Scott, but that animosity caused no problems during the campaign.[37] Generally throughout the campaign, Porter's New York and Pennsylvania militia troops were much less engaged in action than the regulars. At Chippewa, for example, Porter's men cleared the woods of British Indians and militia which had been harassing American pickets. When they ran into British regulars Porter's men did what militia had often done in the war, they took to their heels. At Lundy's Lane Porter's troops were on the left flank of the American lines and suffered fewer casualties than the regulars, but higher casualties in proportion to their number. Only during the sortie from Fort Erie did Brown give the militia a major role in any of the battles of the campaign, when they formed one of the two wings of the attack on British positions. A comparison of the casualty figures during the campaign appears to be the most concrete evidence regarding the militia's relatively minor role before the sortie. Of the 328 casualties at Chippewa only twelve were from the militia. At Lundy's Lane, the militia suffered sixty-seven casualties, but the percentage of militia casualties among the 860 total casualties was quite small. Since only about 150 militia troops fought at Lundy's Lane, their own casualty rate was obviously quite high in that engagement.[38]

During the War of 1812, U.S. army officers often became overly sensitive when they did not think they had been given proper recognition in dispatches or battle reports. The most notable examples of this type of behavior among the officers of the Left Division involved Winfield Scott and Major Henry Leavenworth, both of whom were critical of Brown's failure to give them, or their units, the praise they thought they deserved.

Winfield Scott, who, at times, appears to have been one of the most sensitive officers who ever served in the American army, created the most problems for Brown. When the general order of July 6, 1814 regarding the Battle of Chippewa was issued,[39] Scott expressed his unhappiness in writing even before Brown had written a report of that action. Brown's general order of July 6 had, according to Scott, "repressed his zeal and determined him to resign from the service." He complained that the officers of his brigade had not been noticed at all, and he could not quietly witness their neglect. He, therefore, requested that Brown accept his resignation.[40]

Brown replied to Scott the same day informing him that he highly appreciated Scott's efforts at Chippewa, but that it was not proper to show him his report for reasons Scott would understand when it was issued. Brown went on to urge Scott to let him know immediately if he had left out the names of any officers to whom praise was due.[41] Upon receipt of this mollifying reply, Scott, somewhat chagrined, hastened to apologize for pressing Brown regarding his report, and assured the commanding general that no one knew of his first letter except the aide who had carried it to him.[42] In his official report Brown gave almost the entire credit for the victory at Chippewa to Scott and his brigade, stating that, "to him more than to any other man, am I indebted for the victory of the 5th of July." Brown also praised the regiments of Scott's brigade, saying that, "every officer and every man of the 9th, llth, & 25th Regts did his duty with zeal & energy."[43] Scott, his regimental commanders, and Captain Nathan Towson, who had commanded Scott's artillery, would all be awarded brevet promotions for their services at Chippewa.[44] However, despite Brown's praise for him and his officers, Scott continued to be sensitive about the issue as late as the end of August 1814.[45]

Major Henry Leavenworth of the Ninth Infantry was possibly even more sensitive than Scott at being neglected in official reports, and perhaps with better reason. When he saw Brown's report of Chippewa, Leavenworth also tendered his resignation stating that, "my feeling are injured, my understanding insulted and my country abused." Leavenworth went on to say that he had lost confidence in his commanding general and wished to resign.[46] When he later saw Brown's report of the Battle of Lundy's Lane, Leaven-

Secretary of War A.J. Dallas.

Benson J. Lossing's facsimile of the medal awarded by Congress to Winfield Scott for the Battles of Chippewa and Niagara (Lundy's Lane).

worth was unhappy again, and with good reason. He wrote Brown a lengthy letter to ask the general to inform him if his conduct on July 25 "was such to displeasure you." He trusted his exertions that day "were not I hope of such a feeble nature as to disgust you." Leavenworth concluded by asking Brown if he deserved the "cold neglect" he had received.[47]

Brown had, in fact, neglected to mention Leavenworth and his regiment, or any of his services during the Battle of Lundy's Lane.[48] This was an oversight by Brown as at Lundy's Lane Leavenworth had led his regiment in the thick of the early fighting. More importantly, after Scott's brigade had suffered heavy casualties Leavenworth had consolidated the remnants of the llth, 9th and 22nd regiments into a single unit. Near the end of the action Leavenworth commanded what was left of the first brigade. Brown, for his part, was not on the field during most of the first two hours of fighting at Lundy's Lane and was in no position to have observed Leavenworth's activities early in the evening of July 25.

Despite that, Brown should still have noticed Leavenworth's meritorious conduct in his official report, especially since his regiment had been in the affair from the beginning and had taken severe casualties. On July 26, Leavenworth was the only unwounded commander in Scott's brigade, and his regiment could only muster sixty-four out of its 150 men. For his actions at Lundy's Lane Leavenworth would receive his second brevet, but it was too late to make up for Brown's neglect of him in his report. Generally Brown's report on Lundy's Lane overlooked the officers of Scott's brigade, except for Major Jesup of the 25th who acted independently from the rest of the brigade, which may have made that regiment's performance more noticeable. It is also possible that Brown never received a report from Scott regarding the actions of his brigade because of Scott's severe wounds sustained in the battle, but certainly detailed information would have been available to Brown from other sources.[49]

There seems to have been no reason for Brown withholding praise for Leavenworth, except it was possibly an oversight on the commanding general's part, that was only partially rectified by Leavenworth's brevet promotion. It certainly did not hurt Leavenworth's later career. The incident does, however, serve as an example of the sensitivity of American officers of that time, who, generally, appear to have been very irate whenever they believed they had not been justly praised and were perfectly willing to speak up and tell their superior officers about it.

Any strategic success the Left Division might have had in the Niagara Peninsula depended not only upon the actions of the army, but, more importantly, it depended upon Commodore Isaac Chauncey's fleet controlling Lake Ontario and on cooperation between the two services. As early as May 25, Armstrong had written Scott, then the proposed commander of any Niagara incursion, that everything depended upon naval control of the lake. Without naval cooperation any American force in Niagara could have only lim-

The port of Buffalo in 1813 with American warships at anchor in Lake Erie and the Canadian shore in the right background. From Benson J. Lossing's *Pictorial Field Book of the War of 1812.*

ited success.[50] In June, however, Armstrong was apparently unable to recognize that the army should not advance into the Niagara without first assuring itself of naval support.

When Armstrong rather casually suggested to Brown in a letter of June 10 that Brown cross over the Niagara and be governed by circumstances, Brown did not hesitate to act, as so many other American commanders had during the war.[51] But Brown also believed he would receive naval support and cooperation. The ever-cautious Chauncey, however, procrastinated. He had promised Brown and the government he would sail by July 1. Chauncey, at that time, had a superior force on Lake Ontario. The British fleet, whose eight ships were equal in number to Chauncey, was outgunned 251 to 216, and Chauncey's squadron could throw a 3,352 pound broadside to the British fleet's 2,874 pounds. Furthermore, the British fleet was habitually under-manned and had fewer long guns than Chauncey's ships.[52]

The first part of the campaign went very well. The Left Division crossed the Niagara, took Fort Erie, gained a signal victory at Chippewa, and advanced toward Fort George. When Brown and his army arrived at Queenston, July 10, he fully expected to see Chauncey's fleet. He had written the commodore on June 21 asking Chauncey to meet him about July 10 and to bring additional heavy guns to batter down Fort George. Brown had also asked Chauncey to transport the Rifle Regiment stationed at Sackets Harbor to his army.[53] On July 12, Brown wrote Chauncey from Queenston assuring him the British forces at Kingston were weak and that he should not fear an enemy attack on the naval base at Sackets Harbor. If Chauncey would meet him north of Fort George they could settle on a plan of operations to "break the power of the Enemy in Upper Canada." Brown continued his letter, saying,

> *I have looked for your fleet with great anxiety, since the tenth. I do not doubt my ability to meet the Enemy in the field, and to march in every direction, over his country (your fleet conveying for me the necessary supplies) ... For God's sake let me see you ... There is not a doubt resting in my mind, but that we have between us, the command of sufficient means to conquer Upper Canada within two months, if there is a prompt & zealous cooperation, & a vigorous application of those means. Now is the time, before the Enemy can be greatly re-inforced.*[54]

Brown remained in the vicinity of Fort George

Commodore Isaac Chauncey's inability to coordinate the movements of his Lake Ontario squadron with the advance of Brown's army frustrated the general's hopes of greater success along the Niagara.

trying to entice the British into battle, and waited expectantly for the arrival of Chauncey until July 22 when his need for supplies made it necessary to fall back to Queenston. The next day he received news from General Edmund Gaines at Sackets Harbor that Chauncey was not coming. Chauncey's excuse was that his new 64 gun ship *Mohawk* needed some iron work and blocks before it could sail. On July 15, Chauncey took to his bed with a fever that lasted eighteen days. During that time, he refused to turn over command of his fleet to another officer.[55] In the meantime, the British commander, General Gordon Drummond, was rushing considerable reinforcements to the Niagara area by land and water and assembling the militia of the region.[56] Brown, faced by a continued lack of supplies and naval cooperation, fell back to Chippewa on July 24. In the early evening of July 25 the two armies stumbled into what became the bloodbath at Lundy's Lane.

Chauncey did not arrive off the mouth of the Niagara until August 7, when he wrote Brown telling him that he had always felt that his major duty had been to destroy the British fleet and only to cooperate with the army if he could.[57] A few days later, having returned to the waters off Kingston, he wrote Brown again accusing Brown of unfriendly attitudes for having asserted to the Secretary of War that Chauncey had been pledged to meet him at the head of the lake. He further accused Brown of trying to shift the blame onto him for his own failures. Chauncey stated that the fleet could not have aided Brown in any case because the army had gotten no closer to Lake Ontario than Queenston, and, furthermore the fleet would have been of no use in taking Fort George. Chauncey caustically told Brown that the army might have found the fleet convenient to transport supplies to the army, but that he did not see the fleet as an "appendage" of the army. Chauncey again claimed his higher duty was to seek out and destroy the enemy fleet.[58] Chauncey had forgotten how important the fleet had been only a year earlier in taking Fort George and in the attack on York. His charge that Brown's army had approached no closer to the lake than Queenston was patently false.

Brown, for his part, became incensed over Chauncey's assertions, and what he considered Chauncey's broken promises to aid the army. In his reply to Chauncey, Brown said that the exception the commodore had taken to Brown's letter to the Secretary of War, "would be very reasonable & proper provided the Fleet of Lake Ontario was your private property ... but as it was the property of the Nation, ... and as the Govert [sic] led me to believe that the fleet you command would be upon Lake Ontario to cooperate with my division of the Army ...", he felt he was justified in writing the secretary as he had. Brown went on to say, "You speak of responsibility, I do not desire you or any man, to be responsible for me, - I have endeavoured to execute the orders given me; but I humbly trust in Heaven that the honor of the brave men intrusted [sic] to my command, has & will be, preserved let what may happen."[59] The government found Chauncey's excuses as feeble as Brown had, and issued orders for him to be replaced by Stephen Decatur. The order was later rescinded because Chauncey was already on patrol upon the lake.[60]

Certainly close cooperation between army and navy could very well have changed the outcome of the campaign. The fleet would have prevented reinforcements and provisions from reaching the British forces in the Niagara, and supplied the same items to Brown. It is well within the realm of possibility that Brown might have been able to drive the British out of the peninsula, had he received the support of Chauncey's ships. With the aid of the fleet, perhaps Brown could have mounted an attack upon Kingston before the campaigning season was over.

Brown had advanced into the Niagara Peninsula with a well-trained, adequate force, but, lacking a secure supply line and without naval cooperation, he was forced to draw back to Chippewa. Once the Battle of Lundy's Lane had occurred, however, his army was in no shape to continue because his losses could not be readily replaced. What had started out so auspi-

Maj. Gen. Jacob Brown's Congressional medal for services in the 1814 Niagara campaign.

ciously on July 3 would end up, eventually, as an exercise in vindicating the fighting capabilities and honor of the army.

Brown's problems of command emerge as matters that were largely beyond his control. He could not correct the original flawed strategy which had shifted the campaign westward away from where the main thrust of American energies should have been concentrated. Perhaps it can be argued that Brown helped create that fateful move when he misinterpreted Armstrong's letters back in February, but if Armstrong had made his instructions clear, the way to misconstruing his letters would not have been open.

Maj. Gen. George Izard ended the Niagara campaign by withdrawing American forces to Buffalo in November 1814.

Brown could not correct, either, the lack of logistical support, nor the differences between the capabilities and personalities of his officers, nor the lack of cooperation from the navy. All he could do was handle them as best he could and make the most out of what was an increasingly difficult situation with the materials given him, which he did. The major weaknesses of the American campaign in the Niagara Peninsula in 1814 involved the inadequacies of logistical support and the inability of Brown to replace his casualties. Despite these difficulties, Brown emerged from the war as the best field commander in the army. He had won three of the nine major American victories (Sackets Harbor, Chippewa, and the Sortie from Fort Erie) in the war and fought a tactical victory, but a strategic loss, at Lundy's Lane.

Although the Left Division performed well in the Niagara in the summer of 1814, it could not replace its losses, while British commanders could. The Left Division, or what remained of it, fell back to Fort Erie after Lundy's Lane, and it was never able to recover the initiative in the Niagara Peninsula. Brown's division was reinforced just before the sortie from Fort Erie by New York militia, who proved to be very satisfactory in that engagement. Major General George Izard arrived at Fort Erie in late September with a large reinforcement of regulars, but he was a much less energetic commander than Brown, and withdrew the American forces to Buffalo in November 1814, ending the campaign where it started. Whatever military glory the Left Division obtained it reached while it was under Jacob Brown's command.

NOTES

[1]Donald R. Hickey, *The War of 1812: A Forgotten War* (Urbana, IL, 1989), p. 2; John K. Mahon, *The War of 1812* (Gainesville, FL, 1972), p. 95. The two best Canadian works on the war are the excellent but undocumented J. Mackay Hitsman, *The Incredible War of 1812* (Toronto, 1965) and George F.G. Stanley, *The War of 1812: Land Operations* (Ottawa, 1983) which tends to be more biased to the Canadian side.

[2]For these events see Mahon, pp. 48-54, 76-85, 94-95.

[3]Hickey, p. 151.

[4]Maj. Gen. Henry Dearborn to Secretary of War, Dec. 11, 1812, quoted in Mahon, p. 95.

[5]Hickey, p. 90.

[6]Jeffrey Phillip Kimball, "Strategy on the Northern Frontier: 1814" (Ph.D. dissertation, Louisiana State University, 1969), p. 175; C. Edward Skeen, *John Armstrong Jr., 1758-1843* (Syracuse, 1981), pp. 178-79, 186.

[7]John Armstrong, *Notices of the War of 1812* (2 vols.; New York, 1840), II, p. 213.

[8]*Ibid.,* II, pp. 213-14.

[9]Maj. Gen. Jacob Brown to Sec. of War John Armstrong, March 21, 1814, National Archives and Records Administration, Washington, D.C., Record Group 107 (Records of the Office of the Secretary of War, Letters Received, Registered Series), Microcopy 221, reel 51 (hereafter cited as NA, RG 107, M221, by reel number).

[10]Brown to Armstrong, March 21, 1814, NA, RG 107, M221, reel 51.

[11]*Ibid.,* Brown to Armstrong, March 31, 1814.

[12]*Ibid.,* Brown to Armstrong, April 8, 1814.

[13]Armstrong to Brown, March 20, 1814, National Archives and Records Administration, Washington, D.C., Record Group 107, (Records of the Office of the Secretary of War, Letters Sent by the Secretary of War Relating to Military Affairs), Microcopy 6, reel 7 (hereafter cited as NA, RG 107, M6, by reel number).

[14]Brown to Armstrong, Feb. 24, 1814, NA, RG 107, M221, reel 51.

[15]Skeen, pp. 177-78.

[16]Jeffrey Kimball, "The Fog and Friction of War: The Role of Logistics in the American Offensive Failure During the War of 1812", *Old Northwest,* 6 (1980), 323-43, especially see, 323-30.

[17]General Order of April 7, 1814, New York State Library, Albany, NY, Order Book of the Left Division of the Northern Army from April 7-July 24, 1814 (hereafter cited as Order Book, NYSL); Library of Congress, Washington, D.C., Jacob Jennings Brown Papers (hereafter cited as Brown Papers, LOC).

[18]Brig. Gen. Winfield Scott to Brown, May 22, 1814, Brown Papers, LOC.

[19]*Ibid.,* Brown to Armstrong, June 3, 1814.

[20]Armstrong to Scott, May 25, 1814 and Armstrong to Brown, May 26, 1814, NA, RG 107, M6, reel 7.

[21]*Ibid.,* Armstrong to Brown, June 2, 1814; Brown to Armstrong, June 3, 1814, Brown Papers, LOC.

[22]Armstrong to Brown, June 10, 1814, NA, RG 107, M6, reel 7.

[23]James Wilkinson, *Memoirs of My Own Times* (3 vols.; Philadelphia, 1816), I, pp. 639, 646, 650, 655; Winfield Scott, *Memoirs of Lieut-General Scott, L.L.D.* (2 vols.; London, 1864), I, p. 118.

[24]Jeffrey Kimball, "The Battle of Chippewa: Infantry Tactics in the War of 1812", *Military Affairs,* 32 (1968), 185.

[25]Mahon, p. 276; Stanley, p. 300; Harry L. Coles, *The War of 1812* (Chicago, 1965), p. 139; Russell F. Weigley, *History of the United States Army* (Bloomington, 1965), p. 139.

[26]Brown to Armstrong, June 17, 1814, Brown Papers, LOC.

[27]Brown to Armstrong, Feb. 24, 1814, NA, RG 107, M221, reel 51.

[28]General Orders, July 5, 1814, Order Book, NYSL; Joseph Treat, *The Vindication of Captain Joseph Treat* (Philadelphia, 1815).

[29]General Orders, July 19, 1814, Order Book, NYSL; Stanley, p. 317; Benson J. Lossing, *Pictorial Field-Book of the War of 1812* (New York, 1868), p. 815.

[30]Kimball, "Strategy", 236-37; Scott, I, p. 143; Eleazer W. Ripley, "Facts Relating to the Campaign on the Niagara in 1814" (Boston, 1815), p. 23.

[31]Thomas S. Jesup, "Memoir of the Niagara Campaign", Library of Congress, Washington, D.C., Thomas Sidney Jesup Papers (hereafter cited as Jesup Papers, LOC).

[32]Jesup, "Memoir of the Niagara Campaign", Jesup Papers, LOC; [Jacob Brown], "Memoranda of occurrences and some important facts attending the Campaign on the Niagara", Brown Papers, LOC.

[33]Brown to Armstrong, July 29, 1814, NA, RG 107, M221, reel 59; Brown to Secretary of War, Aug. 25, 1814, Brown Papers, LOC; Jesup, "Memoir of the Niagara Campaign", Jesup Papers, LOC.

[34]For particulars of the sortie, see: Brown to Armstrong, Sept. 19, Sept. 29, 1814, NA, RG 107, M221, reel 59; Brown to Gov. Daniel Tompkins, Sept. 24, 1814; Jesup, "Memoir of the Niagara Campaign", Jesup Papers, LOC; Carl M. Guelzo, "Fort Erie: High Point of a Low War", *Military Review,* 8 (1959), 50-57; L.L. Babcock, "The Siege of Fort Erie", *New York State Historical Society Proceedings,* 8 (1909), 38-59.

[35] Brown to A.J. Dallas, April 30, 1815, Brown Papers, LOC; Draft Court Martial Charges Against General Ripley, Dec. 1815, William L. Clements Library, Ann Arbor, MI, Jacob J. Brown Papers (hereafter cited as Brown Papers, AA); Ripley, "Facts".

[36] [Brown], "Memoranda", Brown Papers, LOC; Nicholas Baylies, *Eleazer Wheelock Ripley of the War of 1812* (Des Moines, IA, 1890); The quotes are from William Crawford to Ripley, June 4, 1816, NA, RG 107, M6, reel 7.

[37] Brig. Gen. Peter B. Porter to Tompkins, July 3, 1814, National Archives and Records Administration, Record Group 98, Records of United States Army Commands, 1784-1821, Letters and Extracts of Letters Received by Daniel D. Tompkins, 1812-1814.

[38] Brown to Armstrong, July 7, Aug. 7, Sept. 29, 1814, NA, RG 107, M221, reel 59; Casualty figures for Chippewa are in Ernest A. Cruikshank, (ed.), *Documentary History of the Campaign Upon the Niagara Frontier in 1812-1814* (9 vols.; Welland, Ont., 1896-1908), I, 43. For Lundy's Lane see C.K. Gardner to Daniel Parker, Casualty Report for Lundy's Lane, July 25, 1814, Historical Society of Pennsylvania, Philadelphia, Daniel Parker Papers.

[39] General Orders, July 6, 1814, Order Book, NYSL.

[40] Scott to Brown, July 10, 1814, Brown Papers, AA.

[41] *Ibid.,* Brown to Scott, July 10, 1814.

[42] *Ibid.,* Scott to Brown, July 10, 1814; Also see Scott to C.K. Gardner, July 15, 1814, NA, RG 107, M221, reel 59.

[43] Brown to Secretary of War, July 7, 1814, Brown Papers, LOC.

[44] *Ibid.,* Brown to Armstrong, July 10, 1814; C.K. Gardner to Jesup, Aug. 9, 1814, Jesup Papers, LOC.

[45] Scott to Edmund Gaines, Aug. 31, 1814, Massachusetts Historical Society, Boston, Jacob J. Brown Papers (hereafter cited as Brown Papers, MHS).

[46] Henry Leavenworth to Scott, July 24, 1814, Jesup Papers. LOC.

[47] Leavenworth to Brown, Sept. 21, 1814, New York State Library, Albany, Charles K. Gardner Papers.

[48] Brown to Armstrong, Aug. 7, 1814, Brown Papers, LOC.

[49] For a full description of Leavenworth's actions at Lundy's Lane, see Leavenworth to Ripley, Jan. 15, 1815, Jesup Papers, LOC.

[50] Armstrong to Scott, May 25, 1814, NA, RG 107, M6, reel 7; Skeen, p. 180.

[51] Armstrong to Brown, June 10, 1814, NA, RG 107, M6, reel 7; Skeen, p. 180.

[52] Kimball, "Strategy", 216; Ernest A. Cruikshank, "The Contest for the Command of Lake Ontario in 1814", *Ontario Historical Society Papers and Records,* 21 (1924), 141.

[53] Brown to Isaac Chauncey, June 21, 1814, Brown Papers, LOC.

[54] *Ibid.,* Brown to Chauncey, July 10, 1814.

[55] Gaines to Brown, July 17, 1814, Brown Papers, MHS; Kimball, "Strategy", 217.

[56] Kimball, "Strategy", 218.

[57] Chauncey to Brown, Aug. 7, 1814, Brown Papers, LOC.

[58] *Ibid.,* Chauncey to Brown, Aug. 10, 1814; also see Armstrong to Brown, July 22, 1814 and Brown to Secretary of War, Aug. 25, 1814, NA, RG 107, M221, reel 59.

[59] Brown to Chauncey, Sept. 4, 1814, Brown Papers, LOC.

[60] Cruikshank, "Contest for Lake Ontario", 141.

Following his distinguished service in the War of 1812, Winfield Scott became commander of the U.S. Army in 1841, led American troops in the war against Mexico and did not retire until 1861.

"I HAVE A HANDSOME LITTLE ARMY..."
A Re-examination of Winfield Scott's Camp At Buffalo in 1814

by
Donald E. Graves

I have a handsome little army ... I am most partial to these regiments. The men are healthy, sober, cheerful and docile. The field officers highly respectable, and many of the platoon officers are decent and emulous of improvement. If, of such materials, I do not make the best army now in service, by the 1st of June, I will agree to be dismissed the service.
Winfield Scott, May 1814

In the early morning of the July 3, 1814, a small American army under the command of Major General Jacob Brown crossed the Niagara River into Canada and invested Fort Erie. In the next seventy-five days, this army, known as the Left Division, inflicted two major defeats on the enemy at Chippewa and Fort Erie and won a tactical victory at the bloody battle of Lundy's Lane.[1] The Left Division's performance during the summer of 1814 earned it the admiration of its opponents. British Major General Phineas Riall noted that the Americans "deployed with the greatest regularity" under fire at Chippewa while, at Lundy's Lane, Lieutenant General Gordon Drummond emphasized the "determined character" of their infantry attacks.[2] A young subaltern of the 104th Foot, who fought throughout that summer thought the Americans has "turned out very good soldiers" and that their "officers were gallant and enterprizing."[3] Commenting after the war, a senior British officer stated it was "but justice to the American soldier to observe that he seems to have wonderfully improved in the last year of the war."[4]

The successes gained by Brown's Left Division went a long way to restoring to American arms a reputation that had become tarnished in the first two years of war. Why was the Left Division so superior to other similar American formations of the War of 1812? The fact that it was led by competent, professional and aggressive senior officers cannot be emphasized too much. Nor should the fact be overlooked that the division won an important victory in its first major action, the Battle of Chippewa, and this provided a tremendous boost to its fighting spirit. But other American armies of the war, notably those of Harrison and Jackson, also enjoyed good leadership and won victories without earning the enemy's praise as did the Left Division. Historians seem generally agreed that much of the credit for the division's success resulted from the training it received at the hands of Brigadier General Winfield Scott in his famous training camp at Buffalo in the spring of 1814.[5] This aspect of the division's history seems worthy of investigation and, in attempting to answer the question posed above, I am going to concentrate on the preparation of Brown's army for battle.

According to Scott, Brown, "though full of zeal and vigor, was not a technical soldier" and "charged" Scott "with the establishment of a camp of instruction ... and the preparation of the army for the field."[6] As Scott tells it in his memoirs, his task included instructing the troops in:

> *... the service of outposts, night patrols, guards, and sentinels ... a sys-*

This is the best War of 1812 period portrait of Winfield Scott. He was brevetted major general for distinguished service at the Battles of Chippewa and Lundy's Lane. *Courtesy, National Portrait Gallery, Smithsonian Institution.*

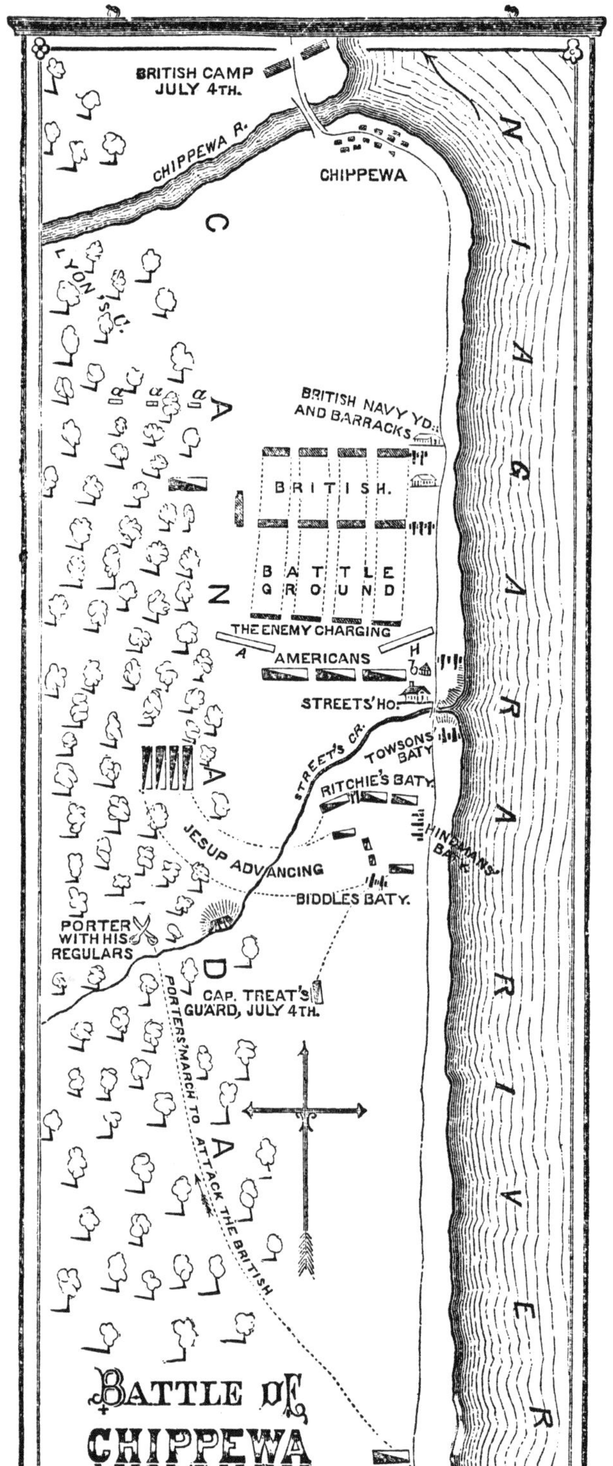

The Battle of Chippewa, fought on July 5, 1814, was the first victory of the Left Division. Canadian sources use the spelling "Chippawa". From Lossing's *Pictorial Field Book of the War of 1812*.

tem of sanitary police, including kitchens, ... rules of civility, etiquette, courtesy - the indispensable outworks of subordination prescribed and enforced, and the tactical instruction of each arm commenced. Nothing but night or a heavy fall of snow or rain was allowed to interrupt these exercises on the ground - to the extent, in tolerable weather, of ten hours a day, for three months.[7]

Scott recorded that his own labors were "heavy and incessant" particularly in regard to infantry training. Noting that since the "Government had provided no text book" for infantry tactics, he adopted the French army drill manual "of which he had a copy in the original." Like Steuben, he began by first drilling the officers until he was satisfied that they were proficient enough to train their men. He continued to take a keen interest in the training of his infantry, spending a few hours each day successively drilling companies, regiments and brigades "to the great delight of the troops." After three months, "confidence, the dawn of victory, inspired the whole line."[8]

This, of course, is familiar stuff. It has become, as Scott perhaps intended it should - the stuff of legend, and later commentators have been quick to expand on this legend. In 1890, Henry Adams wrote that:

> *Scott formed a camp of instruction at Buffalo, and ... personally drilled the officers of all grades. Scott's energy threw into the little army a spirit and an organization strange to the service. Three months of instruction converted ... raw troops into soldiers.*[9]

With one exception, more recent commentators have followed Adams and the story of Scott's camp has become well-established in the historiography of the War of 1812.[10] And what an attractive story it is - the tall, young brigadier general taking a rag-tag collection of green troops and, by discipline, drill and personal example, knocking them into soldiers capable of defeating British regulars in open battle. But much of this story is just that - fiction - and a reconciliation of the legend with the actual facts is required to place Scott's camp in its proper historical perspective.

Based on Scott's memoirs and the embellishments of later authors, the legend of Scott's camp, as it presently stands, breaks down into a number of elements:

> 1. Prior to Scott, American generals had either shown little interest in training their troops or did not make the time available to do so.
> 2. American troops on the northern frontier including the Left Division were, thus, mostly untrained recruits.
> 3. He established strict discipline and sanitary procedures in this camp.

4. During a three month period from April to June 1814, Scott rigorously trained these raw recruits and turned them into regular soldiers.
5. Because the War Department had not issued regulations concerning military duties and camp life, Scott was forced to compile his own.
6. Similarly, because there was not an established drill manual for infantry training, Scott used his own copy of the 1791 French infantry regulations.
7. Like Steuben, Scott began by drilling his officers separately until they were able to drill their men.

There is little doubt that, during the early part of the war, the army experienced tremendous difficulties in properly training its troops. This was partly due to the fact that the regiments sent to the northern border were not prewar regular regiments but units newly raised for wartime service. It was also due to the fact that recruits rarely received any instruction before joining their regiments in the field. Although each regiment had a designated "principal recruiting rendezvous," these were only collection points, not training depots in the British or French sense of the word. In fact, many men did not even pass through these collection points but arrived at the frontier lacking uniforms, weapons and the most elementary military instruction. The result was that the army's field camps also functioned as basic training camps and every commanding general on the northern frontier in the first two years of the war had to first train his troops before committing them to battle. Regardless of their abilities or competence, all of these general officers, without exception, demonstrated a singular interest in properly training their troops for action.

At the outbreak of war, the senior general of the army, Major General Henry Dearborn, was ordered to send all recruits "not otherwise disposed of" to Albany or some station on Lake Champlain to be organized for the invasion of Canada.[11] In the early autumn of 1812, Dearborn began to concentrate at Greenbush near Albany and placed the training of his units in the hands of the inspector general of the army, Brigadier General Alexander Smyth, the author of the current U.S. infantry manual.[12] At the same time, New York militia General Stephen Van Rensselaer established a camp of instruction for his brigade at Lewiston near Fort Niagara where he instituted two hours of company exercises per day and later increased them to four hours after receiving news of Hull's surrender at Detroit. Van Rensselaer also held regular battalion-level drills.[13] In early October, Smyth arrived on the Niagara with a five-regiment brigade of regular infantry and proceeded to encamp them "on an excellent

Maj. Gen. Jacob Brown. From Benson J. Lossing's *Pictorial Field Book of the War of 1812.*

piece of ground for exercise near Buffalo" so as "to devote six hours daily to their training."[14] The site that Smyth chose for this camp was Flint Hill, later the site of Scott's camp in 1814. Despite the efforts of Dearborn, Van Rensselaer and Smyth, the army's level of performance in the first months of the war was inadequate; an inspector described one of the regiments in Smyth's brigade as "mere militia" who "if taken into action in their present state will prove more dangerous to themselves then to their enemy."[15] Major General Morgan Lewis complained to the Secretary of War in early 1813 that "the troops are still as ignorant as when they first enlisted" and the "officers require as much instruction as the men."[16]

In the following year the situation changed for the better. At Saranac Camp near Plattsburg, Brigadier General Zebulon Montgomery Pike, a knowledgeable

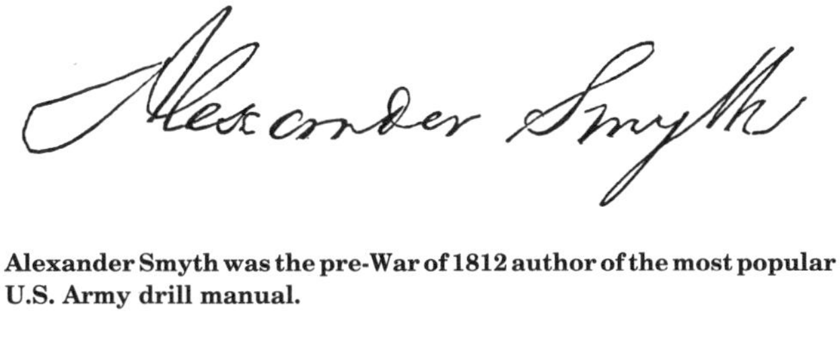

Alexander Smyth was the pre-War of 1812 author of the most popular U.S. Army drill manual.

and professional prewar regular, took over the training of units in the Lake Champlain area.[17] By April, Lewis could report to Washington that the men were progressing rapidly and were "under arms from six to eight hours per day."[18] On the Niagara frontier, the infantry trained two hours daily right through the winter and, in the spring, this was increased to six hours, leading one officer to remark that "we are making such progress that we shall Die with some grace next summer".[19] Further west at Fort Meigs, Major General William Henry Harrison ordered four hours of drill per day for all the troops under his command, both regular and militia.[20] The efforts of these officers paid dividends during the spring of 1813 as their units' performance in action was much improved.

The emphasis on training continued throughout the summer of 1813. Dearborn's successor, Brigadier General John P. Boyd, was ordered by the Secretary of War to "pay the utmost attention to the instruction and disciplining of the troops and engage in no affair with the enemy that can be avoided."[21] Boyd obeyed these orders to the letter and kept his force cooped up in Fort George and besieged by a British force inferior in numbers. When Major General James Wilkinson arrived in August to take over command of the northern frontier, he ordered the troops at Sackets Harbor and Fort George to be drilled "with redoubled energy" and forbade the use of the fife and drum in order to make training conditions more realistic.[22]

The work of all these officers paled beside that of Major General Wade Hampton who established a rigorous course of instruction for his division at Plattsburg in the summer of 1813. Hampton, a strict disciplinarian, ordered his officers to drill their non-commissioned officers separately but, dissatisfied with their progress, instituted officer's training squads and directed that "from the obligation of this drill no Officer of any Corps will be excused without a written dispensation."[23] When these squads had accomplished their purpose, they were replaced with two hours of company drill in the mornings and four hours of regimental exercises in the afternoons.[24] By August 1813, Hampton had progressed to the stage where he could maneuver his entire division.

It can be seen that Winfield Scott was not the only general officer interested in proper training - he had many predecessors. The quality of instruction provided during the first two years of the war is, of course, another matter, but the fact remains that by the spring of 1814 most of the regular units serving on the northern frontier had received some form of training and some it quite intensive. Furthermore, barring casualties, sickness or desertion, the greater part of these trained men would be available in 1814. A return of the troops on the frontier, dated December 8, 1813, which included a break down of their enlistment periods, shows that the terms of service of 5,776 men, or 71.4% of the total of 7,701, extended to 1815 or beyond.[25] In terms of trained men, the army was not nearly as badly off as it has often been portrayed, and the soldiers who marched into the camp at Buffalo were far from being raw recruits.

There is no doubt that they worked hard after they entered that camp. In his memoirs, Scott states that the troops trained continuously during the three months of April, May and June 1814.[26] In actual fact, as recorded in Scott's own order book, instruction did not commence at Buffalo until the 22nd of April.[27] As the division crossed into Canada on July 3, and it would be reasonable to allow at least two days to prepare for this crossing, training was limited to a period of sixty-nine days.

During those ten weeks, Scott pushed his men to the limit. Beginning on the 22nd of April, his regiments drilled between seven and ten hours each day if the weather permitted.[28] Company drill was held in the morning and regimental or brigade drill, usually under Scott's command, took place in the afternoon and, occasionally, in the evenings.[29] As one soldier remembered: "These exercises, continued daily for more than two months, could not fail to make us well acquainted with our business," and it did not take long for the units to achieve a state of near perfection.[30] By June, Scott was satisfied with their progress and drill was reduced to two hours in the morning and two in the afternoon.[31]

Scott enforced strict discipline in the camp. He did not tolerate desertion - the scourge of the wartime army - and, with Brown's permission, executed four men guilty of that crime. He was as hard on officers as he was on enlisted men and, at one point, of the twenty-six prisoners under arrest in the camp, nine held commissions.[32]

But, as Scott himself remarked, "Discipline is but the second object ... first is the health of the troops," and, in this respect, Scott's record was outstanding.[33] Having served at the disastrous Terre aux Boeufs camp where, in 1809, nearly a fifth of the army's enlisted strength was lost through sickness or desertion, Scott insisted on the observance of rigorous sanitary precautions at Flint Hill. The result was very beneficial, only two soldiers died from sickness in three months and, to the amazement of the regimental surgeons, "even the demon diarrhoea appeared to have been exorcised."[34] Scott's interest in the health of his troops extended even to promulgating orders on bathing. Troops under his command were to bath three times a week in Lake Erie and were accompanied by "one officer per company ... to cause the men to wash themselves from head to foot, but not to remain immersed in the water more than five minutes."[35]

In his memoirs, Scott emphasizes the fact that the

War Department's laxity increased his problems. He complained that the department had never issued a "book of general regulations or *Military Institutes* that would guide the conduct of soldiers in camp and in the field" and "this great want he had to supply orally and by written orders."[36] Similarly, because the government "had provided no textbook," he had to use the French regulations to drill his infantry.[37] Both these statement, however, are not quite accurate.

From 1779, the conduct of American troops on the march, in camp, and in garrison was regulated by Steuben's famous little *Blue Book.*[38] At the outbreak of war in 1812, this manual was superceded by Smyth's *Regulations* but Smyth "included as much of Steuben's work ... not relating to drills and manoeuvres as possible."[39] From time to time, the War Department had also issued regulations concerning camp and garrison life and these were collated and published in 1812, 1813 and 1814.[40] Scott's complaint that the War Department had never issued adequate regulations is, therefore, without foundation.

More to the point, it is clear from the orders he issued at Buffalo that Scott, despite his claim to have done so, did not compile his own regulations but adhered to those already issued. On April 22, in the same general order that signaled the commencement of drill, Scott directed that "Everything respecting *camp* duties and the service of Guards will be governed by the Regulations of the War Office and when these are silent by Steuben's tract on *Police.*"[41] Six days later, Scott recommended that officers read those sections in Steuben concerning the march of an army, baggage on a march, the laying out of camps. cleanliness, roll calls, inspections, the maintenance of uniforms, arms and accoutrements, the service of guards, drum beats, and sick calls - in short, nearly all the activities of field service.[42] He also noted that where the published rules and regulations of the War Department differed from Steuben, the former took precedence.[43] In May, he directed his regimental commanders to mark and number their tents in accordance with the system contained in Smyth's *Regulations.*[44] The use of the published regulations at Buffalo did not change when Brown assumed command at that place on June 6 as Brown directed that all of Scott's orders concerning the administration of the camp "be continued and enforced."[45]

A similar case prevails with Scott's claim that, because the War Department had not issued a manual for infantry tactics, he had to adopt the 1791 French regulations.[46] This statement is not entirely accurate. In March 1812, the Secretary of War had authorized Smyth's *Regulations for the Field Exercise, Manoeuvres and Conduct of the Infantry* ... as the manual to be observed by the army but, a year later, replaced it with William Duane's *Hand Book for Infantry.* Duane's manual, basically an elementary

Brig. Gen. Zebulon Pike was one of many regular and militia officers who established camps of instruction.

text for militia, was disliked by regular officers and many, including Scott, refused to use it, opting instead to continue with Smyth or even use other manuals.[47] The result was not as chaotic as it might have been as both Smyth and Duane were basically abridgements of the French regulations and both prescribed similar formations and movements.[48]

Scott's problem at Buffalo was not the absence of an authorized manual, it was that he did not want to use that manual. Instead, he issued orders that all infantry training was to be based on the "French regulations or the system of discipline laid down by Smyth, which are the same."[49] Scott did not adopt the French regulations into the service, he simply authorized for the use of the Left Division an existing manual based on those regulations.

Scott also states that he formed "the officers of all grades, indiscriminately into squads, and personally instructed them in the schools of the soldier and company."[50] This statement, redolent of the gruff old drillmaster Steuben at Valley Forge, with its implication that American officers were not too proud to learn their lessons the hard way, is often included in descriptions of Scott's camp.[51] It should be noted in passing that the use of officers' training squads was not an American innovation but was fairly common practice in the British army during this period.[52]

Unfortunately, there is absolutely no mention of

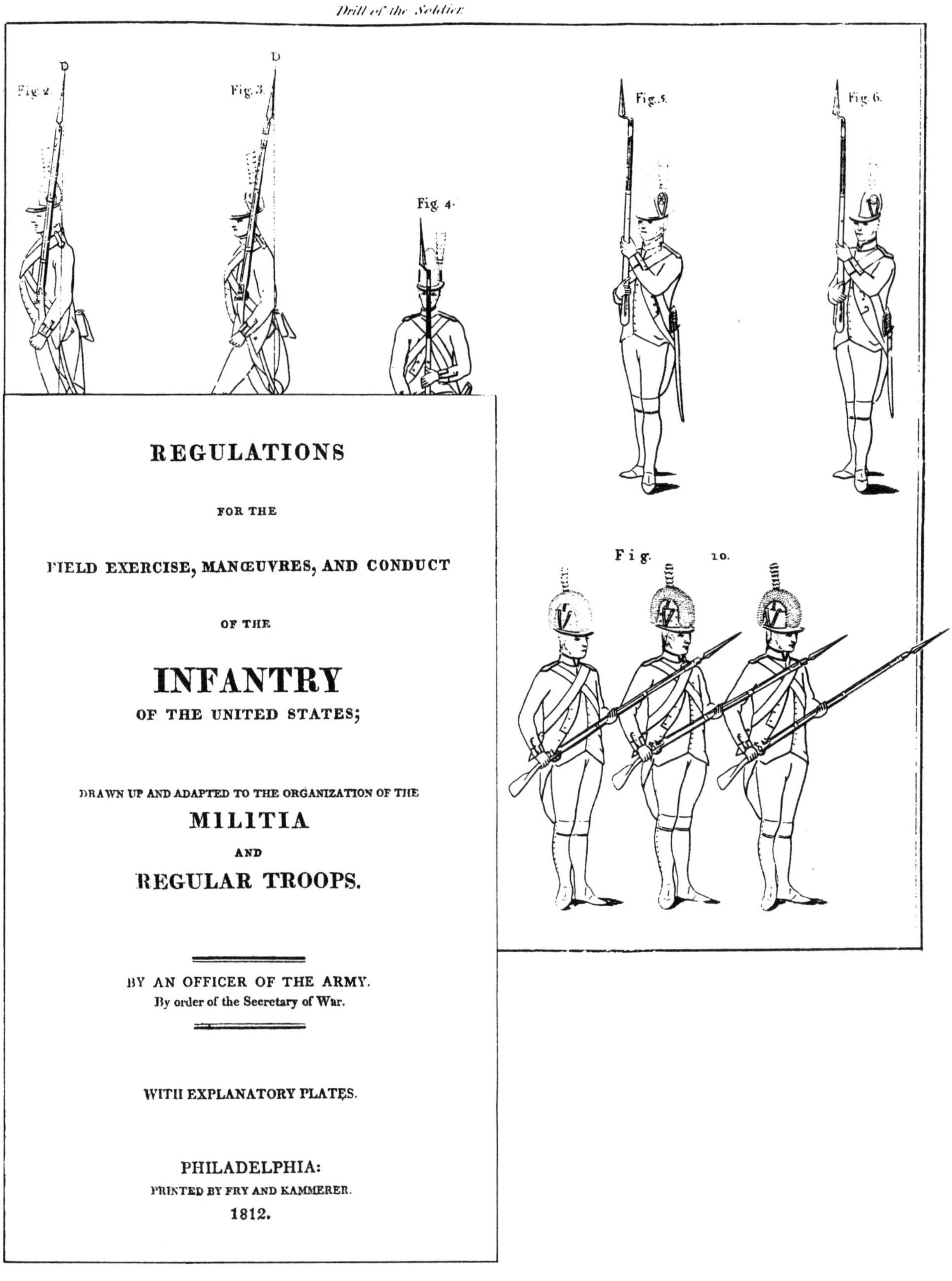

REGULATIONS

FOR THE

FIELD EXERCISE, MANŒUVRES, AND CONDUCT

OF THE

INFANTRY

OF THE UNITED STATES;

DRAWN UP AND ADAPTED TO THE ORGANIZATION OF THE

MILITIA

AND

REGULAR TROOPS.

BY AN OFFICER OF THE ARMY.
By order of the Secretary of War.

WITH EXPLANATORY PLATES.

PHILADELPHIA:
PRINTED BY FRY AND KAMMERER.
1812.

The plates of Smyth's 1812 *Regulations* bore the influence of their French origin. *Courtesy, Frederick C. Gaede.*

these squads in the daily orders issued by Scott at Buffalo from April to June 1814, and their absence is all the more conspicuous because any orders that Scott did issue concerning drill or training were usually very detailed. According to the brigade order book, instruction began on April 22 with company drill in the mornings and regimental drill under Scott's supervision in the afternoons and there are no orders forming officers' squads prior to that date.[53] The absence of such orders is even more puzzling because the orders regarding officers' squads issued by Hampton, who used them in 1813, have survived.[54] There is no reference to such squads in the eyewitness accounts of Scott's camp including that of Major Thomas S. Jesup, commander of the 25th Infantry, who does record other details relating to training.

Since Scott did not use the original French infantry regulations but only Smyth's translation and abridgement of those regulations, there really was no need for special officers' squads. Smyth's manual was familiar to most of the officers present and, as Scott was not introducing a new system, they would have had no need for special training. In the absence of any form of concrete evidence, I am forced to conclude that, if officers' squads existed at Buffalo, they did so only in Scott's mind.[55]

In his memoirs, Scott gives the impression that he trained the entire regular component of the division before it crossed the river to give battle.[56] This impression is not entirely accurate and an examination of just what units in the division were trained by Scott yields some interesting results.

In terms of the number of units belonging to it, the Left Division reached its greatest strength on July 25, 1814, the day of the battle of Lundy's Lane. On that date, the division was composed of two brigades of regular infantry: Scott's 1st Brigade with the 9th, 11th, 22nd, and 25th Infantry and Ripley's 2nd Brigade with the 1st, 21st and 23rd infantry and single "orphan" companies of the 17th and 19th infantry serving with the 21st. Other regular units in the division were a battalion of artillery, a company of bombardiers and a troop of regular light dragoons. New York Militia general Peter B. Porter commanded a third brigade composed of a regiment of Pennsylvania militia, a regiment of New York militia, a detachment of New York militia dragoons and a small party of mounted Canadian volunteers.[57]

Starting with Scott's 1st Brigade - the 9th and 25th infantry, but only part of the 11th and 22nd infantry, attended the camp for ten weeks. In Ripley's 2nd Brigade, only the 21st Infantry was present throughout the life of the camp; half of the 23rd infantry arrived just two days before the division crossed into Canada while the other half, as well as the 1st Infantry, only joined after the campaign had begun. The artillery battalion attended, but the bombardiers and dragoons did not. The militia fared even worse - only Willcocks's renegade unit was thoroughly trained - Fenton's Pennsylvanians got ten days of instruction while the New York units received none.[58]

If we translate this into numbers using the strength returns for July 25, it appears that only 46% - less than half of the troops in the division - were present during the entire period of the camp; 28% received less than two weeks of training while 26% received no instruction at all from Scott. While it is true that the majority of the regular infantry, the backbone of the division, were trained by Scott, the fact that over half of the division received little or no training at Buffalo is striking.[59]

Returning to the elements that form the legend of Scott's camp delineated earlier, we can see that this legend has been somewhat reduced in size. First, contrary to popular belief, Scott was not the only general in the American army who tried to train his troops thoroughly although he may have been the best trainer of men. Most of the soldiers that attended Scott's camp had received previous instruction and were far from being raw recruits. Scott did not train for three months as he claimed - only ten weeks. More importantly, he really trained only half the division, the remainder received little or no instruction from him - an omission that did not seem to adversely affect their performance in battle. Contrary to the statements in his memoirs, Scott did not change the army's infantry manual nor did he have to issue his own regulations on military administration - he relied on existing War Department manuals and regulations. Finally, there appears to be no evidence to support Scott's claim that he commenced by drilling his officer separately.

We are left with the facts that Brigadier General Winfield Scott maintained strict discipline, took proper sanitary precautions and drilled his men as rigorously and as often as possible. This is commendable but it is not so much the stuff of legend that Scott and later historians have made it out to be as it is the work of a professional officer - and Winfield Scott was nothing if not professional. Although I have been critical of Scott, my intention is not to downgrade his role in preparing the division for action but to place that role in proper perspective. I feel that the main reason for the Left Division's superior performance in battle was leadership - not only at the command level as demonstrated by Brown and Scott but also at lower levels.

Historians have paid perhaps too much attention to the senior officers of the division and not enough to the field and company officers. The Left Division was fortunate in that it possessed a wealth of intelligent and talented commissioned manpower which had considerable experience. The division included men like James Miller of the 21st who had won one of the

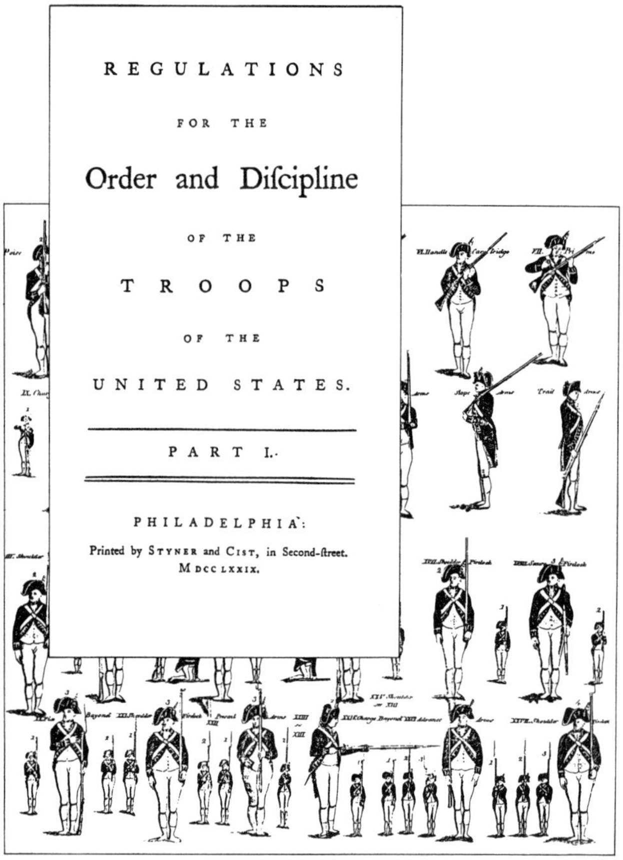

Title page and a plate from the 1779 edition of Steuben's *Regulations*.
Courtesy, Frederick C. Gaede.

army's earliest victories of the war at Magauga in August 1812, Thomas Jesup of the 25th who had seen the wrong way to do things with Hull at Detroit and the right way with Harrison at the Thames, and Hugh Brady of the 22nd who had fought with Wayne in the 1790s and continuously along the border since 1812. Even the weakest regular unit in the division, the hard-luck 23rd Infantry, was commanded by Daniel McFarland and George Brooke, two experienced officers with reputations for bravery. The division was just as fortunate with its artillery and engineers - the two field engineers, William McRee and Eleazer Wood, and the artillery commander, Jacob Hindman, were all veterans of nearly two years service on the northern frontier.[60]

The quality of the junior officers matched that of the field officers. By 1814, the "butterflies" - officers who served only in summer but left their units in winter to advance their careers in the sunnier climes of Washington - who had been so common in the earlier war years were largely gone from the frontier army. Although the division was under strength in terms of officers - Scott's brigade, for example, had only sixty-one of the 170 assigned to it - the junior officers present were highly motivated.[61] Even Scott, always spare with praise, thought them "decent and emulous of improvement."[62] Particularly notable were the gunners, all of whom had served with Scott's former regiment, the 2nd Artillery, which had fought in every major action on the border since October, 1812.

The presence of good and experienced officers and sound and experienced units eased Scott's task of preparing the Left Division for the field and what he provided was not basic training for green recruits but intensive training at an advanced level for veteran soldiers. Although only one half of the division received the full benefit of this training, they provided the steady cadre which formed its backbone. The Left Division was not so much the creation of one man as it was the culmination of two years of schooling in the hard lessons of war and its performance in the summer of 1814 showed that those lessons were well-learned. It is with good reason that a contemporary of the men of the Left Division could remark that they "have done honour to their country and given an imperishable name to the character of the American soldier."[63]

Notes

[1] I am aware that, properly, the Left Division encompassed all the units within the boundaries of Military District No. 9 not just those on the Niagara Frontier, but I have chosen to use the term "Left Division" for the force that fought in the Niagara campaign of 1814 rather than the more common "Army of the Niagara" because this is the term Brown used in his official dispatches and daily orders during the campaign.

[2] Maj. Gen. Phineas Riall to Lt. Gen. Gordon Drummond, July 6, 1814, National Archives of Canada, Ottawa (hereafter NAC), Record Group 8 I, vol. 684, p. 51; Drummond to Sir George Prevost, July 27, 1814, *Ibid.*, p. 235, .

[3] Memoir of General John LeCouteur, Societe Jersiaise, St. Heller.

[4] James Carmichael-Smyth, *Precis of the Wars in Canada ...* (London, 1862), p. 193.

[5] See, for examples, Henry Adams, *History of the United States During the Administration of James Madison* (9 vols.; New York, 1930, originally published 1890), VIII, pp. 28, 34-38; Charles W. Elliott, *Winfield Scott: The Soldier and the Man* (New York, 1937), pp. 146-50; Jeffery Kimball, "The Battle of Chippawa: Infantry Tactics in the War of 1812", *Military Affairs,* 31 (1967), 171-73, and "Strategy on the Northern Frontier", PhD. Thesis, Baton Rouge, 1969, pp. 190-97; James Jacobs and Glenn Tucker, *The War of 1812: A Compact History* (New York, 1969), pp. 130-31; Russell F. Weigley, *History of the United States Army* (New York, 1967), p. 129; John K. Mahon, *The War of 1812* (Gainesville, FL, 1972), pp. 266-67; Pierre Berton, *Flames Across the Border* (Toronto, 1980), pp. 288-90; George F.G. Stanley, *The War of 1812: Land Operations* (Ottawa, 1983), p. 300; D.K.R. Cresswell, "A Near Run Thing on the Niagara: The Battle of Lundy's Lane", in *Sharing Past and Future* (Toronto, 1988), pp. 33-56 and, most recently, Donald Hickey, *The War of 1812, A Forgotten Conflict* (Chicago, 1989), pp. 185-86.

[6] Winfield Scott, *Memoirs of Lieut. General Scott, L.L.D. Written by Himself* (2 vols.; New York, 1864), I, p. 118.

[7] *Ibid.,* I, p. 119.

[8] *Ibid.,* I, p. 121.

[9] Adams, VIII, p. 28.

[10] Stanley, p. 300; Jacobs & Tucker, pp. 130-31; Mahon, pp. 266-67; Weigley, pp. 127, 129; Elliott, pp. 144-60; Cresswell, 42-43. The exception is Kimball, "The Battle of Chippawa".

[11] Secretary of War to Maj. Gen. Henry Dearborn, July 9, 1812, Ernest Cruikshank (ed.), *Documentary History of the Campaign Upon the Niagara Frontier in 1812-1814* (9 vols.; Welland, Ontario, 1896-1908. Hereafter cited as *DH*), III, 119.

[12] Isaac Roach, "Journal of Major Isaac Roach, 1812-1824", *The Pennsylvania Magazine of History and Biography,* XVII, no. 2 (1893), 141-42.

[13] General Orders, Lewiston, August 19, 1812 and General Orders, Lewiston, August 28, 1812, *DH*, III, 195-96.

[14] Brig. Gen. Alexander Smyth to Gen. Stephen Van Rensselaer, October 2, 1812, *Ibid.,* IV, 28.

[15] Report on the State of the 14th Regiment, October 5, 1812, *Ibid.,* IV, 240-41.

[16] Maj. Gen. Morgan Lewis to Secretary of War, February 8, 1813, National Archives and Records Administration, Washington, D.C., Record Group 107, Microfilm 221, reel 54 (hereafter cited as NA, RG 107, M221 by reel number).

[17] John C. Fredriksen (ed.), "'A Poor But Honest Sojer': Colonel Cromwell Pearce, the 16th U.S. Infantry, and the War of 1812", *Pennsylvania History,* 52 (July 1965), 135.

[18] Lewis to the Secretary of War, March 27, 1813, NA, RG 107, M221, reel 54, .

[19] Orders, December 10, 1812, Queen's University, Kingston, Ontario, Fort Niagara Orderly Book, p. 9; Orders, January 18, 1813, *Ibid.,* p. 29; General Order, April 28, 1813, *Ibid.,* p. 78; McFarland to his Brother, February 2, 1813, in John N. Crombie (ed.) *The Western Pennsylvania Historical Magazine,* 51 (1968), 105.

[20] General Order, Fort Meigs, April 22, 1813, in Harlow Lindley (ed.), *Fort Meigs and the War of 1812* (Columbus, 1975), 12; General Order, Fort Meigs, June 15, 1813, *Ibid.,* 31.

[21] Secretary of War to Brig. Gen. John P. Boyd, July 7, 1813, *DH*, VI, 201.

[22] Maj. Gen. James Wilkinson to Gen. Jacob Brown, August 29, 1813, *Ibid.,* VII, 84; General Order, Fort George, September 18, 1813, *Ibid.,* 144.

[23] Regimental Order, 11th and 29th Regiments, n.d. (early July 1813) in "Garrison Orders, Burlington, Vermont, July 13-Aug. 4, 1813", *The Moorfield Antiquarian,* Vol. 1, no. 2 (1937), 82; General Order, Burlington, July 23, 1813, *Ibid.,* 86 .

[24] General Order, Burlington, July 27, 1813, *Ibid.,* 92.

[25] Strength of the Army at French Mills & Chateaugay, December 8, 1813, NA, RG 107, M222, reel 9.

[26] Scott, I, p. 119.

Col. James Miller, 21st U.S. Infantry, distinguished himself at the Battle of Lundy's Lane.

[27] General Order, April 22, 1814, New York State Library, Albany, Ms. 11225, Order Book of the 1st Brigade (hereafter cited as Order Book, NYSL). This document is described as the order book of the U.S. Army during the war on the Niagara Frontier, but it is actually the order book for the camp at Buffalo up to 6 June 1814 and of the 1st Brigade thereafter.

[28] General Order, April 22, 1814, Order Book, NYSL; Thomas S. Jesup, Memoir of the Campaign on the Niagara, Library of Congress, Washington, D.C., Thomas S. Jesup Papers, p. 1.

[29] General Orders, April 22 and May 1, 1814, Order Book, NYSL.

[30] Memoir of Jarvis Frary Hanks, Buffalo and Erie County Historical Society, Buffalo, NY, pp. 15-16.

[31] General Order, June 21, 1814, Order Book, NYSL.

[32] Elliott, p. 150.

[33] General Order, June 23, 1814, Order Book, NYSL.

[34] Elliott, p. 157.

[35] General Orders, June 13, 1814, Order Book, NYSL.

[36] Scott, I, p. 120.

[37] *Ibid.,* I, p. 119.

[38] Baron de Steuben, *Regulations for the Order and Discipline of the*

Troops of the United States (1779 and many subsequent printings).

[39]Smyth to Secretary of War, January 23, 1812, NA, RG 107, M222, reel 6. For a description of the contents of the manuals of Steuben and Smyth, see Donald E. Graves, "'Dry Books of Tactics': U.S. Infantry Manuals of the War of 1812 and After", Part I, *Military Collector & Historian,* XXXVIII, no. 2 (Summer 1986), 50-61.

[40]See *An Act Establishing Rules and Articles for the Government of the Armies of the United States with the Regulations of the War Department ...* (Albany, 1812); *Military Laws and Rules and Regulations for the Armies of the United States* (Washington, 1813); and *The Army Register of the United States* (Philadelphia, 1815) containing the regulations of the War Department to the spring of 1814.

[41]General Order, April 22, 1814, Order Book, NYSL. "Police" is used here in the military sense of camp discipline and sanitation.

[42]*Ibid.,* General Order, April 28, 1814,

[43]*Ibid.*

[44]*Ibid.,* General Order, May 19, 1814.

[45]*Ibid.,* General Order, June 6, 1814.

[46]Scott, I, pp. 119-20.

[47]For a discussion of the army's problems with manuals during the war, see Graves, "'Dry Books of Tactics'", Part I, 50-61.

[48]For a discussion of the introduction of French infantry tactics into the American military, see Donald E. Graves, "'From Steuben to Scott': The Adoption of French Infantry Tactics by the U.S. Army, 1807-1816", *Acta,* XIIIth International Colloquy on Military History, Helsinki, 1988.

[49]General Order, April 22, 1814, Order Book, NYSL.

[50]Scott, I, p. 120.

[51]See, for instance, Weigley, p. 129.

[52]See, for example, "Standing Orders of the 43rd Regiment", 1795 in J.F.C. Fuller, *Sir John Moore's System of Training* (London, 1925), p. 135 and B.W. Webb-Carter (ed.), "The Letters of William Bell, 89th Foot, 1809-1819", *Journal of the Society for Army Historical Research,* XLVIII (Summer 1970), 66.

[53]General Order, April 22, 1814, Order Book, NYSL.

[54]General Order, Burlington, July 23, 1813, "Garrison Orders, Burlington, Vermont", 86; General Order, HQ, Burlington, July 27, 1813, *Ibid.,* 92.

[55]I cannot come to any other conclusion in the absence of any firm evidence for the existence of officers' squads at Buffalo with the exception of statements in Scott's own memoirs which are not notable for their objectivity. Most historians have accepted Scott's word on this matter without question including his biographer, Charles Elliott, who was otherwise only too aware of his subject's shortcomings when describing his achievements, but, as far as I can ascertain, none of these historians has had access to Scott's order book for the camp at Buffalo.

[56]Scott, I, p. 118.

[57]Composition and strength of the Left Division extrapolated from: Strength of the American Army, July 25, 1814 contained in *Facts Relative to the Campaign on the Niagara in 1814* (Boston, 1815); "Strength of the American Army commanded by Major General Jacob Brown on the 23d of July 1814 being the last report of Brigades & Corps prior to the battle of the 25th of that month", Library of Congress, Washington, D.C., Jacob Brown Papers; "Muster Roll of a Detachment of U.S. Volunteers under the Command of Lieut. Colonel Joseph Willcocks ... to the 30th day of June, 1814", NA, RG 94, entry 125.

[58]The arrival of various units in the Left Division has been calculated from the NYSL Order Book, especially from General Orders, May 19, June 16, June 29, June 30, July 10, and Brigade Orders July 13, 1814. Further information has been extracted from: Symmes to Trimble, April 8, 1815 [1st Infantry], State Historical Society of Wisconsin, Madison, WI; Memorandum of Amasah Ford, 23rd Infantry, U.S. Army Military History Institute, Carlisle, PA; Hugh Dobbin Papers [New York Militia and Dragoons and Pennsylvania Militia], Geneva Historical Society, Geneva, NY; John C. Fredriksen (ed.), "Chronicle of Valor: The Journal of a Pennsylvania Officer in the War of 1812", *Western Pennsylvania Historical Magazine,* LXVII, no. 3 (July 1984), 281 [23rd Infantry] and Fredriksen, "The Pennsylvania Volunteers in the War of 1812: An Anonymous Journal of Service for the Year 1814", *Western Pennsylvania Historical Magazine,* LXX, no. 2 (April 1987), 149-51 [New York and Pennsylvania Militia]; Crombie, "McFarland", 119n [23rd Infantry]; Samuel D. Harris, "Service of Capt. Samuel D. Harris", *Buffalo Historical Society Publications,* 24 (1920), 333 [Dragoons]; John T. Horton (ed.), "An Original Narrative of the Niagara Campaign of 1814", *Niagara Frontier,* 46 (1964), 10 [Bombardiers]; Certificate of Maj. W.S. Foster in *Facts Relative to the Campaign on the Niagara in 1814* (Boston, 1815), 42 [11th Infantry]; Narrative of Alexander McMullen, a Private Soldier in Colonel Fenton's Regiment of Pennsylvania Volunteers, *DH,* II, 371-73 [Pennsylvania Militia and Canadian Volunteers]; and Lockwood L. Doty, *A History of Livingston County, New York* (Geneseo, 1876), pp. 317, 320-23 [New York Militia Infantry and Dragoons].

[59]Calculations based on strengths for the units contained in the returns listed in note 57 and in Adams, VIII, pp. 35-37.

[60]For biographical information on the officers of the Left Division, see John C. Fredriksen, *Officers of the War of 1812 with Portraits and Anecdotes* (Lewiston, NY, 1989).

[61]Calculation based on return of the officers in the 1st Brigade contained in Adams, VIII, p. 35 and names of those officers actually assigned to the brigade listed in *The Army Register of the United States* (Philadelphia, 1815).

[62]Scott to Gen. William Winder, May 6, 1814, quoted in Elliott, p. 148.

[63]Walworth to Simmons, Sept. 6, 1814, NAC, Manuscript Group 24, F 16.

A FLEET IN THE WILDERNESS
Shipbuilding at Sackets Harbor

by
Joseph M. Thatcher

One of the most impressive, and yet little known, episodes of the War of 1812 was the massive naval construction program undertaken by both British and American forces on Lake Ontario. Sackets Harbor and Niagara all saw enemy fleets, but apart from some inconclusive running fights like the "Burlington Races," no ship-to-ship combat occurred as happened on Lake Erie and Lake Champlain. Because neither Isaac Chauncey, American naval commander, nor his opponent, Sir James Lucas Yeo, were anxious to engage in a pitched battle without a clear superiority in numbers, their caution led to a tit-for-tat naval arms race, unprecedented in scope, especially considering the location.

When war was declared in June 1812, the British had five vessels, including three converted merchant schooners on the lake. American forces were represented only by the brig *Oneida,* sixteen guns, commanded by Melancton T. Woolsey, built in 1809 at Oswego to control smuggling on the lake. By war's end, in 1815, the British had built or converted fifteen more ships with two large ships of the line on the stocks. Chauncey had built or converted twenty-one ships, with two ships of the line and a large frigate under construction. Completed vessels ranged in size from fifty to ninety tons, to the frigate *Superior,* some 1,580 tons and twenty feet longer than the *Constitution,* and the *New Orleans* and *Chippewa* - 212 feet long and scheduled for 130 guns each - larger than anything America had yet built on the ocean.

The American base, naval and army headquarters and shipyard, was Sackets Harbor, New York, a small village near Watertown with a good harbor protected by a hooked spit of land which became know as Navy Point. As early as 1810, Woolsey had pointed out the value of the harbor should the navy need to build more ships. By late 1814, a system of earthworks, blockhouses and palisades surrounded a core of army and marine barracks, shipyard buildings, magazines, and the launching ways.

To head his ship building program, Chauncey brought Henry Eckford, a master shipbuilder from

The American armed schooners *Hamilton, Governor Tompkins* and *Julia* chase the British schooner *Simcoe* into the shelter of Kingston harbor. Unattributed watercolor. *Courtesy, New York State Office of Parks, Recreation and Historic Preservation, Sackets Harbor State Historic Site.*

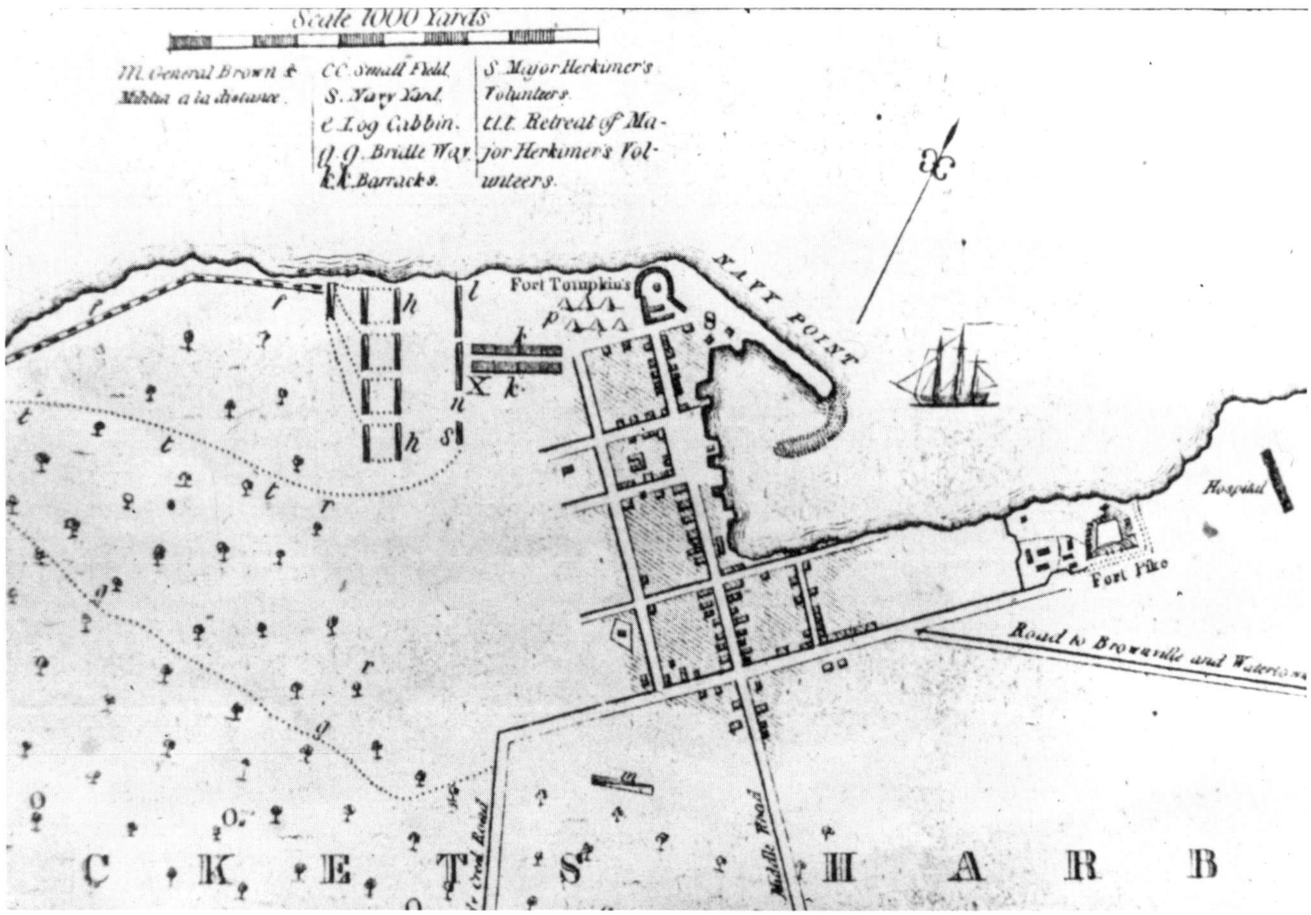

A map of Sackets Harbor, New York, showing the relationship of Navy Point to Fort Tompkins and major elements of the 1813 British attack.

New York, who had supervised the building of the *Oneida* and who built vessels for the navy after the war ended. As the build-up of men and material escalated, Eckford would have over 1,200 shipwrights and carpenters under contract. This figure does not include sailors, marines, soldiers, or support staff in this tightly packed community.

Eckford's first duty was to oversee conversion of two merchant schooners into armed naval vessels. The *Hamilton,* formerly *Diana,* merely had carronades added to her open bulwarks and a pivot gun, affording no protection for gun crews. The *Scourge,* formerly *Lord Nelson,* had its bulwark raised and planked and was armed with six-pounders on conventional carriages. Although the schooners converted by both sides produced a quick increase in fleet size, they were not successful as fighting ships. The weight of the guns severely strained them, and the high center of gravity caused by the guns made them exceptionally tender - sensitive to heeling. In fact, both of these ships sank during a gale in 1813 and still lie on the bottom, virtually intact.

Eckford's principal responsibility was to build new naval vessels, and he entered into this task with a will. Ships were built with a speed which today seems impossible. The *General Pike,* a ship-rigged, flush-decked corvette, rated as a twenty-four-gun vessel, was built and launched in only three months. With a keel of 145 feet and a displacement of 875 to 900 tons, the *Pike* was larger than the thirty-two-gun frigate *Essex* on the Atlantic. She carried twenty-eight long twenty-four-pounder guns and was apparently a handsome and well-finished ship. Chauncey, with an appreciation for quality, used the *General Pike* as his flagship until larger vessels were constructed. Following the launch of the *Pike,* several other small ships were built before two sister brigs were begun in January 1814. The *Jones* and the *Jefferson,* launched in early April, were modeled after the *Peacock,* also designed by Eckford for the ocean navy. They were 118 feet long and mounted sixteen or eighteen forty-two-pounder carronades and either four or two long twenty-four-pounders. A pivot gun planned for their forecastles was removed before their sailing as it caused them to be unstable. The main masts were also moved three feet aft soon after launch to improve their sailing qualities.

How could these ships be built so quickly, especially in a near wilderness? The *Jefferson* now lies on the bottom at Sackets Harbor and is revealing much

The *General Pike*, drawn by Charles Ware, showing the tall rig and large sail area favored by builders of the lake vessels. *Courtesy, National Archives and Records Administration.*

about the techniques which led to such fast construction through careful archaeological excavation sponsored in part by the New York State Office of Parks, Recreation and Historic Preservation and the National Geographic Society.

Accounts tell us that all the ships were built in very short time spans, but the *Jefferson* so far indicates that the work was carefully and neatly done. The ships were shallow draft, with hulls broad in beam but quite sharp - that is, with a steep rise. This would make them speedy but somewhat unstable, especially with the "tall" or large amount of canvas carried. Interior hull space was not important since no fresh water storage was required and food stuffs were only needed for cruises of a few weeks, rather than months.

The principal factor which hastened construction was Eckford's apparent decision to eliminate the use of heavy, shaped knees which, in conventional ships, supplied considerable stiffness and support. Instead, there was only a clamp timber, and the waterway to secure the deck beams. Planks were spiked rather than secured with wooded trunnels. These shortcuts generally were efficient, but the *Jefferson,* caught in a severe storm in 1814, worked badly with the weight of the guns, and the waterway began to separate. After limping into port, diagonal timbers, or riders, were added to help stiffen the hull.

By the end of the war, huge ships of the line were being built by both sides. The British launched the *St. Lawrence* in late 1814, and the Americans had two larger ships, the *New Orleans* and the *Chippewa,* framed and planked in only twenty-nine days. Both of these vessels would have carried 120 guns and dwarfed any ship America had on the ocean. One wonders where they would have berthed on Lake Ontario. Unfortunately, neither ship was finished.

After the war, the ships were placed in ordinary at Sackets Harbor and Kingston. Upper masts were lowered, guns and stores removed and wooden roofs built over the decks to shelter them. At Sackets Harbor, the *New Orleans* was housed in a huge wooden ship house, some 220 feet long, built over the stocks where the ship stood. It was a major tourist attraction in the nineteenth century and created difficulties for the Navy Yard staff who complained that the tourists dropped lit cigars in piles of wood chips and peered into residence windows.

The rest of the ships quickly began to rot. By 1818 the *Jefferson* was sunk and the others were going fast. By the mid-1820s most were sold and removed, al-

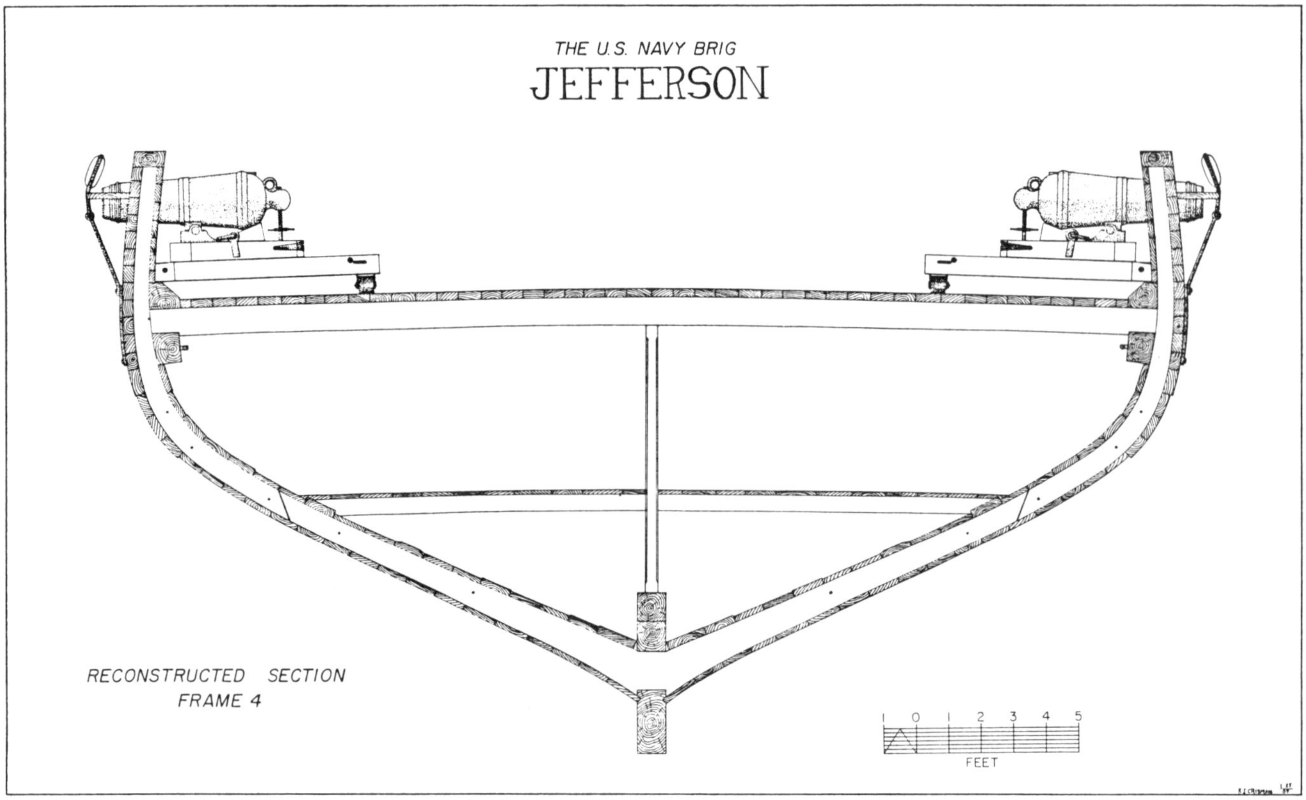

Midships section of the *Jefferson* illustrating the light construction without reinforcing knees. Drawing by Kevin Crisman. *Courtesy, New York State Office of Parks, Recreation and Historic Preservation.*

though some of this history is still unclear. Only the *New Orleans* remained in 1883 when it was finally scrapped, and the *Jefferson,* lying on the bottom and waiting for scientific exploration in the 1980s.

This is an all-too-brief summary of characteristics of the ships, which could not have been built without vast quantities of material and large numbers of men.

Chauncey's former flagship Superior, shown as it appeared decked over and "in ordinary" following the War of 1812.

Both came primarily from New York City and the other East coast population centers - up the Hudson to Albany, across the Mohawk, and then either up the Oswego River and by water to Sackets Harbor, or over land by Oneida Lake and the Black River. Cannon, shot, rope and cable, canvas, paint, and tar all came this way. A single forty-two-pounder carronade weighed almost 2,500 pounds, without slide, tackle or implements. The *Jefferson* carried eighteen of them. On one day, June 22, 1814, while the *Jones* was fitting out, 700 weight of bread, 800 weight of salt beef, 460 weight of salt port, plus flour, cheese, butter, whiskey, rice, peas, vinegar, and candles came aboard and were consumed long before the ship sailed weeks later. Not all of the supplies were military essentials. Chauncey outfitted each ship with a full set of cabin furnishings for the officers including table cloths, pans, decanters, a mirror, and candlesticks.

Most of this material made its tortuous trek from New York. At one point, rebellious teamsters dumped a shipment of cannon in the road near Poughkeepsie and walked off, forcing Chauncey to find new teamsters. The fact that so much reached Lake Ontario is a tribute to the skill and tenacity of the Navy agents.

Ships served primarily as platforms for their cannon, either the long range guns or the short range smashers - the carronades. The carronades were shorter and fired very heavy shot for their length.

The partially built ship of the line *New Orleans* at Sackets Harbor in 1883. The hull was exposed when the ship house which had covered it since 1815 blew down. *Courtesy, New York State Office of Parks, Recreation and Historic Preservation.*

They occupied less deck space and could do tremendous damage to an opponent but limited the vessel to close range combat. Longer range guns allowed a captain to damage his enemy before carronades could be used. Guns and carronades were both muzzle-loading, firing an iron ball with a charge of black powder. Guns, and especially carronades, could also fire cannister - a group of small iron balls packed in a large tin can. When fired, the can burst, spraying the balls along an enemy deck. Some other types of bar or double-headed shot could also be used to damage rigging, making the vessel more difficult to maneuver. Many of the guns used on Lake Ontario were sent from naval vessels idled by the British blockade on the East coast. The forty-two-pounder carronades used on the *Jones* and *Jefferson* had come from the spar decks of the frigates *United States* and *President.* Some of the guns made during the war were of questionable quality. Arthur St. Clair, captain of the *Pike,* reported after an eighteen-pounder burst in battle, killing and wounding some of the crew, that many of the guns were of poor quality, with flaws filled with lead - "an example of Yankee trickery."

Cannon were generally fired with flintlocks, designed for attachment to the gun. Slow match and priming horn were reserved for emergency use, since locks offered faster, surer ignition. Chauncey requested locks for all his cannon and the log of the *Jones* mentions the armorer was on board fitting locks to the guns, and an example of a lock made for a carronade has been excavated at Sackets Harbor.

Small arms were requisitioned as well. Muskets, pistols, boarding pikes, axes, and cutlasses were all requested, and would have been used in close combat when boarding another ship. Cutlasses used by both sides were nearly identical, with straight blades, iron

Dress uniforms worn by United States Navy officers and seamen during the War of 1812. Drawing by H. Charles McBarron. *Courtesy, the Company of Military Historians.*

In a successful combined action, the American fleet landed U.S. troops at Ft. George on May 27, 1813. American-held Ft. Niagara is at left. The vessels, from left to right, are probably the schooners *Julia, Growler, Lady of the Lake,* and *Ontario,* the flagship *Madison,* schooners *Hamilton* and *Scourge,* the brig *Oneida,* and two more schooners, probably the *Governor Tompkins* and *Conquest.* This near-contemporary drawing was published in the July 1817 edition of *Portfolio.*

figure eight guards and cast iron grips. On the sunken *Scourge,* two of these are crossed over each gun port.

One interesting sidelight to the small arms story is Chauncey's request to the New York Navy Yard for fifty each of muskets and pistols, and seven-barrel swivels of the Chambers repeating pattern. These were the so-called "Roman Candle" guns, designed to fire multiple charges one after the other, in an unstoppable sequence. Quick match was inserted in a hole through the center of the bullets, carrying fire to the next powder charge. Chauncey did receive at least some of these weapons and Chambers' son, rated as a gunner, came along to instruct the sailors in their use. Although touted as a super weapon, one of these "Roman Candles" in the hands of a sailor or marine in a rolling top might have had interesting, if not disastrous results.

Benson Lossing's drawing of the bow of the *New Orleans,* still sheltered under its ship house at the time of the Civil War, gives an idea of the massive size of the American ship of the line.

Men were also a problem. When Chauncey was given the lake command in 1812, he quickly sent seven hundred marines and sailors to Lake Ontario. This was to prove a drop in the bucket as the number of ships rapidly increased. The marines, quartered at Fort Tompkins, adjacent to Navy Point, had to be supplemented by artillerymen detailed to man the tops with muskets during action. Sailors were recruited as fast as possible, but many men were reluctant to go into the interior. As ships were blockaded on the Atlantic by the British, however, entire crews were removed and detailed to the west. Charles Ridgeley and the crew of U.S.S. *Erie* were sent to man the newly launched *Jefferson.* Landsmen were also shipped, and merchant sailors were offered extra pay and allowances. Even so, the ships were usually under-manned, and the high disease rate often had as many as twenty percent of a crew on sick call. Nevertheless, by late 1814 there were 2,300 American sailors and marines on Lake Ontario, out of a total naval force of 10,617. At the same time the three vessels at sea had only 450 men between them. It is obvious that the lakes were a major drain on navy resources and were considered important, even though President Madison questioned the wisdom of committing so much to the frontier.

Although there were no uniform regulations for seamen at this time, the slop clothing requested by Chauncey included frocks, trousers, jackets, vests, hats, and handkerchiefs, all common sailor garb. Indications are that the crews were well clothed, even though Chauncey complained that some of the shipments were of sizes too small for his men.

This, then, is an all too hasty survey of the lake navy - a navy which built impressive ships but rarely fought any action - a fleet which never had the recognition of those on Lakes Erie and Champlain but which once ruled the waters of Lake Ontario.

Flintlock firing mechanism for a carronade, found at Sackets Harbor. Commodore Chauncey ordered locks for all the guns of his fleet to insure more certain ignition in battle. *Courtesy, New York State Office of Parks, Recreation and Historic Preservation, A.SA.1988.508.*

SOURCES

Much of the information on the brig *Jefferson* is derived from reports of the underwater archaeology performed by Dr. Kevin J. Crisman and Arthur Cohn with support from the New York State Office of Parks, Recreation and Historic Preservation from 1984 until 1988. Additional information came from files in the Bureau of Historic Sites, and from Gary Ernest and Patrick Wilder, Sackets Harbor State Historic Site.

Manuscript sources include:

William L. Clements Library, Ann Arbor, Michigan.
Isaac Chauncey Letter Books, Volume III

Historical Society of Pennsylvania, Philadelphia, Pennsylvania.
Uselma Clarke Smith Collection, William Jones Papers.

Library of Congress, Washington, D.C.
Naval Historical Foundation Collection, Charles G. Ridgeley Letter Books.

National Archives and Records Administrations, Washington, D.C.
Record Group 45, various entries, Naval Records Collection of the Office of Naval Records and Library.

New York Historical Society, New York, New York.
Isaac Chauncey Letter Books, Volumes I and II.

Royal Military College of Canada Museum, Kingston, Ontario.
Watercolor of Sackets Harbor by E.E. Vidal.

Published sources included:

Cain, Emily. *Ghost Ships.* New York: Beaufort Books, 1983.

Chapelle, Howard Irving. *The History of the American Sailing Navy.* New York: W.W. Norton and Co., 1949.

Crisman, Kevin. *The Eagle: An American Brig on Lake Champlain During the War of 1812.* Shelburne, VT and Annapolis, MD: The New England Press and the Naval Institute Press, 1987.

Roosevelt, Theodore. *The Naval War of 1812.* New York: P.F. Collier and Son, 1882.

William Berczy, Sr. made this portrait of the Mohawk war chief Joseph Brant in the 1790s. Note the scalp lock, rifle, powder horn, hunting pouch, and mix of European and native clothing. *Courtesy, National Gallery of Canada, 5777.*

IROQUOIS WARFARE, 1812-1814

by
Carl Benn

The focus of my presentation is the Iroquois as a military force in the War of 1812. But before I address that topic, I would like to give a brief anthropology lesson on the Iroquois as background to my main discussion.

The Iroquois Confederacy originally was composed of five of the Iroquoian tribes of the Great Lakes region: the Mohawks, Oneidas, Onondagas, Cayugas, and Senecas, who occupied New York State between roughly the Mohawk and Niagara Rivers. About 1722, a sixth Iroquoian tribe, the Tuscaroras, joined the confederacy, hence "the League of the Six Nations". By 1812, the Iroquois were split into three main groups.

The largest group was composed of league members who lived on reservations in New York which had been created following the American Revolution. During the War of 1812, many of these tribesmen fought with the United States, being chiefly engaged in assisting the American army during the blockade of Fort George in 1813 and with Peter B. Porter's brigade in the early phases of the 1814 Niagara campaign. Their greatest success was the defeat of the British-allied native force at the Battle of Chippawa.

The second group was composed of Loyalist Iroquois who had moved to Upper Canada after the American Revolution. Most of these people settled on a reserve along the Grand River just west of the Niagara Peninsula. Men from the Grand River Reserve fought on the British side, primarily at Queenston Heights and throughout the Niagara campaigns of 1813 and 1814.

The third group was composed mainly of individuals whose ancestors had moved to seven French mission settlements along the St. Lawrence River in the seventeenth and eighteenth centuries. Collectively, they were known as the Seven Nations of Canada. Although dominated by the Iroquois, they included non-league Iroquoians such as Hurons, plus non-Iroquoian people, like the Algonkians. They fought with the British in the defense of Montreal in 1812 and 1813 and at Sackets Harbor, Beaver Dams, the blockade of Fort George, and Chrysler's Farm in 1813.

Like the Seven Nations, the New York and Upper Canadian Iroquois included non-league people, such as Delawares, who had come to live with the Iroquois in large numbers, plus people - native, white, and black - who had entered the Iroquois tribes as refugees, as prisoners, or who had simply chosen to live within the league. Likewise, many Iroquois had left their homes and had emigrated to other native communities.

I

Iroquois warfare in the early nineteenth century was influenced by a number of factors. The primary one was culture: modes of fighting were employed which best conformed to Iroquois concerns and priorities. One key priority was the necessity to minimize casualties. Native peoples in the Great Lakes region did not understand why whites thought so highly of dying bravely in battle.[1] For the tribespeople, death was a horrible calamity to be avoided at almost any cost. Furthermore, Iroquois society was small in numbers, and warriors also had roles as husbands and providers. Therefore, Iroquois society could not hope to survive if it suffered heavy casualties.

The underlying personal military aspirations of the chiefs and warriors were other important cultural priorities. When an Iroquois volunteered to take to the warpath, he did so primarily to prove to his community that he was a skillful and fearless fighter. By demonstrating these qualities, he could prove his manhood and win self- and community esteem. Therefore, a warrior fought in a much more individualistic and independent manner than his white contemporaries did; and, once he had proved his warrior skill, he frequently chose to return home rather than stay on campaign. Religion also played a role in preventing the Iroquois from remaining on long campaigns. As the Grand River Mohawk war chief John Norton wrote:

> *One encounter is all that is sought for in an expedition, and when it is met with, they say "This is the fortune, the Great Spirit has prepared for us."*[2]

The second key factor affecting Iroquois warfare was technology. There had been a radical change in

The Mohawk village on the Grand River, drawn in 1793 by Elizabeth Simcoe. *Courtesy, Archives of Ontario, Simcoe Sketch 75.*

native warfare in the two centuries from the Iroquois' first contact with whites in the early seventeenth century as a result of the adoption of more destructive European weaponry.

Fundamentally, what had developed by 1812 among the Iroquois was a form of aboriginal warfare which was very different from both native warfare at the time of initial contact, because of the widespread use of white technology, and from white warfare because of different cultural priorities.

II

The Iroquois used a variety of weapons: muskets, bayonets, rifles, pistols, bows, knives, tomahawks, clubs, swords, and spears. The most common weapons were firearms, tomahawks, and knives. The British gave their Iroquois allies four different types of firearms: common guns or muskets, chiefs' guns, rifles, and pistols.

Common muskets, patterned closely after trade guns, were similar to military firearms but fired a slightly smaller ball and had a somewhat shorter barrel.[3] Common guns cost the Crown about twenty-one to twenty-eight shillings each, which implies they were good weapons since the British Army's Tower musket cost about twenty-five shillings.[4]

Chiefs' guns were better quality weapons than common muskets. They resembled sporting guns, being more elegant than common guns, but usually had the same barrel length and fired the same size ball as a common gun. The wrist of the stocks of these muskets were decorated with an inlaid silver medallion showing the likeness of a native.[5]

The British-issued pistols were similar in design to light dragoon pistols.[6] Pistols seem to have been particularly desirable possessions, perhaps because officers often carried them, which associated these weapons with rank and prestige.[7]

The rifles presented by the British government were constructed in the style of the Pennsylvania Rifle with a longer barrel than a musket and a seven-grooved bore.[8] This rifle had a longer range and was more accurate than the military-issue Baker Rifle, but its killing power was significantly less because the bullets it fired were smaller.[9]

Complete records of weapons issued to the Iroquois do not exist. However, there are some statistics which give an impression of the relative importance of each kind of firearm. The Board of Ordnance supplied the Indian Department with 26,801 firearms between 1813 and 1816 to issue to native allies in the Great Lakes region. Of these weapons, 46.7% were common guns, 37.8% were chiefs' guns, 9.8% were pistols, and 5.7% were rifles.[10] There is the possibility that the percentage of rifles represented by the Board of Ordnance supply was lower than the norm because most early nineteenth century commentators on the British-allied Iroquois spoke of the Iroquois carrying rifles.[11] As well as receiving specially made firearms as gifts, the Iroquois obtained weapons after battles and through trade.[12]

As there are no records of bayonets being issued, it is likely that they were acquired only as battlefield trophies along with soldiers' muskets.[13] Because of the different barrel diameter of native muskets from military arms, bayonets would not have fitted properly onto native muskets. The Iroquois likely did not consider bayonets to be particularly useful weapons since there are relatively few references made to them, although bayonets were used at least occasionally.[14]

Presumably, the range of weapons given to the American-allied Iroquois by the United States gov-

Iroquois gunstock club, date uncertain. *Courtesy, Royal Ontario Museum, 27050.*

ernment was similar to that issued by the British to their native allies. The only major differences were that the New York Iroquois seemed to have been armed overwhelmingly with rifles and the American-issue weapons generally were of poor quality. Issuing rifles in quantity is not surprising as the Americans tended to equip a relatively large portion of their militia and volunteers with rifles. Brigadier General Peter B. Porter, who exercised overall command of the New York Iroquois in American service, even believed that muskets were unsuitable for native warfare.[15]

In 1814, about half of the Iroquois mustered for United States service were armed with their own rifles, and the American army ordered rifles for the rest.[16] These were Pennsylvania-style rifles rather than Harper's Ferry military rifles, and those given by the Americans were considered by American authorities to be both substandard in their manufacture and inferior to the Iroquois' own rifles.[17] The muskets issued by the Americans were very poor as well; but, in an attempt to appeal to native preferences for better-quality British goods, they were made to look like British weapons.[18] Carbines (or short, lighter muskets) also were made for native peoples by the Americans.[19]

Firearms were the Iroquois' primary shooting weapons. Yet, bows still seem to have been used as late as the War of 1812. A traveller among the native peoples in the Great Lakes region saw bows in 1798, and a watercolor from the 1820s shows Iroquois using bows and arrows for hunting.[20] The use of bows in children's socialization for war was common in the early nineteenth century. Bows and arrows, therefore, still were considered to be part of Iroquois military training.[21] From statements on both sides which indicate that not all warriors had firearms, it seems likely that an unarmed Iroquois might furnish himself with a bow and arrows.[22]

At close quarters, the Iroquois' usual weapons were tomahawks, clubs, spears, swords, and knives. Except for clubs and some spears, these weapons were supplied by whites. British inventories of material sent to Upper Canada for the natives included pocket knives, clasp knives, butchers' knives, spears or "Indian lances", chiefs' swords, and hangers (short, often slightly-curved, swords), half axes, and pipe tomahawks.[23]

The tomahawk could be employed as a striking weapon.[24] Alternatively, it could be thrown, as described by William Dunlop of the 89th Regiment of Foot:

> *I ... requested the Chief to show me how he threw the tomahawk. He accordingly cut a small chip out of the bark of a tree, and standing some fourteen yards off, and taking his tomahawk with its pole to the front, he threw it, and it was buried some inches into the oak, with the handle utmost, it having turned round in its flight.*[25]

There are records of both spears being supplied by the British Indian Department and of warriors making their own spears.[26] Although spears could be thrown, they seem to have been used principally as thrusting weapons as was common with contemporary white use of pikes.[27] It seems likely that a spear would have been a particularly desirable weapon in hand-to-hand combat given that most natives did not have bayonets on their firearms and may otherwise have been at a disadvantage against the reach a bayonet on a musket gave a white soldier.

Traditional clubs still were in use at the time of the war.[28] The most common was the ball-headed club, so-called because the striking end was a solid ball of wood. Some ball-headed clubs were made more vicious by the addition of a metal spike at the striking end of the ball. Another traditional club was the carved and painted gunstock club which resembled an inverted gunstock and usually had an iron or steel striking point on its underside.[29] Both kinds of clubs often bore carved representations of the owner's exploits or likenesses of his guardian spirits or spirits associated with war or the underworld and were painted and decorated with feathers.[30]

An American writing of the British-allied natives at the time of the war described a typical warrior's weaponry:

> *The armour of the Indians in time of war, are a rifle, a spear about 18 inches long with a handle 8 feet, a tomahawk, and scalping knife, all of which they use as instruments of death.*[31]

In assessing the abilities of native warriors, John Askin of the Detroit frontier declared that, in the bush, one native warrior was equal to three white men.[32] Although Askin's comment was made in reference to the western tribes, Iroquois warfare fundamentally was the same as that of their western neighbors.[33] As a kind of light infantry force - and it was in light infantry roles that the Iroquois were employed by their white allies - the Iroquois usually surpassed whites, including professional soldiers, even though white regulars possessed more discipline, a much wider range of tactical options, and usually suffered a lower desertion rate in action than the Iroquois. Against less well-trained militia, the Iroquois always demonstrated superior military skills. What mainly gave the Iroquois their advantage was better training.

It seems strange to speak of training when referring to the Iroquois because the concept of military training normally conjures up purely white images; but the Iroquois prepared people for war from childhood, and warlike practices were useful in hunting and other non-combative pursuits, whereas whites rarely possessed any military training before enlistment, and the soldierly arts were mainly useless outside of the military. This combination of a long training period and a more universal application of skills to the broader needs of native society resulted in increased prowess and a higher sense of the value of that prowess among the Iroquois warrior than it did among the rank and file of the American or British armies.

Boys in Iroquois society learned hunting skills at an early age.[34] These skills - stalking, ambush, survival techniques, familiarity with the environment, proficiency with knife and hatchet, and good marksmanship - enabled an Iroquois to feed his family. In warfare, these very same skills were used to fight the enemy. These abilities and warlike attitudes were developed and encouraged through both warlike games among children and by allowing young people to accompany war parties part of the way from their homes.

Adult males were kept fit and trained by the hunt and through leisure activities such as tomahawk throwing and lacrosse. The keen sense of independence and competence in a hostile environment, plus excellent physical development and stamina resulting from the natives' lives, was excellent preparation for the warpath.

One area in which the Iroquois seemed to have been superior to whites as a result of their way of life was marksmanship. As early as the 1660s, Europeans commented on how well the Iroquois handled their firearms.[35] Natives even modified white technology to improve their marksmanship by carving out part of the comb on their gunstocks so that they could sight their weapons better by being able to line up their eyes along the barrels more easily.[36] The Iroquois claimed that whites did not know how to shoot, accusing them of holding "their guns half man high", meaning that whites did not take as careful an aim as natives did.[37] One observer declared that the Iroquois were expert marksmen by the age of ten.[38] A post-war writer believed that it was the "unerring fire of their rifles" which made natives a serious threat to white troops.[39] The Iroquois also may have been the originators of the practice of trying to "pick off" officers in North American battles as they believed "the men will naturally be thrown into confusion when their leaders are dead."[40] They also seem to have supplemented their firepower by adding buck shot to their ball in battle, at least on occasion.[41]

Accuracy in using firearms came with practice from years of hunting. This contrasts markedly with the experience of British and American troops. Few British soldiers, and probably only a minority of American regulars, had ever held a firearm before joining the army. A typical British infantryman, once in the army, might be given as few as sixty blank and thirty ball cartridges each year for musketry practice (although light troops usually were given more).[42] American infantry apparently had even less musketry training.[43] Many American and Canadian militiamen and volunteers from frontier environments had experience with firearms, but it is likely that only a small number of them had as much practice as the

Iroquois. Therefore, the Iroquois generally had much more practice in the use of firearms than whites did. Furthermore, because of their better physical condition, they did not become winded and unsteady when aiming their rifles as often as white troops did.

Another example of Iroquois superiority was in the use of their primary edged weapon, the tomahawk, as compared to white use of the bayonet. There was very little bayonet training provided in the British army, and since the British used their bayonets more often than the Americans did, it may be assumed that there was even less emphasis placed on that weapon by the Americans. In contrast, William Dunlop described a scene in which some natives made skilled use of their tomahawks during the siege of Fort Erie in 1814:

> *When their opponents were from fifteen to twenty yards in advance of them, they threw their tomahawks with unerring aim and great force, burying the head of the hatchet up to the eye in the body of their opponents.*[44]

To be effective, training for battle had to move beyond preparing individuals for combat to include tactical training for the cooperative maneuvering of a force and the control of that force by its leaders. Although there are few records of tactical training among the Iroquois, their performance in the field clearly indicates that such training must have occurred. Previous to European contact in the seventeenth century, the Iroquois employed a double-line tactic which required both leadership and tactical training. In battle, one line, armed with bows, discharged volleys at the enemy. If shock was required, the second line, protected by wooden armor, charged and used clubs to knock down the enemy. The archers, not wearing armor and thus more mobile, then could assist the other line by rushing into the fray to use their clubs against anyone who tried to run away.[45] With the introduction of firearms and iron projectile points for their arrows and spears, armor was abandoned and new tactics were developed to utilize the new technology. Emphasis now was placed on mobility and ambush.[46] However, the Iroquois retained the basic concept of deployment in line which demanded tactical training and a functioning system of command. In the 1750s, one person described Iroquois warfare in a way which assumes tactical training and a certain amount of leadership. He wrote that the Iroquois moved in formation with each man observing the movement of the man on his right. This allowed lines as long at 1,500 metres to travel "for a considerable distance without disorder or confusion," and he noted that the Iroquois were capable of forming circles, semi-circles and squares as required. All of these strongly suggest a high degree of tactical training.[47] (These lines were, of course, not the same as the tight, two or three rank formations of white line troops, but were single or double ranks of spread-out men.) As mentioned earlier, however, warriors acted quite independently once battle had been joined at which time large-scale cooperation became restricted.

In addition to employing their own tactical theories, there is evidence that white tactics were employed by the Iroquois in the early nineteenth century, at least on the Grand River Reserve. Prior to the outbreak of war, one individual wrote, "I have seen the forces of the Six Nations reviewed by Col. Brandt [sic] at their annual parade on the 1st of May."[48] Another recorded that the Six Nations warriors "are exercised in the military use of arms, several times in the year."[49] These events sound very much like typical Upper Canadian militia musters. Even the rank of colonel given to Joseph Brant accords with the image of a militia regimental organization. Furthermore, Major John Norton, the principal Grand River Mohawk war chief between 1812 and 1814, had served in the British army between 1784 and 1788, and may have studied the military sciences while on a visit to England in 1804.[50] Given Norton's background, the militia musters, and the fact that many of the Iroquois had fought closely with Loyalist regiments during the American Revolution, it seems probable that some white tactical doctrine had been absorbed by the Iroquois.[51]

Another aspect of military training was the development of martial attitudes and sensibilities to sustain someone in the terror and confusion of battle. In white armies, a soldier's attitudes and sensibilities were developed through socialization to his regiment, a distinct uniform, traditions, martial music, ceremonies, barrack-room lore, training, and discipline. Likewise, the Iroquois warrior experienced a socialization for war from childhood as part of his military development.

As mentioned earlier, warfare gave a male Iroquois a socially acceptable opportunity to prove his manhood and win self and community esteem, and offered one of the few chances men had of rising to community leadership since most peace chiefs acquired their positions through hereditary succession.[52] The example of advancement based on wartime leadership and the legends and traditions associated with martial ardor which filled an individual's mind, along with the recognition one received for skills which could be applied to combat, were part of the process of socializing warriors for battle. The socialization was cemented further by the desire to conform to the community's ethical and moral standards which acknowledged the value of the warrior spirit.[53] Religion and wartime ceremonial also were rich in emotion and morale-boosting qualities to prepare a man to be an effective warrior.[54]

Iroquois battle dress was part of that socialization and seems to have had many of the same functions as

Detail of a Mohawk from Benjamin West's "Death of Wolfe", painted in the 1770s. West was familiar with the Mohawks and this portrait of a warrior, although idealized, contains interesting information on the appearance of an Iroquois combatant. Unlike military uniforms, Iroquois "battle dress" did not change substantially from the 1770s to the War of 1812. *Courtesy, National Gallery of Canada, 8007.0.1.*

white battle dress, both in practical and cultural terms. It provided suitable costuming in relation to the available technology, boosted the wearer's morale, and intimidated the enemy. A major difference between white and Iroquois dress was that the Iroquois wore far fewer clothes which allowed for greater freedom of movement. This must have seemed exotic to whites in an age when most people covered their bodies extensively and constantly. Iroquois battle dress also gave the warrior greater physical mobility than his less fit white adversary whose equipment might weigh 50% more than an Iroquois'. In close combat, the Iroquois warrior may also have had an advantage over his white opponent by smearing bear's grease on his body, partly as protection against the weather and insects, but mainly to make him slippery and hard to grab.[55]

About all an Iroquois warrior wore in combat was a breech cloth, leggings and moccasins[56] or white soldier's "beef boots"[57] plus his weaponry. To this was added a belt, a powder horn - particularly if he used a rifle[58] - and a pouch, loosely modelled after a white cartridge box but decorated with images of guardian spirits (such as thunderbirds, underwater panthers and horned serpents), for cartridges, spare flints and other necessaries.[59] Ball-headed clubs apparently were worn in the belt in front, whereas tomahawks were worn in a girdle at the warrior's back.[60] Writing after the war, nineteenth century American historian William Stone described the battle dress of the American-allied Iroquois:

> *It was the uniform practice of our Indian warriors, when going into action, to divest their persons of all covering excepting moccasins, perhaps leggings, a breech-cloth, a large tuft of white feathers fastened to the hair on the crown of the head, and a small string plaited line or belt, three or four yards long ... girt about their waist, to secure the tomahawk, knife, powder-horn, &c., and used if necessary to bind their prisoners. Their naked bodies and faces were then painted with bold and gaudy colors, without uniformity, and generally, though not always, without much taste or design* [in Stone's opinion].[61]

Culturally, just as white troops sported uniform features without practical value, but which served to heighten self-esteem and group-identity, Iroquois warriors utilized decoration for the same purposes, such as the body paint and the feather ornamentation just mentioned. Not all the feathers came from domestic birds: imported ostrich and peacock feathers also were popular.[62] Feathers were regarded as signs of war powers received from the thunderbirds.[63]

Warriors usually painted their bodies red and decorated the red with streaks in black (and sometimes with other colors).[64] Red and black were a particularly appropriate combination of colors for warriors because of red's association with life and black's with danger and death.[65]

Mohawks, and possibly other Iroquois, also seem to have used tattoos to ornament themselves. Tattoos usually were applied at puberty after a boy experienced a successful vision quest. They were created by sketching a design on the skin with charcoal or chalk, then pricking the skin with an awl, and finally rubbing whatever color the warrior desired into the wounds. Geometric patterns were common as were representations of guardian spirits.[66]

Another important decorative feature used to boost morale and identify the warrior with Iroquois military tradition was a scalp knot. This was a long, easily grabbed strip of hair on the warrior's otherwise shaved head. It was worn theoretically to taunt an enemy into trying to take it, but probably served more to heighten the warrior's self-esteem and link him emotionally to the Iroquois military tradition.[67] The Iroquois also may have believed that power was concentrated in the scalp lock.[68] It should be noted that the scalp lock was not the famous "Mohawk" haircut of popular imagination running along the centre of the scalp from the front to the back of the head. Rather, it was a circle of long hair located at the centre of the scalp, and often was decorated with feathers, silver, and other ornamentation.

Another ornament was a circular gorget, worn on the chest. Originally gorgets were made of white shell and wampum, but most were silver by 1812. The shape of the gorget was a sun image, an appropriate wartime image because the sun was associated with war. Shell, and its analogue, silver, were considered to be gifts of underworld spirits.[69]

III

When on the warpath, the Iroquois took every precaution to prevent themselves from being surprised and to create a situation in which they could surprise their enemy. As much as possible, they engaged in a reconnaissance of the enemy to assess his strength before committing themselves. Warriors, from their hunting experience, were adept at analysing the number of persons and the length of time an enemy had passed a given spot by examining the condition of the ground over which their opponents had trod, unless the enemy numbers were very small, leaving little trace of their passing, or if rain had obliterated the evidence.[70] Whenever they believed the enemy to be near, scouts were sent out.[71] Unlike most other tribes of the Great Lakes region, the Iroquois also posted sentries at night to avoid a surprise attack.[72]

The classic Iroquois tactic, as was the case with neighboring tribes, was ambush.[73] Traditionally, the Iroquois preferred to surround their enemy in darkness in order to launch a surprise assault at dawn.[74] The purposes of this form of attack were to confuse and over-extend their opponents, thus crippling their ability to respond effectively, and thereby increase the Iroquois' chances of achieving victory with relatively few casualties. Although the Iroquois rarely employed a dawn surprise assault during the War of 1812, Iroquois tactical doctrine was dominated by the underlying principles of over-extending and confusing the enemy in order to upset the enemy's equilibrium so that victory could be attained at little cost.

Another ambush tactic employed by the Iroquois consisted of concealing themselves in a semi-circle across the path of an advancing enemy. Once posted, they would wait until the enemy fell into the trap.[75] Again, the basic philosophy was to confuse the enemy and upset his equilibrium to maximize the potential of success and minimize casualties.

They used these same principles when launching an assault on an enemy in situations where ambush was inappropriate. As the warriors got near their enemy, they usually moved with great rapidity and silence towards their target. To make it difficult for the enemy to outflank them, they divided themselves into several files of men spread over as wide a field as was practical.[76] Communications were sent by means of bird and animal calls which could carry up to one hundred metres. When the target was identified, a shrill-sounding war cry was made and the warriors immediately took cover. Then the leaders of each war party in the force gave the signal to engage by means of a small whistle.[77] The advantage of this form of deployment was that the Iroquois could draw near their enemy unnoticed because of their ability to move quickly and quietly. Once the enemy had been spotted, the war shout served the purposes of bringing all the warriors' attention instantly to the target while unnerving the enemy by the seemingly sudden appearance of the Iroquois. If the Iroquois started firing almost immediately after they found cover, the enemy would not have had time to regain composure completely. Thus the enemy's equilibrium might be upset even as the first shots were fired. Then, according to John Norton, they:

> ... *advance with their guns loaded, which they discharge in their enemy, these are immediately succeeded by others, until they come in close contact, when they use the spear and tomahawk. Against regular troops, they prefer using fire arms, until they have thinned or broken their ranks, before they charge; but against militia, they prefer coming to close quarters, as soon as the situation in which they met will admit, because* ...[the militia] *are good marksmen, but have not discipline to enable them to withstand the impetuosity of an onset.*[78]

According to a witness who described inter-tribal war (but which contains data relevant for studying white-native combat) the Iroquois could be expected to:

> ... *advance leaping from side to side with astonishing agility: This kind of zigzag motion is to prevent the adversary from taking a settled aim with his rifle;... this Maneuvre* [sic] *puzzles even the best shot; sometimes however they are hit when the combatants are come near to one another - they draw their swords & make a desperate Cut or two, one falls, the other takes out his knife, scalps his fallen adversary, hangs the scalp upon his girdle & returns exulting* ...[79]

The principles of preventing casualties and of confusing the enemy are very clear in these statements. Collaboration of this observation is provided by William Dunlop, who described an action in 1814 in which warriors tried to minimize casualties by changing their positions, while upsetting the enemy and boosting their own morale by declaring each casualty they inflicted:

> *I have had an opportunity of seeing bush-fighting in the Indian fashion. It seemed to me to be a point with them at every discharge of their rifle to shift their position, and whenever they knocked a fellow over, their yelling was horrible.*[80]

If the enemy's resistance collapsed, the warriors gave chase. Dunlop continued:

> ... *When the enemy retired the Indians who had shown so much wariness in the fight ... suddenly seemed to lose all their caution, and bounded forward with a horrible yell, threw themselves on the retreating enemy with their tomahawks, and were soon out of our sight; but as we advanced, we saw they left their trace behind them in sundry cleft skulls.*[81]

Dunlop expressed some surprise at the apparent native change from being very concerned about taking cover to exposing themselves to enemy fire when pursuing the Americans. However, the warriors,who, as one observer noted, "depend entirely upon their dexterity in concealing themselves" almost certainly realized that an enemy running away in terror posed little threat to them.[82] Furthermore, this show of bravado provided an excellent opportunity for a warrior to impress his fellow warriors and to inflict more casualties, take more prisoners and scalps, and capture more booty than would be possible with a more timid pursuit of a beaten foe.

If the Iroquois failed to achieve their objectives and were forced to retreat, they tried to minimize their casualties while attempting to prevent a potentially disastrous rout. Lieutenant James Fitzgibbon of the 49th Regiment of Foot, provided this description:

> *The Indians, when retreating and coming to a ravine, do not at once cross the ravine and defend from the brow of the side or hill looking over the ravine to the pursuing enemy; they suddenly throw themselves down immediately behind the bank they first come to, and thence fire on their pursuers, who must then be entirely exposed, while the Indian exposes his head only, and when pressed and compelled to abandon his position, he fires and retires, covered by the smoke and the bank, so that his pursuers cannot tell the course of his retreat, whether to the right or to the left, or directly to the rear, which last the Indian may now do with comparative safety, being for a short time hid by the bank from the view of his pursuers, until he, the pursuer, arrives at the brow of the bank, by which time the Indian has, most probably, taken post in a new position, where he can only be discovered by his next fire.*[83]

According to John Norton, if a war party was pursued, it would pass a river or some other obstacle and post two men to count the pursuers. If the enemy numbers were sufficiently small, the war party then would set an ambush. If the enemy were too numerous, the party would hasten its retreat.[84]

Another description of Iroquois warfare at the time of the War of 1812 is worth quoting at this point. It contrasts somewhat with the statement made earlier that the Iroquois maintained silence until the moment immediately preceding an action. If both statements are correct, as is likely, it seems that the Iroquois simply used whatever approach was more effective for a particular situation to intimidate the enemy and strengthen the Iroquois' own resolve. Also worth noting are the comments made on cooperative movements by different divisions of an Iroquois force, as well as the practical application of the basic principles described earlier:

> *... the way in which they conduct a battle, is both singular & accellent* [sic]*; when they come in sight of the enemy they advance each singing his war song they are made in general extempure* [sic]*; they most commonly signify what they have before done against the people whom they are going to attack, or what they intend to do or what number of scalps they will bring away - when they have advanced far enough to use the rifle they proceed by divisions, so as always to keep up a constant fire - while one division advances & fires while the next is holding & so on ...*[85]

A Grand River Mohawk, painted in 1804 by Lt. Sempronius Stretton. From the center to the outside his face is painted red, black, yellow, black. *Courtesy, National Archives of Canada, C14827.*

IV

As mentioned earlier, these modes of warfare suited Iroquois society where the military virtues included individual heroics and initiative, personal judgement, and flexibility.[86] As well, it was only in employing these methods of fighting that the Iroquois desire to suffer few casualties was at all possible. The Iroquois saw an expensive victory as a defeat. If pressed hard, the Iroquois normally retreated.[87]

Although such action was appropriate for Iroquois society with its small population, these attitudes limited the Iroquois' capabilities and made them vulnerable to disciplined white troops in certain circumstances. It also meant that tactical or strategic objectives took second place to preserving their numbers, and the Iroquois simply withdrew from any action, when possible, at which their enemy threatened to inflict heavy casualties.

In battle, a warrior acted more independently than a white soldier because he hoped to attain personal glory, measured largely by the exercise of individual judgement and daring. An Iroquois who explicitly followed the orders of war chief would subvert a fundamental reason for fighting in the first place. A chief, therefore, could exercise only a limited amount of authority once an action commenced and only his powers of persuasion and personal example could be used to control his men (although the quotations I have read so far warn us not to dismiss too lightly the chief's abilities to lead his men in combat). However, if immediate needs for displaying bravery, or acquiring scalps or plunder were met, an individual was free to go home even though broader strategic objectives had not been achieved. As well, warriors were free to leave their chiefs if they became dissatisfied or if they received a bad omen warning them of disaster.[88] These factors undoubtedly made command difficult and severely limited an Iroquois chief's options once in combat. As a result, it was very difficult to keep a native force together on a longer campaign, which gave white opponents an advantage in achieving their goals even if they suffered defeat in the first battle but were willing to stay in the field.

Professional soldiers, in contrast to natives, were subject to strict discipline which subjugated personal concerns to those of the broader unit. Emphasis was placed on the unit's acquisition of honor and the achievement of the unit's objectives as dictated by its commanders. If properly disciplined, a group of professional soldiers would suffer heavy casualties to achieve the unit's goals and would be capable of changing their focus in unison as the conditions of a battle changed. Therefore, when well-trained professionals went into action against native forces, they could drive off the natives if they could upset the natives' equilibrium by inflicting or threatening to inflict heavy casualties through the judicious use of heavier and more disciplined firepower and/or a cohesive bayonet charge. Once disorganized, native forces had little choice but to retreat because the individual nature of their warfare made it very difficult for chiefs to reform a large body of men for a coherent counterattack.[89] If the natives were forced into a position from which retreat was impossible a devastating defeat could be inflicted.[90] If they or their allies were defeated badly, the Iroquois would reconsider their alliances and could be expected either to withdraw from the war or even switch sides.[91]

Another serious weakness in Iroquois warfare was a high desertion rate when under fire. For example, 50% of the warriors at the first part of the Battle of Queenston Heights and 70% of those at the Battle of Fort George deserted.[92] Even at that great Iroquois victory, Beaver Dams, almost all of the Grand River people deserted, leaving the Seven Nations to fight most of the battle, and the Seven Nations themselves experienced substantial losses through desertion.[93]

Part of the reason for such potentially disastrous hemorrhaging of combat strength was a lack of a disciplinary hierarchical military structure to keep men in the field under fire as existed in white armies (and which was not possible given the fundamentally individualistic quality of native warfare). But there may have been a much deeper problem stemming from the training methods of the tribes which also accounts for so many desertions: the failure of native society to address the genuine and instinctive fear that a human being feels when preparing to engage in mortal combat. At the beginning of the Battle of Fort George, one Iroquois tried to boost flagging morale by saying: "The Warrior knows no anxiety for his safety."[94] This was rhetoric, not the truth; and it may have been dangerous rhetoric from the viewpoint of maintaining morale. Fear, and its attendant physical symptoms, such as trembling or uncontrolled bowel movements, are due to rapid involuntary muscular action designed to warm up the body for the anticipated action, and virtually all combatants experience such symptoms. Yet, in the socialization of the warrior for combat, men seem to have been told only about the fearlessness of their ancestors and the courageous and manly exploits of the war chiefs without any reference to the reality of fear. Therefore, when warriors had to confront their own terror, they only could believe that they were somehow cowardly, were not "men" in their culture's tradition, and responded by fleeing if they could not bring their fear under control. In contrast, soldiers who have been well informed about the naturalness of fear, or who just could discuss it with their friends, are able to recognize its symptoms, place them in context, and, usually, carry on.[95] The Iroquois warrior, who was no less brave than his white counterpart, seems to have been unprepared for this aspect of combat trauma.

V

Torture, massacre, and scalping have been associated with native warfare and with good reason since history provides ample proof that such practices were common. However, they were not common among all native groups and at all times. While the western tribes still tortured prisoners and killed non-combatants as late as the War of 1812, the Iroquois seem to have stopped these practices, at least regularly, by the American Revolution. Much of the reason behind the abandonment of torture and murder is attributable to the influence of British officers who insisted that their native allies obey some of the theoretical constraints of European warfare combined with Iroquois sensitivity to white accusations of barbarism.[96] Scalping, however, was practised through to the end of the War of 1812, but it was not a form of torture because scalps normally were removed from people who were thought to be dead.[97]

Within native culture, scalping was one of three options traditionally associated with the elemental quality of their warfare - the avenging and replacement of the dead. The other two were the capture of prisoners for adoption into the aggrieved family and the capture of prisoners to be tortured and killed to revenge the death. By 1812, adopting captured white soldiers normally was not a viable option and prisoners usually were ransomed for profit. Torture, as already mentioned, generally had died out among the Iroquois. Scalping was the third alternative. Traditionally it was the least favored way of replacing the dead, but by 1812 probably had become the main focus of fulfilling the obligation to avenge a death. Captured scalps sometimes even went through an adoption ceremony similar to the one experienced by adopted prisoners.[98]

The favorite scalping weapons of the Iroquois undoubtedly were the butcher's and pocket knives issued as gifts.[99] An account of how it was done is provided by John Richardson who witnessed a scalping at the Battle of the Thames in 1813. An American rifleman was pursued by a warrior until the warrior got within 15 paces of the American. The native "threw his tomahawk ... with such force and precision ... that it opened the skull" and knocked the rifleman "motionless on the ground." The warrior laid down his own rifle and:

> *... drew ... his knife, and after having removed the hatchet ... proceeded to make a circular incision throughout the scalp. This done, he grasped the bloody instrument between his teeth, and placing his knees on the back of his victim, while at the same time he fastened his hands in the hair, the scalp was torn off without much apparent difficulty, and thrust still bleeding in his bosom.*[100]

Iroquois (probably Mohawk) prisoner tie or "matunip line", pre-1822. This example is 598 cm long, made of braided natural vegetable fiber, dyed black and decorated with red, black and natural white porcupine quills, tin cones and red-dyed moose hair. *Courtesy, Royal Ontario Museum, 918.35.1.*

Richardson remarked with some apparent astonishment or admiration: "All this was the work of a minute."[101]

Once acquired, scalps were highly prized trophies, treasured by warriors for years and displayed in their homes. As gifts to the family of a dead warrior, the scalp, mounted on a little half-moon wooden frame and dyed red around the edges and on the hairless side, became a constant reminder of the departed and an acceptable proof that the dead warrior's life had been avenged.[102]

Scalping, along with the abandoned practices of torture and murder, served another purpose in Iroquois warfare: that of making the Iroquois appear to be ferocious and terrible enemies. Mutilation of enemy corpses was another technique to make the Iroquois appear fearsome.[103] If Iroquois enemies had their morale subverted by exaggerated fears of Iroquois prowess, the Iroquois then could go into battle with a significant psychological advantage which would help overcome the problem of generally being outnumbered by their enemies.[104]

Overall, however, the incidence of scalping and other forms of mutilation seem to have been relatively low. In fact, one American eyewitness at the blockade of Fort George in the summer of 1813 tried to dispel some of the anti-native propaganda then current in the United States. After receiving a letter from the American officer, a Philadelphia newspaper reported that stories of scalpings and atrocities:

> *... were ten-fold exaggerated; that he had been repeatedly informed that so*

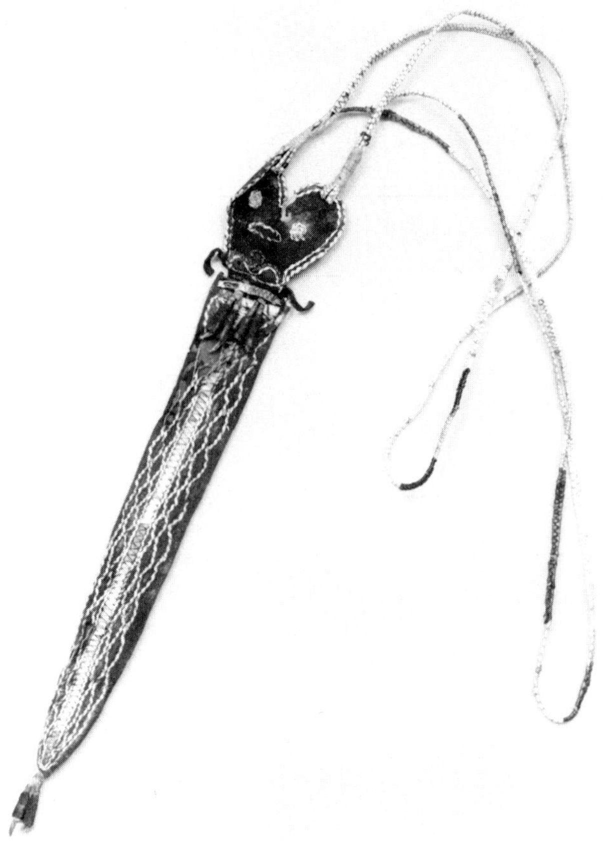

Great Lakes region native knife sheath, collected by Maj. Jasper Grant between 1800 and 1809. It is constructed of black-dyed deer-skin, sinew and natural vegetable fibers and decorated with yellow, blue-green, red, and natural white porcupine quills, metal cones and thongs. *Courtesy, National Museum of Ireland, 1902.339.*

> *far as humane restraint could be laid, it was enjoined by the British soldiers to prevent any act of inhumanity by the savages ... and that they never scalped any but those who were actually dead, and then it was not done when the British officers had the means of preventing it.*[105]

Despite efforts by American and British officers to control those aspects of native warfare they did not like, there was no effort made to contort Iroquois tactical doctrine into white light infantry patterns. On one hand, such an effort would have been counter-productive as the Iroquois were impressive bush fighters and could be used effectively against whites and other natives in a light infantry capacity. On the other hand, the Iroquois simply were unwilling to surrender their own styles of making war to what they considered to be inferior white approaches. As the Seneca war chief, Little Billy, told the Americans following Hull's surrender at Detroit:

> ... [we] *must act under our own chiefs; according to our own customs; be at liberty to take our own course in fighting, we cannot conform to your discipline in camp. So far as we can we will conform to your customs. When you see a boat with a white flag, you do not fire; we shall do the same; But when a boat comes over without one, we shall then begin the attack ... We do not wish you to place us in forts where we cannot act. You know what took place at Detroit; an army was sold. We wish not to be sold.*[106]

Notes

[1] The Sauk chief, Black Hawk, typified native opinion of white warfare when he said, "Instead of stealing upon each other, and taking every advantage to *kill the enemy* and *save their own people,* as we do (which with us is considered good policy in a war chief), they march out, in open day light, and fight, regardless of the number of warriors they may lose! After the battle is over they retire to feast, and drink wine, as if nothing had happened ..." Colin G. Calloway, *Crown and Calumet: British-Indian Relations, 1783-1815* (Norman, OK, 1987), p. 232.

[2] John Norton, *Journal of Major John Norton, 1816* (hereafter *NJ*), ed. by Carl F. Klinck and James J. Talman (Toronto, 1970), p. 129.

[3] Dewitt Bailey, "Those Board of Ordnance Indian Guns - Again", *The Museum of the Fur Trade Quarterly,* 21, no. 1 (Spring 1985), 2-6.

[4] Ross Egles, "Canadian Indian Treaty Guns", Canadian Journal of Arms Collecting, 14, no. 2 (March 1976), 53; Richard Glover, *Peninsular Preparation: The Reform of the British Army, 1795-1809* (Cambridge, 1963), pp. 54-55.

[5] Bailey, 2-3; Egles, 53.

[6] Bailey, 16-17; Egles, 53.

[7] At Beaver Dams, for example, pistols were the most prized items taken from American prisoners by the Iroquois. See Mary Agnes Fitzgibbon, *A Veteran of 1812: The Life of James Fitzgibbon* (Toronto, 1970, originally published 1894), p. 91.

[8] Egles, 54, 58.

[9] Capt. Barber, *Instructions for the Formation and Exercise of Volunteer Sharp-Shooters* (Ottawa, 1968, originally published 1804), pp. 1-3.

[10] Bailey, 11, with modifications from Dewitt Bailey, "Those Board of Ordnance Indian Guns - Again? - Supplement", *The Museum of the Fur Trade Quarterly,* 21, no. 3 (Fall 1985), 6.

[11] M. Smith, *Geographical View of the Province of Upper Canada; and Promiscuous Remarks on the Government* (Philadelphia, 1813), p. 43; Lt. James Fitzgibbon, "Hints to a Son on Receiving his First Commission in a Regiment Serving in the Canadas", 1820s, M. Fitzgibbon, n.p.; William "Tiger" Dunlop, "Recollections of the American War, 1812-1814", 1847, in Carl F. Klinck (ed.), *Tiger Dunlop's Upper Canada* (Toronto, 1967), p. 48; Ms. on Hunting, ascribed as late 18th century, but probably early 19th, judging from internal evidence, Charles M. Johnston (ed.), *The Valley of the Six*

Nations: A Collection of Documents on the Indian Lands of the Grand River (Toronto, 1964), 28.

[12] For example, at the Battle of Queenston Heights, the British captured "435 French carbines" from the Americans, weapons that probably had been issued to American militia. At least some of these probably ended up in Iroquois hands. What the British meant by "French carbines" is unclear. However, they probably meant 1770s-period French infantry muskets rather than short muskets. French muskets (and American muskets which were patterned after them) were about 16.5 mm (.65 cal.) which was the British carbine calibre. Full calibre British muskets were 19 mm (.75 cal.). Return of Ordnance &c. Captured, Dec. 1, 1813 [sic], Ernest Cruikshank (ed.), *Documentary History of the Campaign Upon the Niagara Frontier* (9 vols.; Welland, Ont., 1896-1908) (hereafter *DH*), IV, 75.

[13] Early in the war, for example, John Norton and a small party of Grand River Iroquois chased away an American patrol near Moraviantown and picked up the weapons the Americans left behind. Norton recorded that the muskets "were loaded, and the Bayonets fixed; - this was a Prize to us at that time, as several of the men who had joined us were destitute of guns." *NJ,* p. 298.

[14] There is at least one contemporary painting of a native equipped with a bayonet: "Deputation of Indians from the Mississippi Tribes to the Governor-General", watercolor by Rudolph von Stieger, 1814, in the collection of the National Archives of Canada, illustrated in Ruth B. Phillips, *Patterns of Power: The Jasper Grant Collection of Great Lakes Indian Art of the Early Nineteenth Century ...* (Kleinburg, Ont., 1984), p. 87, fig. II-2.

[15] Brig. Gen. Peter B. Porter to Secretary of War John Armstrong, April 8, 1814 quoted in Allan J. Ferguson, "Notes on the Dress of Indian Allies, 1814", *Military Collector & Historian,* XXXIII, no. 2 (Summer 1981), 85.

[16] Porter to Maj. Gen. Jacob Brown, May 26, 1814, *DH*, II, 398; Lt. Col. Winfield Scott to Porter, May 29, 1814, *DH*, II, 401.

[17] Robert M. Reilley, *United States Martial Flintlocks* (Lincoln, MA, 1986), pp. 126-29; Porter to Armstrong, April 8, 1814, Ferguson, 85.

[18] The Americans used iron furniture (i.e. trigger guards and butt plates) and bands to secure the barrel to the stock. The muskets made for the Iroquois imitated the British practices of using brass furniture and attaching the barrel to the stock with pins. Reilley, pp. 85-89.

[19] *Ibid.,* pp. 224-25. Their overall length was only 123 cm and they weighed only 2.7 kg. Their bore was 14 mm (.54 cal.). Like other U.S. weapons manufactured for the natives, they imitated British manufacture.

[20] George Simon Snyderman, *Behind the Tree of Peace: A Sociological Analysis of Iroquois Warfare* (Philadelphia, 1948), p. 72; "The Seneca Schoolhouse", watercolor by Dennis Cusik, in a private New York collection.

[21] Snyderman, p. 47.

[22] *NJ,* p. 298; Porter to Brown, May 26, 1814, *DH,* II, 398. The western tribes used bows and arrows at the Battle of Tippecanoe in 1811. See Lt. Col. Matthew Elliott to Maj. Gen. Isaac Brock, Jan. 12, 1812, William C.H. Wood (ed.), *Select British Documents of the Canadian War of 1812* (3 vols.; Toronto, 1920-28), I, 281. Tecumseh's followers in June 1812 made bows and arrows as they had no ammunition for their firearms. See Lt. Col. William Claus to Brock, June 16, 1812, Wood, I, 311. Iron points are mentioned by Lewis Henry Morgan, *League of the Iroquois* (Secaucus, NJ, 1972, originally published 1851), pp. 305-06.

Hunting pouch, possibly Delaware, collected by Maj. Jasper Grant between 1800 and 1809. It is of tanned, black-dyed deerskin with orange, blue, black, and white porcupine quill embroidery. The pouch is further decorated with metal cones and red-dyed animal hair. It incorporates leather thongs and a strap of faded green and yellow wool yarn braided in an arrow motif and sewn to the pouch with sinew. The decoration may be stylized representations of horned serpents. It should be noted that there were Delawares living on the Grand River Iroquois Reserve. *Courtesy, National Museum of Ireland, 1902.322.*

[23] Articles sent up ..., 1814, National Archives of Canada (hereafter cited as NAC), Record Group (hereafter cited as RG) 10, Indian Affairs, pp. 172052-53; Requisition for the ... Post of St. Joseph for the year 1813, NAC, RG 10, pp. 171490-91; Requisition of Goods to Supply His Majesty's Indian Stores, Amherstburg ... 1814, n.d., NAC, RG 10, pp. 171772-74; Requisition of Stores for Presents to Indians who resort to Michilimackinac & its dependencies for the Year 1814, n.d., NAC, RG 10, pp. 171438-44; A requisition made on behalf of the people of the River Thames by John Norton, June 24, 1814, NAC, RG 10, p. 1446.

[24] Petition of Robert Livingston, n.d., *DH,* VII, 39.

[25] Dunlop, p. 48; See Morgan, p. 364.

[26] *NJ,* p. 69 and Snyderman, p. 73. Very few Indian lances have survived. The head of one is in the collection of the Toronto Historical Board - Fort York. It resembles a triangular bayonet with a straight grip for attachment to a wooden shaft.

[27] Snyderman, p. 57, quotes a 1750s source describing spears being thrown, but by the American Revolution they seem to have been used principally as thrusting weapons according to " A Visit with Joseph Brant on the Grand River", 1792, Patrick Campbell, *Travels in North America* (1793) in Johnston, p. 63. There is also an account of an American-allied Iroquois thrusting his spear into a Canadian in 1813. See Petition of Robert Livingston, *DH,* VII, 39. Pikes used by white combatants at the same time generally were used as thrusting weapons. See J. Fitzgibbon, M. Fitzgibbon, n.p.

[28] Phillips, *passim.*; William L. Stone, *The Life and Times of Sa-go-ye-wat-ha, or Red Jacket* (Albany, 1866), p. 349.

[29] Phillips. p. 89, fig. 91 illustrates an Ojibway club, c.1800 in the Canadian Museum of Civilization, Ottawa; Morgan, p. 363.

[30] Phillips, pp. 28, 72, 89, figs. 42, 89; Morgan, p. 362. Fig. 42 is an eastern Great Lakes Club, 1800-09 in the collection of the National Museum of Ireland, Dublin; and fig. 89 is a similar example in the Royal Ontario Museum, Toronto. It is possible that the traditional clubs, particularly the ball-headed clubs, were not used much as killing weapons because of the widespread use of the tomahawk. Instead, they may have been used to terrorize the enemy by being left at the scene of a killing and scalping. Since each club bore the distinctive carvings of its owner, leaving a club was an act of bravado and helped to satisfy the need to inform the victim's friends that a death had been avenged. However, ball-headed clubs were perfectly functional and undoubtedly were used to kill opponents long after the tomahawk had become the primary striking weapon among native peoples. A skull excavated by Dr. Michael Gramly of the Buffalo Museum of Science and Technology at a Revolutionary War site, Ft. Laurens, Ohio, clearly shows damage caused by a spiked, ball-headed club, plus trauma caused by the tomahawking of other parts of the skull and knife marks from a scalping. See Skull Number 8, illustrated in Jim Dresslar, "The Ball-Headed Club of the North American Indian", American Society of Arms Collectors *Bulletin,* 55 (1988), 37. Dresslar's article, 33-35, lists sources from 1698, 1774 (two sources), 1779 (two sources), 1792, and 1843 in which ball-headed clubs were left beside the victims. The 1698 reference specifically is to the Iroquois, the others are to natives of the lower Great Lakes region in what is now the United States.

[31] Smith, p. 43.

[32] John Askin to William D. Powell, Jan. 25, 1813, *DH,* V, 50.

[33] Snyderman, p. 56; Anthony F.C. Wallace, *The Death and Rebirth of the Seneca* (New York, 1972), p. 137. However, the Iroquois seem to have been more willing to obey white directives in relation to terrorizing the enemy and therefore were less frightening. As well, the Iroquois lived a more sedentary life compared to that of the western tribes which possibly affected their combat abilities. At the Battle of Beaver Dams, for example, when James Fitzgibbon demanded the American surrender, he told the Americans that a large force of western tribesmen had just arrived who, unlike the Iroquois the Americans had been fighting up to that point in the battle, could not be relied upon to restrain themselves from committing atrocities. Fitzgibbon was not telling the truth. There were no western tribesmen present, and he also knowingly played upon American fears of the western tribes, but this incident illustrates the perceived differences between the two native groups. *Montreal Gazette,* July 6, 1813, *DH,* VI, 118.

[34] John Long, *Voyages and Travels of an Indian Interpreter and Trader describing the Manners and Customs of the North American Indians ...* (Toronto, 1974, originally published 1791), p. 53: "The boys are very expert in *trundling a hoop* particularly the Cahnuaga [Caughnawaga] Indians, whom I have frequently seen excel at this amusement. The game is played by any number of boys who may accidentally assemble together, some driving the hoop, while others with bows and arrows shoot at it. At this exercise they are surprisingly expert, and will stop the progress of the hoop when going with great velocity, by driving the pointed arrow into its edge; this they will do at a considerable distance, and on horseback as well as on foot. They will also kill small birds at fifty yards distance, and strike a halfpenny off a stick at fifteen yards. Spears and tomahawks they manage with equal dexterity." The Caughnawagas, located near Montreal, were one of the Seven Nations of Canada.

[35] Cornelius J. Jaenen, *Friend and Foe: Aspects of French-Amerindian Cultural Contact in the Sixteenth and Seventeenth Centuries* (Toronto, 1976), p. 134.

[36] Conversation with a Toronto collector of early Canadian firearms. Antique weapons associated with native use with carved-out shoulders appear from time to time. It is also possible that the Iroquois, who first owned Dutch muskets which had a low comb on the shoulder, preferred this design to later British and American designs and continued to carve down the comb. The practice seems to have been common over chronological and geographical distances. For example, there is a long arm exhibiting this feature from the Northwest Rebellion of 1885 in the collection of the Toronto Historical Board - Fort York.

[37] Long, p. 29. The expression "half man high" was an exaggeration. Whites did not fire from the waist but from the shoulder.

[38] Ms. on hunting in Johnston, p. 28.

[39] John Howison, *Sketches of Upper Canada, Domestic, Local, and Characteristic ...* (1821) in Johnston, p. 28.

[40] Long, p. 19.

[41] When firing at an enemy, it was common to load a firearm with one bullet or ball. The Americans sometimes fired a ball plus one to three buckshot ("buck and ball"). Buckshot normally would not cause serious injury but could inflict annoying wounds. The British-allied Iroquois were given buckshot. Although most of it was probably used for hunting, the Americans did record buck and ball casualties, possibly from Iroquois weapons. James Mann, *Medical Sketches of the Campaigns of 1812, 13, 14* (Dedham, MA, 1816), p. 215. Furthermore, U.S. buck and ball (2,810) and buckshot (3,140) cartridges were captured by the British at the Battle of Queenston Heights, and it would seem logical for the British to have issued that ammunition to militia and natives along with captured weapons. Return of Ordnance, &c. Captured, Dec. 1, 1813 [sic], *DH,* IV, 75.

[42] Glover, pp. 126, 141. Larger amounts of ammunition may have been used during intensive training according to J.A. Houlding, *Fit For Service: The Training of the British Army, 1715-1795* (Oxford, 1981), pp. 335-37.

[43] Jeffrey Kimball. "The Battle of Chippawa: Infantry Tactics in the War of 1812", *Military Affairs,* 32 (1968), 172, n. 22.

[44] Dunlop, p. 48.

[45] Harry Holbert Turner-High, *Primitive Warfare: Its Practice and Concepts* (Columbia, SC, 1949), p. 55.

[46] Keith F. Otterbein, "Why the Iroquois Won: An Analysis of Iroquois Military Tactics", *Ethnohistory,* XI (1964), pp. 56-61.

[47] *Ibid.*

[48] Dr. Gideon or Sylvester Tiffany quoted in the *National Intelligencer,* January, 1813, *DH,* V, 25. The Tiffanys were Americans who resided in Upper Canada before the war.

[49] Smith, p. 40.

[50] *NJ,* p. xxvii; J. McE. Murray, "John Norton", *Ontario History,*

XXXVII (1945), 12.

[51] The Grand River Iroquois even may have learned some of the rudiments of arms drill. At the burial of Gen. Brock in 1812, the route of the funeral procession "was lined by a double row of militia and Indians, resting on their arms reversed." Lt. G. Rideout to his mother, Oct. 21, 1812, *DH,* IV, 147.

[52] In Iroquois society, civil leadership fundamentally was hereditary whereas military leadership normally was attained through battlefield performance. Sometimes, as in the case of Joseph Brant, military leaders could rise to power over civil leaders. There were, however, two hereditary war chiefs in the Seneca tribe and there was a class of peace chiefs, the pine tree chiefs, who were a sort of appointed group of advisors to the peace chiefs or sachems. Some pine tree chiefs were able to exercise considerable influence.

[53] Barbara Graymont, *The Iroquois in the American Revolution* (Syracuse, 1972), pp. 20-23; Morgan, p. 72.

[54] *Ibid.,* p. 21.

[55] William Smith, *An Historical Account of the Expedition Against the Ohio Indians, in the Year 1764, Under the Command of Henry Bouquet, Esq. ...* (1765) reprinted as *Expedition Against the Ohio Indians* (Ann Arbor, MI, 1966), p. 39.

[56] Snyderman, p. 79.

[57] Various inventories list "beef boots" as being issued during the war to natives who fought with the British, such as NAC, RG 10, p. 171833. In 1814, shoes were requested for U.S.-allied natives. Porter to Armstrong, March 27, 1814 in Ferguson, p. 85.

[58] In loading a rifle, it was important to use a finer grade of powder to prime the weapon and to use a more carefully measured charge than was necessary with a musket; therefore, reliance could not be placed on the pre-made cartridges used by musketmen; and hence, the use of powder horns in which loose powder was kept.

[59] Phillips, *Patterns ...*, p. 26; Ruth B. Phillips, "Like a Star I Shine: Northern Woodlands Artistic Traditions", *The Spirit Sings: Artistic Traditions of Canada's First Peoples* (Calgary, 1987), p. 83. One is illustrated in the latter article, fig. 76. It is in the Natural History Collection of the Town of Winterthur, Switzerland.

[60] Morgan, pp. 262-63.

[61] Stone, p. 333, n. 1.

[62] Robin May, "King George's Indians, 1775-1783", *Military Illustrated,* Oct.-Nov. 1987, 40.

[63] Phillips, "Like a Star ...", 81.

[64] Note of Goods Remaining in His Majesty's Indian Storehouses, Upper Canada, early 1812, NAC, RG 10, p. 1232, lists vermillion dye supplied by whites. George Heriot, *Travels Through the Canadas* (2 vols.; Toronto, 1971, originally published 1807), II, p. 292 mentions red and yellow found locally by the natives. Snyderman, p. 57, describes black being applied to a red-colored base.

[65] Phillips, "Like a Star ...", 83.

[66] Heriot, II, pp. 292-93; William N. Fenton, "Northern Iroquois Culture Patterns", Bruce Trigger (ed.), *Handbook of North American Indians,* vol. 15, "The Northeast" (Washington, 1979), p. 303; Phillips, Like a Star ...", 83.

[67] Daniel J. Glenney, "An Ethnohistory of the Grand River Iroquois and the War of 1812", M.A. Thesis, University of Guelph, 1973, p. 30. There are numerous illustrations of scalp locks. One of the most famous is William Berczy's 1790s portrait of Joseph Brant in the National Gallery of Canada, illustrated in Johnston. Another is Peter of Buffalo, drawn by the Baroness Hyde de Neuville in 1807 in the collection of the New-York Historical Society, illustrated in Phillips, *Patterns ...*, p. 92, fig. II-3.

[68] Phillips, "Like a Star ...", 81.

[69] *Ibid.,* 80. The only known surviving example of a wampum gorget, an 18th century Mohawk one, is illustrated in as fig. 71 in this article. The gorget is in the Museum of Anthropology and Ethnography, Leningrad. Silver gorgets are fairly common and are found in many museum collections, such as that of the Royal Ontario Museum, Toronto.

[70] *NJ,* pp. 126-27.

[71] *Ibid.,* p. 129.

[72] *NJ,* pp. 128, 322; Heriot, II, pp. 406, 466-67. John Norton's journal provides instances which confirm that the Iroquois did post sentries at night. Heriot was one of a number of contemporary witnesses who expressed surprise at the general lack of care other natives took while camping, claiming that they were "incautious with respect to their encampments at night, even in an enemy's territory" since they placed no sentries and often fell "a sacrifice to their indolence." In their own defense, natives expressed the view that they needed their rest. Heriot believed that only the Iroquois placed guards at night.

[73] Snyderman, p. 56.

[74] John K. Mahon, "Anglo-American Methods of Indian Warfare, 1676-1794", *The Mississippi Valley Historical Review,* XLV (1958-59), 259.

[75] Heriot, II, p. 431.

[76] Morgan, p. 340; *NJ,* p. 129.

[77] Snyderman, p. 57.

[78] *NJ,* pp. 129-30.

[79] Ms. on warfare in Johnston, p. 32.

[80] Dunlop, p. 48.

[81] *Ibid.*

[82] W. Smith, p. 41.

[83] J. Fitzgibbon, M. Fitzgibbon, n.p.

[84] *NJ,* pp. 127-28.

[85] Ms, on warfare in Johnston, p. 33.

[86] Snyderman, p. 48; Graymont, pp. 21-22.

[87] John Sugden, *Tecumseh's Last Stand* (Norman, OK, 1985), p. 16; Glenney, pp. 7, 32; Mahon, 257.

[88] Glenney, p. 30; Graymont, pp. 21-22; Sugden, pp. 16-17.

[89] Wiley Sword, *President Washington's Indian War: The Struggle for the Old Northwest, 1790-1795* (Norman, OK, 1985), p. 181; Mahon, pp. 254-75; See also Kimball, 169-86. At least as early as the 1750s, whites understood native warfare when British Colonel Henry Bouquet identified three principles of native tactics: fight scattered, surround, and give ground when hard-pressed. To prevent surprise or envelopment, white armies travelled so they could deploy quickly in a square or a rectangle to defeat native attempts to surround them, and scouts and light troops were deployed around a body of troops to prevent surprise. At one battle, Bushy Run near Fort Pitt in 1763, scouts informed Bouquet that a native force was surrounding his troops. He formed his men into a square under cover and was able to prevent the Indians from upsetting his equilibrium. However, Bouquet was outnumbered and had to do more than sit still. Therefore, he formed some of his men within the square for a counter-attack. The he directed others on his perimeter to appear to give way. When the natives rushed the apparent weak spot, Bouquet's reserve dashed out and dispersed the enemy at bayonet point. What Bouquet had done was take the European square, designed to enable infantry to defend themselves against cavalry (by eliminating vulnerable flanks or a rear against which the quick-moving cavalry could attack) and add a counter-attack element which was possible against opponents on foot but not those on horses. The principles of this tactic were to combine the firepower and cohesion of disciplined troops via the square with quick but strong movement in a bayonet charge. In much of North American popular history, the image of the independent white frontiersman is held up as the supreme model of the successful "Indian fighter". The reality, however, was that it was well-trained and disciplined professional troops who stood the best chance of defeating native forces. Ironically, U.S. Maj. Gen. Arthur St. Clair, whose force of ill-trained men was crushed by the natives in 1791, observed correctly, "It has been often proved that the savages if violently attacked will always break and give way - and when once broke, for the want of discipline, will never rally." Sword, p. 101.

[90] Mahon, pp. 254, 264, 274-75. A contemporary writer explained the Iroquois' vulnerability when their families were present at an engagement: "in these cases the battle was always bloody, for when the Women could see the fight, every young man was anxious to show his courage ... but it produced the most fatal consequences if the enemy gained any advantage; for ... [when] the Ladies were not present, they pursued the measures dictated by prudence & instead of maintaining a disadvantageous contest, would secure their safety by flight - but humanity compelled them ... to expose their own lives for the purpose of letting the Women escape ..." Ms. on warfare in Johnston, pp. 33-34.

[91] A significant portion of the Grand River Iroquois seem to have contemplated switching to the American side following the American victory at Fort George in May 1813 in order to preserve their community from American reprisals for fighting with the British. However, the British success at Stoney Creek reversed fortunes on the Niagara Peninsula by June, and the Grand River Iroquois continued to support the British. Unfortunately, the documentary evidence is scattered and unclear, as if the eyewitnesses did not want this fact to "get out". However, between *NJ, passim.*, and other sources, I believe the proof is fairly conclusive. Ms. in preparation: Carl Benn, "The Last War Dance: The Iroquois in the War of 1812", chapter 5.

[92] *NJ,* pp. 306, 323-24.

[93] Capt. Dominique Ducharme to *La Bibliotheque Canadienne,* June 5, 1826, *DH,* VI, 127; Journal of Maj. Isaac Roach, n.d., *DH,* VI, 147; M. Fitzgibbon, p. 86.

[94] *NJ,* p. 323.

[95] Richard Holmes, *Firing Line* (Hammondsworth, UK, 1987), pp. 206-08. For example, in World War II, the British Army experienced a lower psychological casualty rate and fewer desertions in units which had been fully briefed on the nature of fear before going into action than in those which had not.

[96] Wallace, p. 137.

[97] Isabel Thompson Kelsay, *Joseph Brant, 1743-1807: Man of Two Worlds* (Syracuse, 1984), p. 21. There are numerous accounts of people surviving scalpings. After the American defeat on the Wabash River in 1791, some scalped people who survived the ordeal were seen seated on the ground, propped up against trees, with their heads "smoking like a chimney" in the cold November air, according to Lt. Micah McDonough. Others were found retreating from the battlefield, staggering, with blood oozing from their scalped heads. Survival was possible because scalping removed only the skin, tissue and hair from the top of an individual's head, leaving the scull intact. Sword, pp. 186, 190. Long, p. 22, wrote: "There are instances of persons of both sexes, now living in America ... who, having been scalped, by wearing a plate of silver or tin on the crown of the head, to keep it from cold, enjoy a good state of health, and are seldom afflicted with pains."

[98] Wallace, p. 102.

[99] E.g. General Abstract of Indian Stores in the [British] Indian Department serving with the Centre, between 25th June and 24th September 1813, n.d., NAC, RG 10, p. 171597.

[100] John Richardson, "A Canadian Campaign by a British Officer", *The New Monthly Magazine and Literary Journal,* 17 (1826) in Sugden, p. 131.

[101] *Ibid.* There is a forensically authenticated pre-1815 scalp in the collection of the Toronto Historical Board - Fort York.

[102] Kelsay, p. 22; George F.G. Stanley, *The War of 1812: Land Operations* (Ottawa, 1983), p. 153. Sometimes scalps served other purposes. In 1791, for example, after the western tribes destroyed the American army on the Wabash, the scalp of a famous American soldier was sent to Joseph Brant to chide the Six Nations for not participating in the action. Sword, p. 191.

[103] Kelsay, p. 216; Glenney, p. 30.

[104] W. Smith, p. 38.

[105] *American Daily Advertiser,* Aug. 3, 1813, *DH,* VI, 262. It should be noted that whites, particularly Americans, scalped people too. In the autumn of 1812, Brig. Gen. Alexander Smyth offered $40 (equal to several months wages for a private soldier) for native scalps. Smyth to the Soldiers of the Army of the Center, Nov. 17, 1812, *DH,* IV, 216. Lt. Col. George McFeely of the 22nd Regiment of Infantry described what he saw at Fort Niagara while entertaining a recently paroled prisoner: "[Captain Ballard] ... had two Indian scalps that he had taken at Frenchtown, and had concealed them in the waist band of his pantaloons while a prisoner. While in the fort with us he ripped open his waist band, took out the scalps, fleshed them with his knife, salted them, and set them in hoops in true Indian style. He said he had twenty scalps at home, and these two would make thirty he had taken off with his own hands in his time, and that he would raise fifty scalps before he would die." John C. Fredriksen (ed.), "Chronicle of Valor: The Journal of a Pennsylvania Officer in the War of 1812", *The Western Pennsylvania Historical Magazine,* 67, no. 3 (July 1984), 256.

[106] Minutes of a Council held at Buffalo, Sept. 8, 1812, *DH,* IV, 20-21.

PROPAGANDA IN UPPER CANADA IN THE WAR OF 1812

by
R. Arthur Bowler

When in June 1812 the government of the United States declared war on Great Britain, it did so with the intention of waging that war against Britain's North American colonies, particularly Upper and Lower Canada. A number of reasons lay behind the choice of the Canadas as the war objective, the most important of which was the conviction of Madison and his administration that the Canadas had become a vital part of the British imperial system and that their loss would force Britain to negotiate her policies with respect to neutral trade.[1] But also important was the belief that the conquest of the Canadas would be relatively easy. The *National Intelligencer,* the informal voice of the Madison administration, appraised the situation in an article on December 3, 1812: the population of the Canadas was small, just over 300,000 (compared to the 7.5 million of the United States), and for its defense Britain, deeply engaged in Europe, could spare only a few thousand of her regular troops; in the event of war these troops would keep the fortress of Quebec and abandon everything to the west. "The distance of Great Britain - the ice of the St. Lawrence - the difficulty of recruiting and supporting an army - the ease with which it might be outnumbered from the United States and the impossibility of retreat in case of disaster will prevent Great Britain from sending any considerable army into the interior." And to make the task even easier, most of the people, it was believed, had no loyalty to Britain. The French Canadians were described as "disaffected ...

Isaac Brock's death at Queenston in 1812 elevated him to the status of "the saviour of Upper Canada".

partly from an hereditary national antipathy; and partly from viewing her in the light of a conqueror." As for the English Canadians, "20,000 or 30,000 may be considered as European or American Tories - the latter most incorrigible. The residue are a mixed multitude having few predilections, except those created by interest and consequently leaning on the side of America."[2]

There were many errors in this assessment of the Canadas but much also that was valid, especially as it pertained to Upper Canada. The population was no more than 90,000 and although the first large group of settlers was Loyalists of the American Revolution, a branch of the stream of westward-moving Americans had also found its way into the province and by 1812 constituted some two-thirds of the total. They were in overwhelming majority in the area west of Burlington. What is more, the garrison of British regulars in the province numbered less than a thousand and their commander was convinced that there could be no defending the province without popular support and the enthusiastic participation of the militia. But the general population could recognize a hopeless cause when they saw it and made it clear that they would not willingly participate. It was this situation which led some of the members of the small conservative and largely Loyalist elite of Upper Canada to angry despair,[3] and which prompted some Americans to assert that the capture of that province would involve little more than the formality of taking possession of it.[4]

Here was a situation made for propaganda: by the Upper Canadian elite to stir up patriotism and the will to resist and by the Americans to maintain acquiescence and defeatism. A few people on both sides took up the challenge. The means they had for spreading their messages were meager - word of mouth and a handful of manual flatbed presses whose limited output could be distributed only as fast as a horse could walk or a ship sail. Even at that some of the presses were destroyed during the war and supplies of paper were erratic. Nevertheless, significant propaganda was produced and a careful examination of it can help us to understand the war and the societies involved in it.

I

If many of those in authority in Upper Canadian society are to be believed, American attempts to undermine their society began long before the War of 1812. Lieutenant Governor John Graves Simcoe's policy of encouraging settlers from the United States had initially drawn little opposition in Upper Canada, but as early as 1799 Richard Cartwright in Kingston began to express his fear that these settlers would not become loyal members of the structured and conservative society which he and others of the elite wished to establish in Upper Canada. Rather, he suspected they would become transmitters of the corrupting democratic ideas which had helped bring on the American Revolution and were already rotting the American Republic from within. "It is not to be expected," he wrote to Lieutenant Governor Peter Hunter,

> *... that a man will change his political principles or prejudices by crossing a River; or that an oath of allegiance is at once to check the Bias of Mind, and prevent the predilection for Maxims and Modes of estimating and conducting the concerns of the Public to which he has been trained from displaying itself, even without any sinister purpose, whenever an opportunity shall be presented.*[5]

What Cartwright meant was demonstrated in a letter from a settler on Young Street to David Smith, the Surveyor General:

> *I am sorry to find in the disposition of several of the inhabitants of Young Street, and in particular those from the Northern States, that they show a very great contempt to the Officers of our Government, both civil & military, as it is their whole desire to have the election of all of their own officers ... As for Fiske and little Hide, the Schoolmasters, they use all their efforts to poison the minds of the Youth, by teaching them in republican books, in particular the 3d part of Webster's History ... Youths educated in said books, by & by, will have the privilege of voting members for our Assembly, & filling the house with their own kind, & when that is the Case, what may the Governor and Council of this Province expect - trouble too much - as I had the misfortune to live in Maryland, before the rebellion in America, I was an Eyewitness to the Steps they took - makes me dread anything that may lead to any innovation in Government.*[6]

As relations between Great Britain and the United States worsened, the effect of the presence of these people was more and more deplored. At the time of the *Chesapeake-Leopard* affair, Lieutenant Governor Gore confided to Governor Craig in Quebec that he had little confidence in any of the settlers west of Kingston except those who had fought for the British during the Revolution.[7] By early 1812 the governors of both the Canadas were convinced that the United States had dispatched agents to their provinces whose task was to "seduce the inhabitants ... from their allegiance."[8] Governor Sir George Prevost of Lower Canada was more fearful of the effect of these spies and secret agents than American armies and wrote in code to warn General Isaac Brock in Upper Canada. Brock discussed the matter with his executive council, who felt the matter was serious enough to warrant a proclamation warning that "diverse persons have recently come into this Province with seditious intent to disturb the tranquility thereof and to endeavour to alienate the minds of His Majesty's Subjects from His Person and Government."[9] Brock remained convinced of the presence of American agents in Upper Canada and reported to Lord Liverpool that part of the reason for General Hull's early success in the western tip of the province was the presence of "numerous and active" emissaries.[10]

But, despite the warnings and fears, there is no evidence of paid American emissaries being sent to the Canadas.[11] There was no need for them. Enthusiasts for the ideas of democratic republicanism and the American cause - largely but not entirely recent immigrants from the United States - were everywhere in Upper Canada. They constituted a potent if unorganized propaganda machine which twice in 1812 frustrated Brock's attempts to get emergency war powers for his government.[12] The assembly refused to approve the necessary bills but even had they passed, wrote an astute observer "there is no doubt but that a rebellion would have taken place."[13] Brock himself made a very revealing assessment of the population of the Niagara region. "There can be no doubt," he wrote, "that a large portion of the population of this neighborhood are sincere in their profession to defend the country, but it appears likewise evident to me that the greater part are either indifferent to what is passing, or so completely American as to rejoice in the prospects of a change of governments."[14]

Direct American propaganda of the war in Upper Canada was the product of American military men and their staffs and consisted entirely of proclamations, usually prepared on the occasion of the occupation of a portion of the province. The most famous and most important of these was that issued by General William Hull on July 12, 1812 when he took his army across the Detroit River into Upper Canada. Hull's proclamation was designed to convince Upper Canadians not to oppose his army, and its inspiration was, in part, the product of the American perception of the composition and loyalty of the Upper Canadian population. It also, though, clearly said that Upper Canada was to become a part of the United States and sought to explain the attractions of that fate. It is worth examining in some detail both for its effectiveness as a piece of propaganda and for what it conveys about

Gen. William Hull issued the first and most influential of several proclamations to be made by American officers leading invasions of Upper Canada.

American perceptions of themselves and their country.[15]

The most important theme of the proclamation is an invocation of the values of the American Revolution and their contrast with the situation in which Upper Canadians supposedly lived. "I tender you," wrote Hull, "the invaluable blessings of civil, political and religious liberty." Linked with this, though, was an appeal based on that growing prosperity in the United States which even then was being compared favorably to the situation in the Canadas; the liberties he offered them, Hull assured Canadians, carried with them as a "necessary result," "Individual and general prosperity."

Although it was printed in both French and English, a recognition of the character of the population of the southwestern tip of Upper Canada, the proclamation was directed at the English-speakers and appeals were made to both the Loyalists and post-Loyalists settlers. To the post-Loyalists the values of the Revolution were particularly involved: "Many of your fathers fought for the freedom and independence we now enjoy," and now they in turn would be "emancipated from tyranny and oppression." "Raise not your hand against your brethren" was the plea. For the Loyalists and other settlers, Hull emphasized that the war was against Great Britain, not the "peaceful, unoffending inhabitants" of Canada. "I come to find enemies," he declared, "not make them." The Canadians, in the view of the Democratic Republicans, had no reason to support Britain: "Separated by an immense ocean and an extensive wilderness from Great Britain, you have no participation in her councils, no interest in her conduct." The rule of Britain brought only tyranny and injustice: the Americans had come to relieve Canadians of this burden.

The gifts Hull offered, however, were balanced by a warning. Those who took up arms with the British would be treated as enemies "and the horrors and calamities of war will stalk before you." Moreover, Britain was sure to employ her Indian allies in the war and that would bring even greater horrors: "the first stroke of the tomahawk - the first attempt with the scalping knife will be the signal of one indiscriminate scene of desolation. No white man found fighting by the side of an Indian will be taken prisoner."

Finally, it was pointed out that those who wished to join the American force would be welcome but all that was required of Canadian was that they remain quietly at home. There their lives and their property would be preserved. "The United States," he concluded, "offer you *Peace, liberty,* and *security* - your choice lies between these and WAR, *Slavery* and *Destruction.*"

This proclamation, although it has a certain bombastic quality to modern ears, was a skillful piece of writing which Prevost called "artful and insidious."[16] In the following days Canadian militiamen deserted by the hundreds to join Hull or seek his parole. The militia of Norfolk County, when called up, turned out only reluctantly and then refused to march, and many of the inhabitants of Westminster Township signed a petition inviting Hull to advance to them and promising to join with him when he arrived. It was at this time that Brock approached the legislature of Upper Canada for the second time with a request that the militia law be revised and *habeus corpus* suspended: he was again refused. "A more decent House has not been elected since the formation of the Province," he asserted, but they feared reprisals.[17]

It cannot, of course, be asserted that all this was the result of Hull's proclamation; the proclamation was, after all, delivered by an army. Nevertheless there are indication of its effect. Brock, for instance, felt it necessary to immediately compose a counter-proclamation in which he not only asserted that he was going to fight, which would have been all that was required if he believed the presence of the American army had brought about the disaffection and desertions, but deemed it necessary to counter the ideological arguments which Hull made and point out the benevolence and generosity of Britain and the prosperity of her subjects. He also warned that the likely fate of Canada in the event of an American victory would be reannexation to France.[18] There also exists a letter from an informant in Canada to General Stephen Van Rensselaer which asserts that Hull's proclamation had its effect because it promised security for private property. The best evidence, though, comes from one of Hull's officers, who noted in his journal that when they landed in Upper Canada "the inhabitants all fled in different directions from us. The General immediately circulated his proclamation which gave great satisfaction to the inhabitants and caused many of them to return and apply for protection."[19]

Had Hull followed his proclamation with military success, propaganda might well have become a standard American weapon in the war. As it was, his humiliating surrender to Brock led to public condemnation of himself and his methods. Federalist newspapers ridiculed "War by proclamation" and soon carried advertisements for the biting satire *The War of the Gulls,* the third chapter of which showed how "a certain doughty General of the Gulls goes forth to play the game of Hull-Gull in Upper Canada

'and from the pinnicle of glory,
Falls headlong into purgatory.'"

As a result, while there were four more proclamations or addresses to the people of Upper Canada by American military commanders, none had the broad propaganda content which was there is Hull's.[20] General James Wilkinson, as he began his ill-fated expedition down the St. Lawrence in late 1813, informed the inhabitants of Canada that he had come to "subdue the forces of His Britannic Majesty, not to war against his unoffending subjects" and promised protection for the person and property of those who remained peaceful but left it at that.[21] Lieutenant Colonel James Preston, when he took command of the American forces at Fort Erie in late May 1813, found that there were local people anxious to join him. He quickly issued a proclamation which seemed to take the position enunciated by Hull at Detroit and later by General Smyth in a general order to his troops at Buffalo, that Upper Canada was to become a part of the United States. The proclamation promised the the security of property and personal rights to all who voluntarily sought the protection of the United States but warned that those who "obstinately continue inimical" were bringing on themselves "the most rigorous and disastrous consequences."[22] Later that same fall, General George McClure, left in Command on the Niagara frontier, also found it necessary to issue an address to the inhabitants of Upper Canada. Long and rambling, it was largely a condemnation of the British for employing Indians and an assertion that "our Free republican government" would assure the security and protection of all who remained peaceable.[23]

II

In contrast to the American effort, British propaganda in the War of 1812 was extensive and relatively sophisticated. Newspapers which in times of peace were usually dull compilation of advertisements, extracts from foreign newspapers about the war in Europe and local tidbits became on occasion little more than patriotic handbills, featuring editorials and prominently displayed letters to the editor developing patriotic themes and exhorting the reader to patriotic endeavors. Important speeches and addresses as well as sermons which developed patriotic ideas were also featured in newspapers and sometimes printed up as handbills. This was the case in August 1812 when a carefully composed address of the House of Assembly to its constituents, which condemned the actions of the American government and praised the system which Canadians had inherited from Britain, was ordered printed in five hundred copies and distributed about the province. Lesser number of a patriotic sermon by the Reverend John Strachan were ordered at the same time.[24] When the war reduced the number of newspapers in the province to one, the *Kingston Gazette,* the Upper Canadian establishment still managed to print proclamations and addresses commenting on and giving official explanations of what was happening and distributed them through much of the province. Prevost had a reply to the proclamation of Lieutenant Colonel Preston so distributed in June 1813, and in 1814 sent out a handbill justifying the British destruction of the settlements on the American side of the Niagara River.[25] For most settlers west of the Bay of Quinte such handbills along with the army general and district orders were often the only source of news for most of the war.

Direct arguments and exhortations were not the only form of Canadian propaganda, however. The material that went into newspapers was usually very carefully managed in order to present the "proper" view. The issue of war hotly divided Federalists and Democratic Republicans in the United States and the Upper Canadian conservative elite was anxious that the population should understand this and its effect on the ability of that nation to wage war. Hence Upper Canadian papers regularly republished articles from Federalist newspapers which denounced Madison's government and its war policy. The "Old Farmer" letters originally printed in the *Boston Gazette* were regular features of the *Kingston Gazette* and prominent place was given to particularly juicy items such as Hull's and Van Rensselaer's letters explaining the reasons for their failures at Detroit and Queenston, and Colonel Cass's letter accusing Hull of cowardice.[26] When the declaration of war produced riots in Baltimore in which a Federalist newspaper was destroyed and several of its supporters killed or badly injured, the *Kingston Gazette* was happy to print the news under the headline "BALTIMORE MOBS! or Democracy Unveiled." The same paper also explained the Federalist satire *The War of the Gulls* to its readers and even offered copies of it for sale.[27] Earlier it had placed on its front page the complete text of the address of the Massachusetts Assembly to the people of that state shortly after the declaration of war, which concluded that the war was "a wanton sacrifice of your best interests."[28] The *York Gazette* in its issue of October 24, 1812 printed an article from a Vermont paper which reported the unwillingness of the militia of that state to have anything to do with the war.

Sir George Prevost, Governor of Canada answered American proclamations with handbills and general orders detailing British victories. *Courtesy, Metropolitan Toronto Reference Library, J. Ross Robertson Collection.*

On the other hand, important information from the Democratic Republicans was likely to be distorted. The editor of the *York Gazette* in the issue of December 5, 1812 summarized a speech made to Congress by President Madison the previous month. The summary is almost a masterpiece of distortion by subtle change, overemphasis and rearrangement. Madison's introduction, which in the original "invites attention to the providential favors" bestowed on the country, becomes a blasphemous "He begins by congratulating his country and complimenting Providence on the health and abundant harvest of the year" and went on from there. After several columns he announced that "this subject generally defeats all calm reasoning and the editor indignantly drops it."

Clearly, also, military commanders and newspaper editors together managed the war news presented to the public in general orders and newspapers. For instance, the official account of the battle of Stoney Creek, the only account made public during the war, not only greatly exaggerated the extent of the American defeat but neglected to mention the number of British casualties, which was high.[29] The timing of the release of news was also manipulated to produce the best effect. The American incursions of 1813, which began with the capture of Fort George on May 27, was not even noticed officially - and then only obliquely - until the general order of June 28 announcing the Canadian victory at Beaver Dams. The actual admission of the fall of Fort George was not made until July 13 when it was combined with the report of the victory at Stoney Creek. In contrast, the retaking of the fort on December 12, 1813 was the subject of a general order of December 14, which was printed in the *Kingston Gazette* only four days later. Similar delays are found in the announcements of the fall of York and the disasters at Put-in Bay and on the Thames while the battle at Chrysler's Farm was reported within the week.

It is also possible that Canadians engaged in a bit of black propaganda, that is propaganda which attempts to conceal its source. The *York Gazette* published two letters in 1812, one in February and one in September, which seem to fit this category. The February letter purported to be a note to a friend from a Quaker recently arrived in Upper Canada. It had been brought to his attention, the editor noted, and was published because it contained worthwhile ideas "unbiased by political or party spirit." The second letter, addressed to "Americans residing in Canada" and signed "An American," was reprinted from the *Canadian Courant*. In both letters the ideas and arguments are so close to the establishment line that it is impossible to believe that they were not planted.[30]

The origins of this barrage of propaganda are not too difficult to find. In part, of course, they lay in the desire to see "truth" set up against "falsehood" and in the very natural instinct to conceal failure and advertise success. But it is possible to go beyond that. By late 1811 developments in British-American relations made it clear that war was almost inevitable and steps were taken to prepare both of the Canadas for that eventuality. In Upper Canada, Lieutenant Governor Francis Gore was sent on leave and General Isaac Brock installed as military commander and administrator of the civil government, the feeble regiment of British regulars in garrison was replaced by a well-trained and up-to-strength one, and the fortifications and stores of munitions rehabilitated and replenished. From Quebec, Prevost also sent to Upper Canada Captain Andrew Gray, an assistant deputy quartermaster general. Gray's task was to make an assessment of the provincial marine establishment at Kingston and then proceed to York. At Kingston, Gray met Richard Cartwright, the most distinguished member of the Upper Canadian Loyalist elite. This elite had, on a number of occasions since the election of Thomas Jefferson as President of the United States, taken to the press in letters to the editor to warn Canadians of the danger to the United States and to themselves of the rising tide of democratic republicanism, and Cartwright informed Gray that he had again taken up his pen; he would shortly begin publishing a series of letters under the *nom-de-plume* "Falkland" in the *Kingston Gazette*. A few days later Gray was in York and in the report he sent to Prevost from there he noted not only Cartwright's plans but the fact that "We intend to let fly a drive official at them in the next *York Gazette* as the Genl. thinks it may have a good effect on both sides."[31] The February 4 issue of the *Gazette* contained Brock's patriotic speech on the opening of the legislature the previous day, a copy of an attack on the policy of the American government from the *Quebec Gazette,* and as a special supplement, a passionate analysis of the war addressed to the "Inhabitants of Upper Canada" and signed "A Loyalist." This was the opening gun of a propaganda campaign which faltered occasionally but never entirely failed through the war years.

To the campaign a number of people contributed in important ways. Of these Brock was certainly the most significant. Not only were his speeches, proclamations and general orders important but he probably initiated the campaign and, as will be discussed shortly, he developed one whole line of propaganda himself. The Reverend John Strachan was also deeply involved in the effort. In 1810, in an attempt to arouse patriotism and loyalty (and probably also to demonstrate his own commitment), he published *A Discourse on the Character of King George the Third,* a long patriotic pamphlet which also damned the United States. When in the summer of 1812 he took up the post of rector of York and chaplain of the garrison and of the Legislative Council, he plunged immediately into the fray. He published two of his more patriotic sermons during the war and claimed to have written the "Address of the House of Assembly to the People of Upper Canada" adopted by that body at the end of their session in August 1812 and printed and distributed throughout the province.[32] That address was both a call to patriotic duty and a strong denunciation of the United States and is particularly interesting because the assembly which adopted it had just refused to suspend *habeus corpus* and amend the militia act to punish the avoidance of duty more severely. Strachan was never one to hide his light under a

The "Upper Canada Preserved" medal, produced by the "Loyal and Patriotic Society of Upper Canada" was never issued, as intended, to Canadians who had distinguished themselves in the defense of their province.

bushel and he noted to a friend that, in addition to the above, he had "many opportunities when preaching & my general knowledge of the people [sic] to preserve and increase the spirit of Loyalty which principally saved the Province during the first two years of the war."[33]

There were, of course, others who were involved in the Canadian propaganda campaign but they remain anonymous, some because a name was not attached to their work and others because they chose, like Richard Cartwright, to write under *noms-de-plume* such as "A Loyalist," "A Loyalist's Son," and "Camilus."

III

From the time of his death, Canadians regarded General Isaac Brock as a hero. That elevation was based on his military exploits but it is clear that his propaganda efforts are equally deserving of recognition. In late 1811, shortly after he arrived in the province, Brock prepared a report on his situation for his superior, General Prevost. He noted that the people were much heartened by the appointment of himself - a military man - to administer the government, and by recent additions to its military establishment. He also reported that although there were in the province "improper characters ... whose principles diffuse a spirit of insubordination," he had been to Niagara where he found the principal inhabitants to be firmly loyal and determined to support the government and was assured that a large majority of the population would "prove faithful."[34] Over the next months, however, Brock became more and more pessimistic about the population. The first shock came in February 1812 when the Assembly, which he had confidently assumed would pass bills to give the government emergency powers, refused to cooperate. The reason, he felt, was "the great influence which the vast number of settlers from the United States possess over the decisions of the Lower House."[35] Over the next months evidence of the reluctance of large parts of the population to participate in the defence of the province continued to come in. When war was declared and Hull brought his army into Upper Canada, the worst fears came true. From all over the western part of the province reports came in of militiamen who refused to answer the call to arms or, when they did turn out, deserted at the first opportunity. The great shock, though, came from the newly elected assembly. Called into session immediately to consider Brock's emergency measures it, like its predecessor, refused to pass them. At the end of July Brock summed up his position:

> *My situation is getting each day more critical ... The population, although I had no great confidence in the majority, is worse than I expected to find it, and the magistrates, &c, &c, appear quite confounded and decline acting - the consequence is the most improper conduct is tolerated. The officers of militia exert no authority. Everything*

> *shows as if a certainty existed of a change taking place soon ...*
>
> *A more decent house* [of Assembly] *has not been elected since the formation of the Province, but I perceived at once that I shall get no good of them. They, like the magistrates and others in office, evidently mean to remain passive. The repeal of* habeas corpus *will not pass and if I have recourse to the law martial I am told the whole armed force will disperse. Never was an officer placed in a more awkward predicament. The militia cannot possibly be governed by the present law - all admit that fact, yet the fear of giving offence will prevent anything effectual from being effected.*[36]

Brock was sure that this situation could be cured by stationing more regular troops in Upper Canada and on numerous occasions he pleaded with Prevost for such reinforcement. This of course, was impossible until Lower Canada itself was reinforced so Brock had to turn to other strategies. One of these was to assure the population on every possible occasion that Britain would never abandon a colony which she so highly valued and that he intended to devote all his energy to its defense.[37] Another was to ensure that good tidings were quickly disseminated. When Hull withdrew his army from Upper Canada, Brock immediately put that news into a general order, along with the first details of the capture of Michilimackinac, and directed commanding officers to make certain that it and all other general orders were read to militia units. The general order also praised the militia and noted that "if the enemy is thus made to sustain severe losses at the Threshold of our Territory by a small but determined band of United Troops, what has he to expect from the whole Physical Force of the Province actuated by an ardor and Loyalty worthy of their Sires?"[38] Brock also made sure that the American prisoners of war from Michilimackinac and Detroit were paraded in front of as many Upper Canadians as possible.[39]

Nor was Brock above a bit of bribery. In May 1812 he suggested to the Executive Council that permission be obtained from the home government to place on the United Empire Loyalist list the names of all militiamen, provincial mariners, and regular soldiers in Upper Canada killed, maimed or disabled in defense of the province. This would make them and their families eligible for land grants. The counsellors were too jealous of Loyalist privileges to permit the dilution of the Loyalist list, but they did approve of the idea of land grants and only four days later a militia general order announced the plan. This idea was further developed by John Strachan at the end of 1812 when he brought together the "Principal Inhabitants of York and its Vicinity" to found "The Loyal and Patriotic Society of Upper Canada." The Society, supported by donations, announced that it would provide relief for the distressed families of militiamen and provide aid for those disabled in service. It also sought to "reward merit, excite emulation and commemorate glorious exploits by bestowing medals or honorary marks of public approbation."[40] Publicly Strachan stressed the benevolent aims of the society but privately he emphasized its propaganda function. Reporting in 1814 to the directors of the Society in his capacity as treasurer, he noted that,

> *... as it is a principal object with the Society, to nourish affection for the Government, and a determined resistance to the enemy; the committee will carefully attend to that part of the constitution, which excludes all those who have deserted their posts, or have given just cause of suspicion from participating in their bounty.*[41]

General Sir Roger Sheaffe, who succeeded Brock as military commander and civil administrator in Upper Canada, thought the Society was a marvellous idea and helped to ensure that copies of the constitution were distributed, particularly into the western part of the province, as soon as possible.[42]

Brock's most subtle - and arguably his greatest - contribution not merely to the propaganda campaign but to the war itself was the public stance he maintained in the face of the widespread defeatism and disaffection he found in Upper Canada. As he became aware of its extent he could well have adopted a defeatist attitude himself and lashed out at the popular failings. The approach he took was daring and imaginative. In a letter to Prevost in December 1811 he laid it out. "It is certain that the best policy to be pursued, should future circumstances call for active preparations," he wrote, "will be to act with the utmost liberality, and as if no mistrust existed."[43] He maintained this policy even through the worst of times. Thus, although he wrote to Prevost on July 20 complaining of the poor conduct and lack of enthusiasm not only of the militia but of the population in general, when he opened the legislature a few days later he painted a very different picture in his speech:

> *Our Militia have heard* [the voice of loyalty] ... *and obeyed it. They have evinced by the promptitude and Loyalty of their conduct that they are worthy of the King whom they serve and the Constitution which they enjoy; and it affords me particular satisfaction that while I address you as Legislators I speak to Men, who in the day of danger, will be ready to assist*

not only with their Counsel but with their Arms.[44]

And although he informed the legislature that "the disaffected ... are few," he gave the Executive Council a more candid report. The militia, he told them, "was in a perfect state of insubordination ...; had refused to march when legally commanded ...; had insulted their officers, and some, not immediately embodied, had manifested in many instances a treasonable spirit of Neutrality or disaffection."[45] From the meeting of the legislature Brock hurried to Amherstburg to oppose General Hull. There the desertions from the militia were impossible to ignore but Brock merely issued a general order in which he expressed surprise at them and stated his willingness to believe that they were motivated by a desire to return home to bring in the harvest, not by "a predilection for the principles or Government of the United States."[46] His treatment of the often-reluctant militia of the Niagara peninsula in the weeks that followed was equally gentle. Brock's successors were wise enough to carry on his policy and although there were occasional warning to the public to beware of cowards and traitors, not until well into 1813 was there any public notice of the extent of defeatism and disaffection or any hint that the militia had not valiantly and to a man carried out its duty. By that time the British forces in the province were being reinforced and the situation in Europe gave promise of more troops being available for Canada shortly. In November the government had no hesitation in announcing the capture of "a band of Traitors who in violation of their allegiance and of every principle of Honor and Honesty had leagued themselves with the Enemies of their country" and to try them publicly for treason at Ancaster the following year.[47]

Brock's policy was clearly the origin of the militia myth which was for so long a part of Upper Canadian history.[48] According to it, from the very beginning of the war the American invaders were turned back by the Upper Canadian militia, assisted on occasion by a few hundred British regulars. The myth took hold even before the end of the war. In a letter to Dugald Stewart in 1814 John Strachan attributed the preservation of the province to the militia and in a sermon predicted that:

... it will be told by future Historians, that the Province of Upper Canada, without the assistance of men or arms, except a handful of regular troops, repelled its invaders, slew or took them all prisoners, and captured from its enemies the greater part of the arms by which it was defended.[49]

When John Clarke, a captain of militia during the war, wrote his memoirs sometime after 1837, he bragged that the declaration of war had been "a signal for the loyal inhabitants to rush *en masse* to the frontiers of the country to repel invasion" and quoted from some of Brock's more outrageous inventions to back up his statement. By the late nineteenth century when Egerton Ryerson, in an effort to establish the place of the Loyalists as the moral founders of British Canada, wrote *The Loyalists of America and Their Times,* the myth had become the truth and he could confidently assert that Upper Canada had been saved by "spartan bands of Canadian Loyalist volunteers,

The second monument to Gen. Isaac Brock, drawn by Benson J. Lossing in 1860. By that time Brock's reputation and that of the Upper Canada militia were well established.

aided by a few hundred English soldiers and civilized Indians."[50] Brock would have been pleased.

IV

By modern standards all of the Upper Canadian efforts made only a very modest propaganda campaign, but given the times and the frontier and pioneer character of most of the province its extent was really quite extraordinary and is understandable only in terms of the apprehensions of the Upper Canadian elite about the willingness of the population to resist an American invasion and even about its basic loyalty. The aim of the overwhelming bulk of the propaganda which they produced was to convince Upper Canadians that they must resist an American invasion and the arguments which they used in their attempt to achieve this end are worth examining in some detail.

Some of the arguments used were simplicity itself. A number of writers, for instance, invoked the pride of the settlers in their British heritage of freedom and independence and called for a recognition of the debt they owed Britain for their generous inheritance from her in land, law, and government.[51] Combined with this, though, could be warnings and even veiled threats. Brock cautioned the assembly in a speech that without Britain's support, Upper Canada, "from its geographical position, must inevitably sink into comparative poverty and insignificance," and "A Loyalist" suggested that although the Americans might win some initial battles, the nation which was trouncing Napoleon on land and sea was not likely to "suffer a parcel of peddling land jobbers to wrest from her a foot of territory."[52]

The mainstream of the propaganda, however, had as its focus the causes of the war. The Upper Canadian conservative elite were quite sure they knew why American relations with Britain deteriorated to the point of war. For these people, some of them victims of Patriot mobs during the American Revolution, the great illusion of the age was democracy - turning over to the mass of the people the power to choose their own governors and the course society would follow. The illusion lay in the belief that the masses were wise or knowledgeable enough to handle this power responsibly. The conservative elite believed that history had proved in ancient Greece and Rome and time and again since - most recently in Revolutionary France - that the mass always misuses its power to force conformity on minorities and itself eventually succumbs to the wiles of demagogues who soon installed themselves as tyrants. So it was that once free, happy, and prosperous societies were reduced to poverty and misery. These people did not deny that democracy had a place in society - indeed they were sure that it was an essential component of any society that aspired to liberty. They believed, rather, that democracy must be offset by responsibility and that the liberty it could bring must be a restrained and judicious liberty. In practice this meant that the leadership of society must be conceded to men of education, wealth, and proven judgement who would deny the popular will when it was necessary to do so.[53]

For the Upper Canadian elite, avid observers of the nation to the south, the American experiment in democratic republicanism had succeeded in the 1790s because it had been led by the Federalists, whom they identified as the men of wealth and education. In the last years of the century, however, the process of decay set in, in the form of Thomas Jefferson and his followers.[54] When Jefferson was elected president in 1800, the conservative elite were sure that the decline of American society would be rapid and complete. Two things in particular condemned the Jeffersonians. First, they had split away from the Federalists and formed an opposition party, which to conservative minds of the time meant they had placed their own selfish interests ahead of the interests of the nation. Equally important, though, in the great war going on between France and England, the Jeffersonians leaned towards France while the Federalists favored England. This was no trivial distinction. In conservative eyes Britain was the champion of Liberty who was devoting her treasure and the flower of her menfolk to the defeat of Napoleonic tyranny. The "Virginia Oligarchy" demonstrated its true colors when it adopted pro-French policies and thus sided with tyranny.[55] Particularly after the *Chesapeake-Leopard* affair, the Upper Canadian elite were sure that the Jeffersonians were becoming more tyrannical in their policies and more influenced by Napoleon. The tyranny was demonstrated in the trade restrictions so devastating to the New England merchant economy and denounced by the Federalists as "unconstitutional, ruinous and tyrannical."[56] The influence of Napoleon was apparent in attitudes and policies which seemed designed to bring on war with Britain. As the war neared and then was declared, the Canadian propagandists repeated this analysis again and again. "The President," wrote "Camilus,"

> *... together with the majority of the members of Congress, are composed of southern epicures, whose bodies and whose minds have become enervated by idleness, intemperance, and every species of excess, and whose hearts have become callous to the feelings of humanity by the daily habits of tyranny and cruelty, which they are exercising over their slaves 'who fan them when they sleep,' and by whose toil and sweat they are supplied with all*

> *the luxuries the palate of an epicure could suggest.*[57]

It was these people who, once they had the power of the state in their hands,

> *... trampled on the rights and liberties of their constituents, destroyed their commerce, ruined the merchant, disheartened the farmer, palsied every incitement to industry, and threw the whole nation into a kind of apathy and despair.*[58]

It was these people who were the natural allies of Napoleon. In joining the war against Britain they were following his bidding and becoming a part of "the most formidable conspiracy against the civilization of man that ever was contrived."[59] That their motive in declaring war was not the freedom of neutral trade put forward by President Madison in his war message was made perfectly clear when the British cancellation of the offending Orders-in-Council was not followed by an American peace initiative. "The American government," wrote Sir George Prevost in a widely circulated general order, "has proclaimed in language not to be misunderstood that other objects independent of those held out to the American people as grounds of the war were originally in their contemplation."[60] When a copy of an address of the American General Alexander Smyth to his troops in Buffalo fell into his hands, one Canadian pounced on it in a letter to the editor of the *York Gazette.* Smyth had told his troops that they were going to "conquer Canada" and the writer found in that phrase the true reason for the American declaration of war.[61]

The propagandists also went on to lay out just what Canadians could expect from an American invasion. For "A Canadian" it would mean joining America in her social and political degeneration. Canadians, he said, had the great fortune to participate in the British constitution which was protection against such a fate. "We have," he argued, "real liberty grounded upon the most wise and equitable laws," protection of property, personal safety, and prosperity, but all that would be lost "should the enemy succeed in persuading the Canadian people that they are come to fraternize and regenerate them, by blinding their understanding with a dose of republican Jargon."[62] Others saw an even worse fate for Canada, reannexation to the dominion of France. That was the price of France's aid to the United States in the Revolution "and the debt is still due."[63] Just what that meant was made clear in a report in the *York Gazette* of August 22, 1812, which printed a list of the cargo of a French ship captured at the time of Napoleon's attempt to invade Britain. The cargo included 50,120 thumb screws, 44,201 toe vices, 25,040 pair of fetters, and 479 racks. The editor commented that

> *... many of these instruments of torture, which were unquestionably intended to facilitate the discovery of property, had the words Liberty, at full length; and others, the initials L.E. Liberty and Equality stamped on them.*

The political situation in the United States also gave the propagandists a vision of the kind of war that would be fought. Jane Errington and George Rawlyk point out in their valuable article, "The Loyalist-Federalist Alliance of Upper Canada," that the propagandists were careful not to condemn all Americans: the war, they said, was opposed by all the best parts of American society. But that led to another conclusion: the American army would be made up of "the refuse and scum of the earth ... Our Fertile plains, and the fruits of our industry are no doubt temptations every way calculated to excite their avarice, and gratify their abominable and licentious passion for plunder and rapine."[64] Richard Cartwright in one of his early "Falkland" letters was sure that the Loyalists would be particularly singled out for ill-treatment by invading American democrats.[65] When the war came, it brought opportunities for atrocity stories and they were seldom neglected.[66]

V

This examination of the propaganda of the War of 1812 raises a number of questions. The most obvious is whether or not the propaganda was intentional. Propaganda may be defined as the attempt to control people's actions by controlling their attitudes but much that could be thus defined could be unintentional; a teacher in the course of his or her work is often an unintentional propagandist. Intentional propaganda "arises ... from interested motives, is consciously and systematically carried on, and its primary purpose is to obtain public support for a particular idea or course of action."[67] That this was the case with both the limited American effort and the extensive Canadian one is obvious. The intent of the various authors to persuade Upper Canadians to resist or not resist the American invasion is apparent in the content of many of the pieces, but even where it is not, other evidence exists. As already noted, Cartwright, Strachan and Brock all made clear their intentions at one time or another and Prevost established his credentials as a propagandist when he recommended to Brock in July 1812 that the news be widely disseminated that the British government had repealed the Orders-In-Council. "Although I much doubt," he wrote,

> *... whether this step on the part of our government will have any effect upon that of the United States, the circulation of the paper evincing their con-*

ciliatory disposition may tend to increase & strengthen the divisions which exist among the people upon the subject of war.[68]

We can also ask if the propagandists themselves believed the ideas they put forward. There are two commonly held but erroneous ideas about propaganda: that it is essentially lies and that it is something that the bad guys engage in and which the good guys counter with "the truth." In reality, the chief characteristic of propaganda is that is seeks to achieve its aim not by the use of reason and balanced and objective arguments but by appeals to emotion and by the use of one-sided arguments and partial information. Most commercial advertising is propaganda. The best propagandists themselves believe the ideas they put forward, but it is not their belief or lack of it which makes them propagandists - it is their methods.

With the obvious exception of such things as Brock's "militia myth" campaign, it seems likely that the propagandists of the War of 1812 believed the basic ideas they propounded, for most of them can be found in peacetime settings which had no propaganda intent.[69] But it is also clear that on occasion propagandists modified or exaggerated ideas to increase their impact. Good examples of this can be found in two pieces written by the Reverend John Strachan.

In 1814 Strachan published a sermon celebrating the surrender of Napoleon. It included an account of the war and of Britain's heroic role, in the course of which he expressed directly and obliquely his very conservative views about government and society. There are, for instance, lower and superior orders of society and the latter are the natural governors; if on occasion the governors make mistakes, they should be seen as merely a failing to which all human beings are prone and not taken as a cause to incite rebellion; misery is "inseperable from mortality," and "no great and decided amelioration of the lower classes of society can be expected." He also attributed the salvation of Canada to the Loyalist population and denounced the "shortsighted and mistaken policy" - that which had opened Upper Canada to American settlers - for introducing "traitors and false friends."[70]

Strachan wrote the sermon in the confident expectation that British troops, freed from their European duties, would quickly bring the North American conflict to an end. Two years earlier, however, when General Hull was in Upper Canada and promising the people liberty, prosperity and happiness without end, Stachan wrote another public address, the "Address of the House of Assembly to the People of Upper Canada." In it he examined the war and explained the virtues of the government which Upper Canadians had been given in the Constitution of 1791. He avoided, however, discussing any of the very conservative provisions of that document, such as the clergy reserves, the expanded power of the governor, and the provision for a hereditary aristocracy, and never once mentioned the conservative social theory so prevalent in his 1814 sermon. As for the many recent settlers from the United States, although they "would naturally lean against us," their inclinations were "in the main good."

Finally, we can ask how effective the propaganda was. Unfortunately this question is impossible to answer with any significant degree of accuracy. Not only is there no objective evidence from which "before" and "after" measurements can be made, but in any particular case there are always extraneous factors. General Hull's proclamation comes across as the most effective single piece of propaganda of the war, but it must be asked how much of what can be seen as its effect was in fact due to the already notorious reluctance of Upper Canadians to resist an American invasion. As indicated earlier, there is evidence of the effectiveness of Hull's proclamation but even then it can be asked whether Upper Canadians were responding merely to Hull's promise to protect private property, as the slim evidence available would indicate, or to the many other appeals in the proclamation as well.

The degree of success of Upper Canadian propaganda is even more difficult to assess. On the surface it would seem to have been an exercise in futility, since the propaganda campaign which began in February 1812 could not even by August bring the agreement of a newly elected legislative assembly to Brock's emergency measures. To be sure, there was a marked decline in disaffection and defeatism in the autumn of 1812 but that could be expected as a result of the astonishing victories over the Americans at Detroit and Queenston. The fact that disaffection increased again in 1813 when the Americans forces achieved a series of victories would seem to clinch the case, were it not that Canadian propaganda declined markedly at that time as a result of paper shortages and the disappearance or destruction of several presses, including that at York. There are also a few pieces of evidence which indicate that the message of the Canadian propagandists did get through to some. The best of these is a letter from one Isaac Wilson, a settler in the York area and a private in the York militia, to his brother in England. He wrote as follows:

> *The war is likely to prove a very disastrous one to the States. It was a foolish measure for their government. It is wholly attributed to the intrigues of the French. Many people feel they will lose their independence but how it will end no one can tell. The people in this country are very much divided in their political principles. Many of them*

are friendly to the States and wish the country to fall into their hands and where the Americans conquer they have no mercy on the property of the other party.[71]

Unfortunately for the historian there are not enough Wilson letters about.

There is, however, another way to appraise, although tenuously, the effectiveness of the propaganda. The basis of this is an understanding that the potential success of propaganda is limited by a number of factors. In his book *Techniques of Persuasion,* J.A.C. Brown writes:

Propaganda is limited by prevailing interests, social trends and prejudices; it is encouraged by ignorance of the facts and is more likely to succeed when it flows with the social current than when it flows against it ... the propagandist can accelerate or retard a trend in public opinion but he cannot reverse it.[72]

Clearly Hull's proclamation went with the flow and was correspondingly successful; had it been followed up, the outcome of the war for at least parts of Upper Canada might have been different. Canadian propagandists, on the other hand, were going against the flow and achieved correspondingly meager results. It can be argued, though, that the military successes of the fall of 1812 did provide a base on which to build, and as a result the defeatism and disaffection which reappeared in 1813 were neither as pervasive nor as threatening as in 1812.[73]

But if we cannot gauge with any degree of accuracy the effect of Upper Canadian propaganda during the war, it is possible to speak more authoritatively of later years. As noted earlier, Brock's efforts produced the enduring militia myth but it was by no means the only part of the propagandists' efforts to survive the war. Their whole interpretation of the war was passed on and lasted for more than a century. A generation after the Treaty of Ghent, Gilbert Auchinleck published in Toronto a history of the war which contained all the essentials of the Canadian propagandists' version of it. He found, for instance, that the "reflecting portion of the community" in the United States was opposed to the war and that although Madison was not a traitor to the United States as some claimed, he was nevertheless "entangled in the toils of French intrigue." It was French gold, he surmised, which was behind the "idle speculation" that Canadians were anxious to escape the tyranny of British rule. When the United States persisted in the war despite the British repeal of the offending Orders-in-Council, it did so "for want of a better excuse," on the ground of the Impressment question. He also found that while there were in Upper Canada American settlers who were "everywhere disseminating their evil counsels," when the war came the people of Upper Canada demonstrated their loyalty to Britain. Hull's proclamation, he noted, "failed in producing its anticipated effect." That Auchinleck should come to such conclusions is not surprising since he quotes liberally from such propaganda pieces as Brock's proclamation, his speech to the legislature in August 1812, and Strachan's "Address of the House of Assembly."[74]

Although there were occasional modifications, this interpretations persisted with Canadian historians through the remainder of the nineteenth century and well into the twentieth. Not until Ernest Cruikshank began his monumental investigations into the War of 1812 was the propaganda version challenged. Cruikshank began to publish his multi-volume documentary history of the war in the last years of the nineteenth century but James Hannay's *History of the War of 1812,* published in 1905, still relied extensively on the propagandists for its interpretation of the war. Cruikshank's "A Study of Disaffection in Upper Canada in 1812-15" appeared in 1912 but in 1930 George Wrong could still hint darkly that the issues of impressment and neutral trade were only the "ostensible" reasons for the American declaration of war and that Canada was defended by its own people with merely "the aid" of British regulars.[75]

At the beginning of this essay it was suggested that propaganda can be revealing of the society which produced it. The very fact that propaganda was used as a weapon and the ways in which it was used are themselves revealing, but a few particular conclusions and speculations also emerge. Because there was so little American propaganda, the revelations which can be drawn from it are few and tenuous. They are nevertheless interesting. For one thing it demonstrates that there were Americans who looked to the addition of Canada to the Union as an outcome of the war. This is nowhere more explicit than in an address by General Alexander Smyth to his army at Buffalo but which was immediately available across the border. In urging them to be moderate in their treatment of Canadian civilians, he wrote:

... you will enter a country that is to be one of the United States. You will arrive among a people who are to become your fellow citizens.[76]

The propaganda also demonstrates an early version of that peculiarly American conceit, that people everywhere yearn for the chance to become American citizens, and the idea from which it springs, that true liberty and happiness and the prosperity which they necessarily bring exist only in America. In just a few decades these ideas would be joined with others and sanctified with the name "Manifest Destiny."

The Canadian propaganda is even more revealing. It demonstrates the deep conservatism of the Upper

Canadian elite and its fundamental distrust of democratic and republican ideas because they would undermine the structured society which they believed was at the root of social order and "rational liberty." It is also evidence of the shock of the elite when the war revealed how little control it had over the population. We can understand, if not sympathize with, the determination of the Family Compact in the postwar years to suppress democratic influences in general and American influences in particular, whenever they raised their heads in the province. It is also possible to see in the propaganda a basis for some ideas long held in Upper Canada and subsequently Ontario. One was that the British connection was essential. The other emerges from the direction of most of the propaganda. Explicitly or implicitly it was directed at the Loyalists while the later American settlers - who in fact composed the majority of the population - were often ignored or at best treated as a small group who could be controlled with warnings of the price of treason. The picture that can emerge, especially when the image this can create is combined with the militia myth, is one of Upper Canada as a Loyalist province. When people such as Egerton Ryerson later looked back to the beginnings of the province they could find, if they so wished, a society of Loyalist heroes created by the propagandists of 1812.

Notes

[1] J.C.A. Stagg, *Mr. Madison's War* (Princeton, 1983), ch. 1.

[2] *National Intelligencer,* Dec. 3, 1811. This was one of three articles entitled *The Canadas*. All are printed as an appendix in Stagg.

[3] Isaac Brock to Sir George Prevost, Feb. 25 1812, printed in William Wood (ed.), *Select British Documents of the Canadian War of 1812* (hereafter *SD*) (3 vols.; Toronto, 1920-26), I, 169; Brock to Prevost, Dec. 3, 1811, National Archives of Canada (hereafter NAC), Colonial Office Papers (CO), 42/352; J.B. Glegg to Thomas Talbot, March 12, 1812, printed in James H. Coyne (ed.), "The Talbot Papers", *Proceedings and Transactions of the Royal Society of Canada,* Third Series, vol. I (1907).

[4] Ernest Cruikshank, "A Study of Disaffection in Upper Canada in 1812-15" in Morris Zaslow (ed.), *The Defended Border* (Toronto, 1964), p. 206; Statements of Henry Clay and William Eustis quoted in Ferdinand Brock Tupper, Family Records; containing the Memoirs of Major-General Isaac Brock (Guernsey, 1835), p. 133.

[5] Richard Cartwright to Lt. Gov. Peter Hunter, Aug. 23, 1799, Douglas Library, Queen's University, Kingston, Ont., Richard Cartwright Letter Books.

[6] Maj. Graham to D.W. Smith, March 29, 1802, NAC, Record Group (RG) 1, Upper Canada State Papers.

[7] Lt. Gov. Francis Gore to Craig, Jan. 5, 1808, NAC, CO 42/136.

[8] The initiative here came from Governor Prevost who received warnings to that effect from British consuls in New York City and Philadelphia. See Thomas Barclay to Prevost, Jan. 22, 1812 in Ernest Cruikshank (ed.), *Documentary History of the Campaign Upon the Niagara Frontier in 1812-1814* (hereafter *DH*) (9 vols.; Welland, Ont., 1896-1908), III, 34 and Cruikshank, "A Study of Disaffection ..."

[9] A.W. Cochran to his father, June 23, 1812, quoted in Cruikshank, "A Study of Disaffection ..."; Upper Canada Executive Council Minute Book, Feb. 18, 1812, NAC, RG 1; Proclamation published in the *York Gazette,* March 4, 1812.

[10] Brock to Lord Liverpool, Aug. 29, 1812, NAC, CO 42/352.

[11] There is, however, a report by a commissioner to the Indians on the Grand River of the arrival there of Indians from the Buffalo area of New York. They were representatives of the Seneca chief Red Jacket and their purpose was to dissuade the Grand River Iroquois from joining the British in the coming war. J.B. Rousseau to Col. Claus, July 7, 1812, NAC, RG 1, E 3, Upper Canada State Papers, 79.

[12] In January and again in early August the assembly refused, by narrow margins, to pass bills which would have suspended *habeus corpus* and, among other things, demanded from members of the militia an oath abjuring all other loyalties.

[13] Michael Smith, *A Geographical View of the Province of Upper Canada,* 3rd ed. (Philadelphia, 1813), p. 83.

[14] Brock to Prevost, Feb. 25 and July 12, 1812, *SD,* I, 169, 352; Brock to Liverpool, March 23, 1812, NAC, CO 42/352.

[15] The proclamation can be found in a number of sources. It is reprinted in Arthur Bowler, *The War of 1812* (Toronto, 1973), p. 52 and in *SD*, I, 355. The *Kingston Gazette* printed it on August 18, and there is an original copy in NAC, CO 42/147.

[16] Prevost to Liverpool, July 30, 1812, NAC, CO 42/147.

[17] Daniel Springer to Brock, July 23, 1812, Talbot to Brock, July 27, 1812, Brock to Prevost, July 28, 1812, Brock to Baynes, July 29 and Aug. 4, 1812, *SD,* I, 375-76, 382, 386-87, 396, 409; Upper Canada Executive Council Minute Book, Minutes of Aug. 3, 1812, NAC, RG 1; Henry Adams, *The History of the United States Under the Administration of James Madison* (New York, 1880), p. 303.

[18] *Kingston Gazette,* July 31, 1812. It is also printed in Bowler, pp. 53-55 and *SD*, I, 371-74.

[19] *DH,* III, 268.

[20] It did occur to others, though. Governor Tompkins of New York felt that the very appearance of an American army on the Niagara Frontier would end the war, especially if it were accompanied by a proclamation "extending the hand of fellowship" to the Canadian militia, which would revolt against Great Britain. He made the suggestion in a letter written on July 12, 1812, the day Hull issued his proclamation. Stagg, pp. 243-44. See also p. 201.

[21] *SD,* II, 441.

[22] Declaration of the American Commandant of Ft. Erie, May 30, 1813, NAC, CO 42/151.

[23] Address to the Inhabitants of the Province of Upper Canada, Oct. 16, 1813, *DH,* VIII, 65. The fourth proclamation is one mentioned by Cruikshank in "A Study of Disaffection", but I have been unable

to find it. It was issued by General Harrison and Commodore Perry to the people of the Western District.

[24] NAC, RG 5, Upper Canada Sundries, 6532.

[25] NAC, CO 42/151; *DH,* IX, 112.

[26] For the *York Gazette* see, for example, March 18, July 28, Aug. 29, 1812.

[27] *Kingston Gazette,* Aug. 18, Dec. 19, 1812.

[28] *Ibid.,* July 28, 1812.

[29] General Order, June 8, 1812, *DH,* IX, 63.

[30] *York Gazette,* Feb. 26, Sept. 12, 1812. The *Canadian Courant* was published in Montreal by Nahum Mower, a man noted for his enthusiastic loyalty.

[31] Andrew Gray to Prevost, Jan. 29, 1812, *DH,* III, 35-38. Gray was killed the next year in the assault on Sackets Harbor.

[32] John Strachan to Lt. Col. Clifford, April 26, 1816 in George W. Sprague (ed.), *The John Strachan Letter Book, 1812-1834* (Toronto, 1946).

[33] *Ibid.*

[34] Brock to Prevost, Dec. 3, 1811, NAC, CO 42/352.

[35] Brock to Prevost, Feb. 25, 1812, *SD,* I, 169.

[36] Brock to Prevost, July 28, 1812, *DH,* III, 148.

[37] See, for instance, *Kingston Gazette,* Feb. 19, 1812, Brock's speech on opening the Legislature; Militia General Orders, July 4, 1812, NAC, RG 9.

[38] *SD,* I, 407-08.

[39] The prisoners from Michilimackinac and Detroit were also brought through Fort Erie, in full view of Buffalo, with the intent of disheartening the American forces assembled there. See Stagg, p. 247.

[40] After the war Strachan published a *Report of the Loyal and Patriotic Society of Upper Canada, with an Appendix and a List of Subscribers* (Montreal, 1817). The constitution of the society was also printed in the *Kingston Gazette,* Feb. 23, 1813.

[41] Strachan, *Report of the Loyal and Patriotic Society,* p. 325. Although the document is undated, its position in the correspondence printed makes a date in the first half of 1814 fairly certain.

[42] Gen. Roger H. Sheaffe to W.D. Powell, Dec. 20, 1812, *DH,* V, 20.

[43] Brock to Prevost, Dec. 2, 1811, *SD,* I, 272.

[44] *Ibid.,* I, 390.

[45] Brock's representation on the state of the Province & Council minutes, Aug. 3, 1812, NAC, RG 1, Upper Canada State Papers, 7.

[46] District General Order, Aug. 14, 1812, *SD,* I, 459.

[47] Militia General Orders, Nov. 25, 1813, NAC, RG 9.

[48] C.P. Stacey, "The War of 1812 in Canadian History", in Zaslow, p. 332.

[49] Sprague, p. 58; Strachan, *Report of the Loyal and Patriotic Society,* p. 365.

[50] Egerton Ryerson, *The Loyalists of America and Their Times* (2 vols.; Toronto, 1880), II, p. 379. Ryerson printed excerpts from Clarke's memoirs in his work. This is not to deny that the militia played an important role in the war, merely that they were not the essential core of the forces defending Upper Canada. The role of the militia is described in George F.G. Stanley, "The Contribution of the Canadian Militia to the War" in Philip Mason et. al., *After Tippecanoe: Some Aspects of the War of 1812* (Toronto, 1963).

[51] See, for instance, the "Falkland" letters printed in the *Kingston Gazette,* Feb. 18 and March 3, 1812, Brock's proclamation in response to Hull, *ibid.,* July 28, 1812 and Strachan's "Address of the House of Assembly", *ibid.,* Sept. 5, 1812.

[52] *York Gazette,* Feb. 4 and Feb. 18, 1812.

[53] This understanding of the world-view of the Upper Canadian elite was first developed by Prof. S.F. Wise and is developed fully in his two essays in S.F. Wise and R.C. Brown, *Canada Views the United States* (Toronto, 1967).

[54] See particularly the address by "John Bull jun," to "The Independent Electors of the County of Frontenac" in the *Kingston Gazette,* May 26, 1812.

[55] This paper can only touch on the complex reaction of the Upper Canadian elite to events in the United States in these years. For the full story the reader is referred to the very perceptive article by Jane Errington and George Rawlyk, "The Loyalist-Federalist Alliance of Upper Canada", *The American Review of Canadian Studies,* XVI, no. 2 (Summer 1984), 157-76.

[56] *Upper Canada Gazette,* Jan. 12, 1808 quoted in *Ibid.,* 165.

[57] *Kingston Gazette,* Dec. 12, 1812.

[58] *Ibid.,* May 26, 1812.

[59] *York Gazette,* Sept. 5, 1812, "Address of the Assembly".

[60] *Kingston Gazette,* Sept. 19, 1812.

[61] Dec. 12, 1812. Smyth's address is reprinted in the *Kingston Gazette,* Dec. 26, 1812.

[62] *York Gazette,* Feb. 4, 1812. See also the *Kingston Gazette,* Feb. 18, 1812, both "A Loyalist" and "Falkland" letters.

[63] *York Gazette,* July 28, 1812, Brock's proclamation in reply to Hull.

[64] *York Gazette,* Feb. 4, 1812.

[65] *Kingston Gazette,* Feb. 18, 1812.

[66] See, for instance, *Kingston Gazette,* Sept. 26 and Oct. 24, 1812 and Aug. 10, 1813. See also the handbill and proclamation printed in *DH,* IV, 313 and IX, 112.

[67] Philip Davidson, *Propaganda and the American Revolution, 1763-1783* (Chapel Hill, 1941), xiii. A good discussion of propaganda and propaganda techniques can also be found in Leonard W. Doob, *Propaganda: Its Psychology and Technique* (New York,

1935), J.A.C. Brown, *Techniques of Persuasion* (New York, 1963) and James T. Boulton, *The Language of Politics in the Age of Fox and Burke* (London, 1963).

[68] Prevost to Brock, July 12, 1812, NAC, MG 24, Brock Correspondence.

[69] For instance, Admiral Berkley, British commander on the North American station noted in a letter to Lt. Gov. Gore in 1807 that he had information of a secret agreement which provided that if Canada were captured by the United States in a war with Britain, it would be transferred to France. D. Brymer, *Report on the Canadian Archives, 1896* (Ottawa, 1896), p. 29.

[70] The Rev. John Strachan, D.D., *A Sermon Preached at York, Upper Canada, on the Third of June, being the Day Appointed for a General Thanksgiving* (Montreal, 1814).

[71] Isaac Wilson Diary, Dec. 5, 1813, Ontario Archives.

[72] Brown, p. 77.

[73] Cruikshank, "A Study of Disaffection"; Gerald M. Craig, *Upper Canada: The Formative Years* (Toronto, 1963), p. 77.

[74] Gilbert Auchinleck, *A History of the War Between Great Britain and the United States of America During the Years 1812, 1813 and 1814* (London, 1972, originally published 1855), pp. 42-49.

[75] Cruikshank's "A Study of Disaffection" was first published in the *Transactions of the Royal Society of Canada,* series three, section two (1912). Professor Wrong's 1930 work is *A Study of the Canadian People* (Toronto), see pp. 142-43, 151. Ryerson's *The Loyalists of America and Their Times* carries the propaganda interpretation in pristine form as does J.G. Bourinot's *Canada* (London, 1897). More detailed works, such as William Kingsford's *History of Canada* (London, 1895, see vol. VIII) and Adam Shortt and Arthur Doughty, *Canada and Its Provinces* (Toronto, 1913, see vol. III) managed largely to escape from the propagandists, especially when they examined the causes of the war, but even they succumbed to the militia myth.

[76] Frank Severance, "The Case of Brigadier General Alexander Smyth", *Publications of the Buffalo Historical Society,* 18 (Buffalo, 1914), 227-28.

THE POLITICS OF ENDING THE WAR OF 1812

by
J.C.A. Stagg

It is a commonplace to observe that the causes of war are studied far more frequently than the causes of peace. Certainly this is true with respect to the War of 1812. In Richard Burns' recently compiled bibliographical *Guide to American Foreign Relations since 1700* there are listed more than one hundred and fifty titles dealing with the coming of the War of 1812; on the ending of the war there are a mere eight.[1] And since the publication of the Burns *Guide* in 1983, there have appeared several more titles on the causes of the war, but none of any significance relating to its termination.[2] A variety of reasons might be adduced to account for this imbalance in the literature, but they might as well here be effectively reduced to the observation that historians have found the reasons for ending the War of 1812 to be as simple and obvious as they have found its causes to be obscure and controversial. So simple and obvious, in fact, that the ending of the War of 1812 is not usually regarded as a matter that requires any explanation at all.

As is well known, attempts to end the War of 1812 began right at its outset and continued intermittently throughout its duration. Moreover, it was the United States rather than Great Britain that always showed the greater interest in making peace. It was the United States that made the first overtures for peace in June-July 1812. It was the United States that seized at the Russian offer to mediate the conflict in

An allegorical picture, reproduced by Lossing, entitled "The Peace of Ghent, 1814, and Triumph of America". It emphasized American heroes and victories of the War of 1812. The latter however, required only the small pedestal at lower left.

President James Madison.

1813 and then clung to a hope in its efficacy long after Great Britain had made it clear that it had no interest in the business. And in addition to these official efforts to seek peace, the United States either prompted or encouraged a number of proposals for armistices, sometimes in conjunction with prisoner of war negotiations, only to see all of them fail.[3] Great Britain, by contrast, offered an armistice only once,[4] and although it took the initiative in November 1813 in proposing the negotiations that finally led to peace, it did so more to rid itself of the importunities of prospective Russian mediators than to make haste in ending its disputes with the United States.

Throughout the final year of the war, too, Great Britain was very slow to define its approach to making peace with the United States, a tardiness that was appropriately symbolized by the late arrival of its trio of negotiators in Ghent where their American counterparts had been awaiting them for weeks. And once in Ghent, the British seemed intent only on ending the peace talks by making demands that the Americans could scarcely even discuss, let alone accept, before they finally agreed, under the pressure of events in both Europe and America, to settle on Christmas Eve, 1814, for a peace based on the *status quo ante bellum.*

There is therefore an element of paradox that requires an explanation in any account of the ending of the War of 1812. Why did the United States appear to be so keen to end a war that it had declared and whose success was always dependent on its ability to carry the fight to the enemy? Most accounts of the war offer very simple answers to this question, to the extent that they bother to offer answers at all; and all would agree that the American quest for peace reflected two basic problems in the War of 1812: a distinct lack of public enthusiasm for the conflict, coupled with serious practical difficulties experienced in prosecuting it effectively. And since evidence of American disenchantment with the war and of military weakness in its conduct is not difficult to find, and once it is all put in context - the hesitations of the politicians, the incompetence of the generals, the undisciplined nature of the armies, and the financial and administrative chaos of the organization for war - it is scarcely to be wondered that the United States should have tried to extract itself from the war almost as soon as it got into it. The politics of peacemaking, in short, represented sober American second thoughts about the imprudence of the policy of war. Or, to paraphrase a theme that runs throughout Bradford Perkins' classic account of Anglo-American relations between 1812 and 1823, as the United States mismanaged its limited military resources between 1812 and 1814 to uphold its grossly unrealistic diplomatic pretensions, the Republican administration of James Madison gradually and painfully learned to temper the "idealism" of its policies with the "realism" of its Federalist opponents.[5] And by finally making peace at Ghent, the Madison administration, if it did not achieve its wartime foreign policy goals, at least laid the political and diplomatic foundations for the Era of Good Feelings.

Such is the conventional wisdom about the American search for peace after 1812, and it is *not* the purpose of this paper to suggest that it is either wrong or even somewhat misplaced. There is much truth in it, and the diplomatic and military aspects of the War of 1812 are sufficiently complex that no historian of the subject can successfully become a revisionist merely by standing old orthodoxies on their head. However, throughout the War of 1812 matters were seldom so simple and obvious at the time as they have seemed to historians writing after the event. This statement holds as true for the efforts to disengage from the conflict as it does for all the accounts that deal with its origins and progress. There is a good deal of evidence to suggest that the American quest for peace after 1812 arose not simply from a failure to win the war but reflected instead a variety of quite complex considerations. It is therefore important to review some of that evidence.

I

The first efforts to disengage from the war were made between June and September 1812. It cannot be plausibly argued, however, that they originated in disillusionment or in difficulties in waging the war. Let us briefly recall the events here.[6] On the day war was declared - June 18, 1812 - Secretary of State James Monroe summoned British minister Augustus Foster to his office, where, over a pot of tea, Monroe stated the American requirements for peace. These were the repeal of the orders in council and a settlement of the impressment dispute. The first issue was to be resolved, Foster recorded Monroe as saying, by Great Britain agreeing to a treaty containing "a definition of blockades according to the [Anglo-] Russian treaty" of 1801; while the second was to be placed beyond the realm of future controversy by a mutual agreement, to be embodied in British and American law, that the two nations would forgo the employment of each other's seamen in their merchant marines.[7] Monroe subsequently issued two sets of diplomatic instructions to Jonathan Russell, then chargé d'affaires in London, in June and July, offering essentially the same terms to the British government. Lord Castlereagh rejected both offers.

Admittedly, the United States did not open the Canadian campaigns of 1812 auspiciously, but this first effort to seek peace reflected neither sober second thoughts about the war nor any unusual difficulties in waging it. None of the practical problems of waging war was then acutely felt by the administration, and the news of the first serious disaster in the war, the fall of Detroit, did not reach Washington until the end of August 1812.[8] Rather, this first overture is best understood as a continuation of the politics and the diplomacy that had preceded the declaration of war. Just as the United States did not prepare for war after November 1811 without leaving open the chance of terminating the preparations if terms could be negotiated, so too it did not wage war without always leaving open the possibility of peace. This approach revealed, as much as anything else, President James Madison's carefully measured temperament as a diplomatist. When he took major decisions, he often carefully hedged his bets as he did so. But, more importantly, this approach also reflected his administration's understanding of the situation of Great Britain at the time of the declaration of war.

It is worth stressing here that the administration had grounds for believing that the war would succeed. It was not known in America in June-July 1812 that Great Britain was about to repeal the orders in council, but it was known very shortly after the declaration of war that the most ardent proponent of those orders, Prime Minister Spencer Perceval, had just been assassinated; and this news was accompanied by reports of social unrest in Great Britain on a truly alarming scale.[9] That British policies toward the United States would have to accommodate these unpleasant realities sooner or later was taken for granted by most Republican advocates of the war, and this was so even without their contemplating the difficulties that Napoleon's anticipated success in his invasion of Russia in 1812 would cause for Great Britain's diplomatic and commercial interests. On this last subject there is no need to refute at length the details of the Federalist charge that Madison had sought war with Great Britain in 1812 in order to serve the interests of French foreign policy,[10] but there is also little reason to doubt that both Madison and Monroe believed that Napoleon's Russian campaign would be successful, at least to the extent of restoring enough vigor to the Continental System to heighten the value of North American markets and resources to an already critically distressed British economy.[11] In fact, the administration may have hoped that the mere shock of the declaration of war itself, even before the results of any Canadian invasions were felt, would be sufficient to bring Great Britain to the negotiating table. As Monroe remarked on the eve of the war: "I have great hope that [the] decision here will at an early day rid the British nation of its present ministry, and that an accommodation will soon follow the change."[12]

For its part, the British ministry rejected these first initiatives, not because it was unconcerned about the pressures on it that might result from a successful American war in Canada combined with impact of Napoleonic success in Russia, but more simply because it felt it did not have to make any concessions at this time to restore peace. It should be recalled here that Great Britain repealed the orders in council on June 23, 1812, and the ministry assumed that this news alone, once it reached America, would be enough to stop any fighting. It therefore rejected Russell's overtures, made in August and September 1812, and only went so far as to empower its own agents in Canada, principally Admiral Sir John Borlase Warren, to arrange armistices that would secure Canada against invasion. At this time, Great Britain had no reason to suppose that the United States would continue the war over grievances other than the orders in council; and certainly not for impressment, which, although a very great injustice to Americans, had not been a topic of serious negotiation between the two governments for nearly five years before the declaration of war.

This first effort to end the war failed therefore as a result of the same sort of misunderstandings, erroneous preconceptions, and accidents of unfortunate timing that had contributed to the very outbreak of the conflict. The various transactions involved in the negotiations are thus better understood more as a comment on the causes of the war than they reflect an effort to disengage from a conflict that was already going wrong. On the British side particularly, there was a reluctance to accept the fact that there was a war, and before October 1812 the ministry did not so

John Quincy Adams served as U.S. Minister to Russia.

much refuse to make peace as, more simply, try to abort a conflict which it belatedly realized as it repealed the orders in council was likely to be a mistake.

II

The next effort to end the war centered round the Russian mediation of 1813, a interesting episode in the annals of early American diplomacy that has never quite received the scholarly attention it deserves.[13] The offer of mediation originated in St Petersburg in September 1812 with Czar Alexander I, who was concerned both to prevent his British ally from diverting resources to North America at the height of Napoleon's invasion and to maintain the Russian-American trade that had begun to flourish shortly before the Anglo-American conflict. The offer reached Washington by the first week of March 1813 and was formally accepted by the administration on March 11, 1813. The administration's motives for accepting, in most accounts of the war, are usually depicted as sheer desperation, if not something worse. Madison is invariably described as clutching in indecent haste at the offer of mediation in order to make peace, very much as a drowning man clutches at a straw to preserve life itself.[14]

The evidence to support this description is, on the face of it, substantial. By February 1813, the opening campaigns of the war had all clearly been disastrous for the American cause - from the fall of Detroit, through the fiascos on the Niagara Peninsula and at La Colle Mill, to James Winchester's tragic misfortunes at the River Raisin. The administration itself had been depleted with the forced resignations of the navy and the war secretaries, the Treasury was virtually empty, while Congress was balking at the cost of carrying on the war for the future. Adding to the sense of gloom that pervaded Washington over the winter of 1812-1813 was Madison's own reduced electoral majority in the election of 1812, a result which, in turn, reflected the greatly increased political influence of the Federalist opponents of the war, particularly in New York and New England. Just as bad too, from the Republican point of view, was the news of Napoleon's failure in Russia; and although Madison and his colleagues had at first discounted the stories of the destruction of the French army, by March 1813 the magnitude of the disaster could no longer be denied.[15] British diplomatic and commercial interests now seemed relatively secure for the foreseeable future, while the new ministry formed under Lord Liverpool after Perceval's assassination had found its hand strengthened in its dealings with the United States. This was because the British opponents of the American war had rallied to the flag once it was known that Madison had failed to accept the repeal of the orders in council as a basis for peace.[16] Madison, by comparison, was to enjoy no such similar political benefit; his refusal to make peace after the repeal of the orders in council and his attempt to continue the war for the sake of impressment increased rather than lessened domestic discord about the legitimacy of the war.

Considering all this, Madison's acceptance of the Russian mediation scarcely requires explanation. And that he seemed desperately eager for peace might be further deduced from his choice of commissioners to go to St Petersburg. John Quincy Adams, James Ashton Bayard, and Albert Gallatin were all men who were known to have reservations, to say the least, about the wisdom of the war. The prospect that these men might settle the war, under the agency of a foreign emperor, in a city about as far removed from Washington as it was possible to be, led most ardent Republican supporters of the war to conclude that their president was altogether too eager for peace,[17] and their opinions on this score have duly found their way into the historical literature.

All this seems true enough, but in reality the politics of the Russian mediation were far more complex than this scenario allows for, and the episode meant very different things to different members of the administration. To Gallatin, the mediation certainly offered the best chance for the United States to get out of a bad war. It also gave him a personal opening to escape from intra-party political feuding, his distaste for which had reached breaking point after John Armstrong took over the War Department in February 1813 and had begun to organize the war effort according to priorities distinctly unfriendly to the concerns of the Treasury Secretary.[18] But for both Gallatin and other members of the administration, the main advantage of the Russian mediation was financial. It enabled the administration to obtain from moneylenders, notably John Jacob Astor, Stephen Girard, and David Parish, the funds to fill the government's loans and thus continue operations for the remainder of the year. These loans had not been filled before the offer of mediation was accepted, and Gallatin regarded his negotiation of the loans under its prospect as a personal pledge that the administration was now committed to ending the war as soon as possible.[19]

But where Gallatin saw the chance to end the war, others, particularly Monroe and Armstrong, saw opportunities to continue it on an extended scale. How else are we to account for the ambitious schemes of military conquest that flitted through the minds of these two cabinet members throughout 1813; and how else are we to explain the instructions that Monroe then wrote for the mediation commissioners? These instructions called not only for Great Britain to accept American terms on the issues of blockades and impressment as these had been defined in 1812, but also for Great Britain to cede large portions of Canada to the United States and to accept as well the American claim to East Florida, thereby committing the ministry formally not to obstruct any future American measures to acquire that Spanish province.[20]

Where the President himself stood on this spectrum of possibilities is difficult to ascertain, mainly because Madison never appears to have committed himself explicitly to one set of outcomes as opposed to another. Yet one of the attractions of the mediation offer, surely, was that he did not, in fact, have to do so. Nonetheless, it is not credible to assume that Monroe drafted the ambitious instructions for the mediation commissioners without Madison's approval, if not explicit direction, and at least two members of the administration gained the distinct impression that Madison suspected - possibly on the basis of his reading of a particular sentence in John Quincy Adams' despatch announcing the Russian offer - that the mediation had been prompted by Great Britain as a way of escaping from the American war.[21] Though Madison also told Jefferson that it would be wise not to presume openly too much on that score, it is evident that he did not entirely dismiss the possibility from his mind at this time either.[22]

As for the anti-war, or pro-peace, cast of the mediation commission, that was more the result of accident than deliberate design. John Quincy Adams would have to participate by virtue of his position as minister to Russia, and there was nothing at all unusual about the inclusion of an opponent of the administration, who, if nothing else, would have to testify to the sincerity of its efforts to negotiate a settlement. Here Madison narrowed the range of his choice down to Rufus King, Harrison Gray Otis, and James Ashton Bayard before he finally settled for the last.[23] For the third place on the commission, the President's first inclination seems to have been for Henry Clay, who was surely the most logical candidate to represent the interests of the Republican majority in Congress.[24] The position only went to Gallatin because the Treasury Secretary requested it, and his wishes here were strongly reinforced by the lobbying of the Russian diplomat, Andrei Dashkov, who argued that Gallatin's nomination would favorably impress the Czar.[25] Considering all these matters, then, it seems at least plausible to suggest that Madison in 1813, the obvious difficulties of his position notwithstanding, was rather more optimistic about his ultimate prospects for success than many historians have realized. The Russian mediation was not simply an escape hatch from an unwinnable war; it offered the United States a positive opportunity to win that war and then to withdraw from it on the best possible terms.

James Ashton Bayard.

III

The final efforts to end the War of 1812 began in the first week of January 1814 and culminated in success at the charterhouse of Ghent almost a year later. Before January 1814, however, the progress of the American war had not been sufficient to sustain the hopes that Madison and his colleagues had allowed themselves when they accepted the offer of Russian mediation. To be sure, William Henry Harrison and Oliver Hazard Perry between them had more than redeemed William Hull's loss of Detroit in the first year of the war, but the campaigns of Henry Dearborn, James Wilkinson, and Wade Hampton in the summer and fall of 1813 had done nothing of real consequence to extend American power into Lower Canada. And as the new year opened, the problems of organizing future invasions of Canada as well as maintaining adequate domestic support for them were obviously increasing. These difficulties were underscored in the week after December 24, 1813, when British forces raided upstate New York and laid waste the communities of Black Rock, Buffalo, Lewiston, and Niagara.

On the diplomatic front, the worst news was that Great Britain had rejected the Russian mediation. It was highly unlikely, of course, that Great Britain would have accepted mediation in any event, and almost certainly not when the business involved submitting issues of naval power and maritime rights to the interposition of a sovereign who was regarded as notoriously unsound on these matters anyway.[26] But more than merely long-standing tensions in Anglo-Russian relations were involved in the failure of the mediation. Napoleon himself had muddied the waters here by proposing after the battle of Bautzen in May 1813 that there should be a European congress to arrange a general peace, including disputes over maritime rights, and for that purpose the French emperor wished to invite delegates from the United States.[27] This prospect could only have stiffened Lord Castlereagh's resolve that under no circumstances should American and maritime problems ever be entangled with the problems of negotiating the settlement of Europe.

It is possible to go even further and argue that Lord Castlereagh did not want the settlement of any fundamental issues, be they European, maritime or American, before Napoleon had either been overthrown or confined so securely within France's pre-Revolutionary boundaries that he could never again disturb the peace. But even if this is what Castlereagh ideally would have liked, he was not in any position to obtain it, not even after Napoleon's defeat at the battle of Leipzig in October 1813. The future shape of Europe at that time was still too uncertain to give the British ministry any clear-cut advantages, either diplomatically or militarily, in its dealings with the United States.[28] The best Castlereagh could do as he labored to reconstruct Europe was to keep European and American problems apart, and to that end he offered in November 1813 to hold peace talks with the United States, either at London or at Gothenburg, and then only on the basis of Great Britain's understanding of international law and its own maritime rights.[29] But as Castlereagh made this offer to the United States, he was, whether he liked it or not, tacitly admitting that Great Britain would now have to start dealing seriously with the problem of the American war. What was unclear at the time was how he would do so.

The British offer reached the United States on December 30, 1813 and was accepted by Madison within the week.[30] Again, it is possible to read into the President's actions the counsels of despair, but there are also reasons for not taking so extreme a view. In the first place, Madison could hardly have turned the British offer down under any circumstances, at least not unless he wanted to provide further ammunition for his Federalist opponents to charge that he was waging a war of aggression instead of a war to defend American neutral rights against British outrages. And given the fact that Madison had never attempted to deal with domestic dissent by any means of restraint or censorship, one of the few tactics he had to disarm his Federalist critics was to demonstrate that the United States was always willing to seek peace while casting the odium for not achieving it on British obstructionism. In short, the politics of justifying the war at home compelled Madison to enter into the process of negotiation.[31]

Secondly, the position of the United States at the beginning of 1814, although certainly not one of great strength, was not one of total desperation either. Madison countered Castlereagh's offer to negotiate on the basis of the maritime rights of Great Britain with the pledge that he would respect the rights of both powers "as sovereign and independent nations."[32] What this language really meant was that Madison realized, as Castlereagh must also have done, that there was now going to be some hard fighting and tough bargaining over the disputes dividing the two nations, principally impressment. And Madison saw no need to start the process by making concessions in advance. The diplomatic instructions for the American negotiating team in 1814 remained essentially unchanged from those given to the mediation commission the previous year;[33] and it is also evident, despite the failure of the Russian mediation, that Madison had not yet abandoned all hope of the Baltic powers being able to restrain British maritime pretensions in ways that would serve American interests.[34] The more immediately important question at the beginning of 1814 was whether the United States would be able to implement military strategies to sustain its diplomatic pretensions in Europe.

As events developed throughout 1814, American military efforts did prove, *in the last analysis,* to be adequate to sustain American diplomacy, but this was so only *after* that diplomacy had been radically revised to the extent of abandoning the American demands for peace that had been stipulated in 1812 and 1813. The process whereby these readjustments were made has been narrated repeatedly by Henry Adams, Fred Engelman, Bradford Perkins, and Frank Updyke, and it would be tiresome merely to repeat their accounts here.[35] All these authorities, rightly so, place a heavy emphasis on European events, particularly the collapse of Napoleonic France and the ensuing likelihood that Great Britain would "give Jonathan a good drubbing" as the phrase ran, in compelling Madison to redefine his diplomatic goals. The gloomy prospects for 1814, in turn, led to the series of administration decisions, the last of them being made by June 27, 1814, to settle for a peace on the basis of the *status quo ante bellum.*[36] In this fashion, the administration had already abandoned its wartime diplomatic goals, including the lingering hope of some sort of intervention by the Baltic powers on maritime rights, even before the talks at Ghent had begun. For the remainder of 1814, Madison and his colleagues, as their diplomats in Europe had warned them to do, simply buckled down to fight out a long and bloody summer for survival, trusting all the while that good fortune and their own efforts would permit them to emerge with the *status quo ante bellum* at the end.[37] As they did so, the American war against Canada was transformed from a means of coercing Great Britain into a strategy for defending the republic against aggression; and it was in this context that the nation's military efforts, particularly on the Niagara Peninsula, at Plattsburg, and at Baltimore, were ultimately adequate for its diplomatic needs.

At this point, though, the question about how the war was terminated might be redefined to ask why it was in 1814 that the United States was not able to launch a more extensive series of campaigns against Canada than it did and thus attempt to compensate for the diplomatic and military advantages that Great Britain was drawing from the changing European situation? To pursue this inquiry would open up several very large questions about the politics of the war as a whole and the roots of American military weakness in the conflict in particular. It would require historians, to mention only one matter, to explore more extensively than they have the recruitment and organization of the U.S. Army;[38] but in passing by these larger issues, it should be noted that there was one very serious problem arising from Madison's decision to enter peace negotiations that did hobble the American military effort in the final year of the war. That problem was the President's

Henry Clay represented the Republican majority of Congress on the American delegation.

quarrel with John Armstrong, and the tensions and difficulties between the two men became an open breach with Madison's decision to accept Castlereagh's offer of negotiations.

Armstrong opposed the decision to negotiate for peace, or, more accurately, he disagreed with Madison's efforts to seek peace while attempting to continue the war at the same time. His reason for doing so was that it would be difficult, if not impossible, to organize the nation for the conquest of Canada if it became generally assumed that peace might be negotiated in Europe at almost any time; and events later in 1814 did, more or less, confirm his apprehensions on this score. Leaving aside here Armstrong's propensity to turn his worst suspicions into realities and without going into every detail of his relationship with Madison, there is, nonetheless, abundant evidence of the unfortunate impact of the quarrel between the two men on almost every aspect of the Niagara campaigns in 1814 - from disagreements and misunderstandings over strategy, over the choice and extent of commands, and over the relations between the military and naval forces involved in the operations. These quarrels did contribute to limiting the extent and the success of the Canadian campaigns of 1814, just as they also contributed to the fiascos that allowed invading British forces to capture and burn Washington at the end of the summer.[39] Thereafter it was to fall to Monroe, coming into the War Department when Armstrong

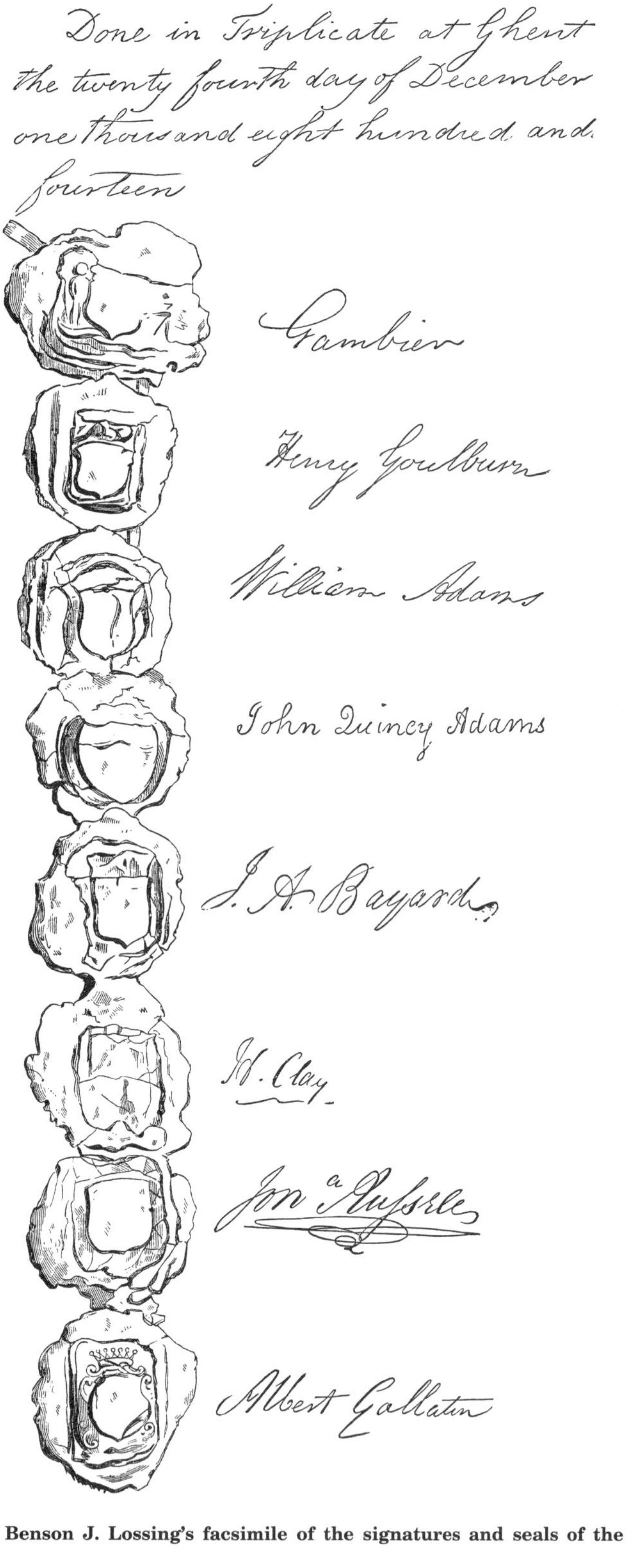

Benson J. Lossing's facsimile of the signatures and seals of the British and United States negotiators of the Treaty of Ghent.

resigned in September 1814, to revive more extensive and ambitious schemes for the conquest of all of Canada in an effort to bring heavier pressure to bear on Great Britain. Had all of Monroe's plans come to fruition, there can be little doubt that Great Britain would have been embarrassed by the American war in ways that it never was between 1812 and 1814; but whether Monroe would ever have been able to turn his ambitious schemes into realities is, perhaps,a very open question.[40]

But, leaving aside the organization of a war for 1815 that did not have to be fought, the real key to understanding the politics of peace-making in 1814 lies not so much in American behavior as it does in that of the British; and here we might wish that the historical literature was more helpful than it is. The fundamental question is: what sort of peace with America did Lord Castlereagh and his colleagues, principally Earl Bathurst and Lord Liverpool, envisage when the ministry made its offer of negotiations in November 1813? The answer, rather surprisingly, is precisely the sort of peace the British negotiators eventually signed at Ghent on Christmas Eve, more than one year later. In a cabinet memorandum dated December 26, 1813, the ministry recorded that it was "ready to sign a peace with the United States, in a general peace on the *status quo ante bellum* without involving in such Treaty any decision on the points in dispute at the commencement of hostilities."[41] The exact considerations that led the ministry to reach this conclusion at this time were not spelled out, but they can be easily enough surmised: continuing concern over the European situation; an unwillingness to put any definitions of maritime rights into a treaty that might later be used against Great Britain, especially by the United States; and some more pragmatic concerns as well. These last concerns were best summed up by Lord Liverpool when he observed that while an American war in the context of a general European conflict certainly had its uses in justifying British policies to break up or to control all American-European trade, the continuation of such a war after Europe was at peace was only harmful to British commercial and diplomatic interests.[42] So, all things considered, the ministry decided that a treaty that appeared to settle nothing at all was the best possible outcome for Great Britain.

The time at which the ministry was prepared to reveal to the United States that it would settle for the *status quo ante bellum,* however, was left to depend on circumstances; and the circumstances of Great Britain changed so drastically in the first six months of 1814 that the ministry was tempted to believe that endless procrastination was the best way to serve the nation's interests. As it did so, the ministry flirted with, although it did not actually adopt, a whole range of proposals for an American peace that were thrust upon it by very disparate groups of lobbyists, including Canadian merchants, West Indian traders, old Tories seeking revenge for the past, and Indian agents of one sort or another. Each of these groups had an agenda, and if these were considered collectively, they

A view of the city of Ghent from the River Scheldt, drawn by Benson J. Lossing.

coalesced into a formidable set of proposals designed to restructure the pre-war patterns of Anglo-American relations, as well as to punish the upstart republic for having had the temerity to declare war in the first place.[43] The ministry's problem was that it was never able to find reliable ways of assessing which parts of these various agendas stood the best chance for success, either on the battlefield or at the bargaining table. And the British ministers, it should be stressed, never lost sight of two essential facts: that whatever concessions might be extracted from the Americans, they had to be achieved within the temporal and fiscal limits of the 1814 campaign; and that if they were to have a central purpose, it should be to improve Canada's position to resist future American aggression.[44]

It was these circumstances that produced the four and one half months of confrontation at Ghent, a diplomatic encounter that was both longer and more dramatic than either government really wanted. The British ministry, under great pressure from European events, omitted to draw up fully detailed instructions to guide its three negotiators in opening the proceedings at Ghent, and gave them instead only a series of headings designed to probe what the Americans might, or might not, concede. A certain lack of subtlety on the part of these British diplomats at Ghent then led them to reshape these headings into a number of demands and *sine qua nons* that the Americans were not even remotely authorized to discuss, and which Earl Bathurst and Lord Liverpool later had to retract in order to avoid the collapse of the negotiations.[45] The American negotiators played their part by remaining united despite their not inconsiderable personal conflicts and differences, and by not revealing that by now they had nothing to concede anyway. In the last analysis, of course, the fundamental American and British positions were never so far apart as the exchange of their diplomatic notes at Ghent suggested. Each nation was ultimately prepared to settle for the *status quo ante bellum,* and it proved to be only a matter of time before the pressure of events in the latter half of 1814 revealed this essential similarity of interest.

In considering the significance of those events after August 1814, it seems doubtful that any single factor or episode can truly be said to have been decisive in producing the peace. There was no single turning point, not even the battle of Plattsburg in September 1814 as is sometimes claimed,[46] in the

Commemorative medal of the treaty of peace which ended the War of 1812. From Lossing's *Pictorial Field Book of the War of 1812.*

dialectic of exchanges that finally led to the signing of a treaty on Christmas Eve. Rather there was simply a process of attrition to expose the hard core of mutual self-interest behind the positions that the two governments had reached in different ways before the talks began; and in this process of exposure historians have generally agreed that the British were compelled to make some more embarrassing concessions than were their American counterparts. And if the ultimate purpose of the British maneuverings at Ghent had been to improve the position of Canada vis-a-vis the United States in any way, there can be no denying that the ministry did not make very much progress on this front at all.

The reception of the Treaty of Ghent in the two nations therefore was governed much more by circumstances surrounding the timing of its arrival than it was by the empty contents of its relatively few provisions. And in this context, the timing of the peace was much more favorable for the Americans than it was for the British. For the latter, the peace of the *status quo* came after a prolonged period of heightened expectations for an important British victory. These were then deflated by the release of Parliamentary papers which displayed the embarrassing retreat of the British diplomats at Ghent, as well as highlighting the enormous costs of a campaign that had been waged for no significant gains. For the former, the news of peace came after the trials of the summer of 1814, the prospect of disunion as presented by the Hartford Convention, the fruitless deliberations of the third session of the Thirteenth Congress which failed to furnish means for carrying on the war for the future, and finally the British defeat at New Orleans. Under these circumstances, it is hardly surprising that few Americans bothered to contemplate the real meaning of the Treaty of Ghent, which might more properly be designated as only an armistice in the ongoing rivalry after 1783 between the imperial mother country and her former colonies.[47] The real winners were the future generations of the British and the American peoples who have never had the occasion since to break the terms of that armistice.

Notes

[1] Richard Dean Burns (ed.), *Guide to American Foreign Relations Since 1700* (Santa Barbara, CA, 1983), pp. 184-92.

[2] For two recent works on the coming of the war, see Ronald H. Hatzenbuehler and Robert L. Ivie, *Congress Declares War: Rhetoric. Leadership, and Partisanship in the Early Republic* (Kent, OH, 1983) and Steven Watts, *The Republic Reborn: War and the Making of Liberal America, 1790-1820* (Baltimore, 1987). Although there have been no significant recent studies of the ending of the war, notice should be made here of Paul R. Pillar, *Negotiating Peace: War Termination as a Bargaining Process* (Princeton, 1983). While not devoted exclusively to the diplomacy of the War of 1812, Pillar's study does draw on the history of that conflict in its endeavor to systematize scholarly understanding of the ways in which nations disengage from war.

[3] In April 1813, the Russian minister, Andrei Dashkov, proposed an armistice to British Admiral Sir John Borlase Warren, evidently with the administration's knowledge; while in April of the following

year Madison authorized William Henry Winder to negotiate for an armistice during his meetings with British officials in Lower Canada on the exchange of prisoners of war. See J.C.A. Stagg, *Mr. Madison's War: Politics, Diplomacy and Warfare in the Early American Republic, 1783-1830* (Princeton, 1983), pp. 300, 384-86.

[4] British Adjutant General Edward Baynes offered an armistice to Henry Dearborn on August 8, 1812. Dearborn accepted the proposal, but the administration repudiated it. See E.A. Cruikshank (ed.), *Documentary History of the Campaign Upon the Niagara Frontier in 1812-1814* (9 vols.; Welland, Ont., 1896-1908), I, 169.

[5] Bradford Perkins, *Castlereagh and Adams: England and the United States, 1812-1823* (Berkeley and Los Angeles, 1964), pp. 20, 150-53.

[6] For the events described in the following paragraphs, see Perkins, pp. 3-19 and Frank A. Updyke, *The Diplomacy of the War of 1812* (Baltimore, 1915), pp. 125-42.

[7] Augustus Foster, Journal entry, June 18, 1812, Library of Congress, Washington, D.C. (hereafter cited as LOC), Augustus Foster Papers.

[8] The Washington, D.C. *National Intelligencer* printed the first news of the fall of Detroit on Sept. 1, 1812.

[9] Perceval's assassination was reported in the *National Intelligencer,* June 25, 1812. Accounts of conditions in Great Britain were published along with the news of the campaign for repeal of the orders in council. See *ibid.,* Aug. 6, 1812 and also the *Baltimore Weekly Register,* Aug. 15 and Sept. 19, 1812.

[10] For a discussion of this issue, see Lawrence S. Kaplan, "France and Madison's Decision for War, 1812", *Mississippi Valley Historical Review,* 50 (1964), 652-71.

[11] For Monroe's views, see Augustus Foster, Journal entry, May 24, 1812, Augustus Foster Papers, LOC.

[12] James Monroe to John Taylor, June 13, 1812, James Monroe Papers, LOC.

[13] Frank A. Golder, "The Russian Offer of Mediation in the War of 1812", *Political Science Quarterly,* 31 (1912), 380-91. See also Nikolai N. Bolkhovitinov, *The Beginnings of Russian-American Relations, 1775-1815,* Elena Levin, trans. (Cambridge, MA, 1975), pp. 304-33.

[14] Henry Adams, *History of the United States During the Administrations of Jefferson and Madison* (9 vols.; New York, 1891-96), VII, 30, 33-41. See also Perkins, p. 20.

[15] See Stagg, pp. 270-74.

[16] *Ibid.,* pp. 295-97. See also Perkins, pp. 2, 15-18.

[17] For Republican criticism of Madison's acceptance of the mediation see the Philadelphia *Democratic Press,* March 20, 30, 1813; the Richmond *The Enquirer*, March 26, 1813; the Baltimore *The Whig,* March 10, 1813; the Philadelphia *Aurora General Advertiser,* April 10, 22, 1813.

[18] Gallatin particularly resented Armstrong's appointment of the Treasury's most severe critic, William Duane, as adjutant general for the Fourth Military District. See Gallatin to James W. Nicholson, May 5, 1813 and Gallatin to William Few, May 9, 1813 in Carl Prince and Helen Fineman (eds.), *The Papers of Albert Gallatin* (microfilm ed.).

[19] Gallatin to Madison, March 5, 1813; Gallatin to Alexander James Dallas, March 19, 1813; Gallatin to David Parish and Stephen Girard, April 7, 1813; John Jacob Astor to Gallatin, April 5, 1813; Parish and Girard to Gallatin, April 5, 1813, all in *Gallatin Papers.* For details of the loan see Donald R. Adams, Jr., *Finance and Enterprise in Early America: A Study of Stephen Girard's Bank, 1812-1831* (Philadelphia, 1978), pp. 30-34.

[20] Monroe to Adams, Bayard and Gallatin, April 15, 27, 30 and June 23, 1813, National Archives and Records Administration, Washington, D.C. (hereafter cited as NA), Record Group (RG) 59 (Diplomatic Instructions: All Countries). For the military plans of Monroe and Armstrong, see Stagg, pp. 278-79, 284.

[21] In conveying the offer of mediation, John Quincy Adams mentioned that the Russian foreign minister, Count Nikolai Rumianstev, had told him that the subject "had already been suggested to him by the British ambassador, Lord Cathcart, who had the day before dispatched it by messenger to his court." See John Quincy Adams to Monroe, Sept. 30, 1812 in Worthington C. Ford (ed.), *The Writings of John Quincy Adams* (7 vols.; New York, 1913-17), IV, 391.

[22] Madison to Thomas Jefferson, March 10, 1813, Madison Papers, LOC. See also William Jones to Dallas, March 10, 1813, Historical Society of Pennsylvania, Philadelphia (hereafter cited as HSP), George Mifflin Dallas Collection and Elbridge Gerry to Mercy Warren, April 4, 1813, Massachusetts Historical Society, Boston, Elbridge Gerry Papers.

[23] Madison to Gallatin, April 5, 1813, Gallatin Papers; Charles Jared Ingersoll, *Historical Sketch of the Second War Between the United States of America and Great Britain* (2 vols.; Philadelphia, 1845), II, pp. 248, 289.

[24] "Gallatin's Mission", Charles R. King (ed.), *The Life and Correspondence of Rufus King* (6 vols.; New York, 1894-1900), V, 320.

[25] Dashkov to Rumianstev, March 16, 1813, Archives of the Russian Foreign Ministry for 1809-16, microfilm copy, LOC.

[26] Charles K. Webster, *The Foreign Policy of Castlereagh, 1812-1815: Britain and the Reconstruction of Europe* (London, 1931), p. 162. For Lord Liverpool's remarks that he feared "the Emperor of Russia [was] half an American," see Liverpool to the Duke of Wellington, Sept. 27, 1814 in Arthur R. Wellesley (ed.), *Supplementary Despatches, Correspondence, and Memoranda of Field Marshall Arthur Duke of Wellington* (13 vols.; London, 1858-71), IX, 291.

[27] Webster, p. 147.

[28] See *ibid.,* pp. 166-89.

[29] Castlereagh to Monroe, Nov. 4, 1813 in Walter Lowrie and Matthew St. Clair Clarke (eds.), *American State Papers: Foreign Relations* (6 vols.; Washington, 1832-59), III, 621.

[30] Monroe to Castlereagh, Jan. 5, 1814, *ibid.,* 622-23.

[31] For discussions of Madison's rhetorical techniques in justifying the war, see Stagg, pp. 110, 305, 436-37.

[32] Monroe to Castlereagh, Jan. 5, 1814, *American State Papers,* III, 622-23.

[33] Monroe to Adams, Bayard, Henry Clay, and Jonathan Russell, Jan. 28, 1814, NA, RG 59.

[34] Monroe to Adams, Bayard, Clay, and Russell, Feb. 14, 1814, *ibid.;* See also Jones to Dallas, Jan. 4, 1814, Dallas Collection, HSP.

[35] Adams, IX, pp. 1-53; Fred L. Engelman, *The Peace of Christmas Eve* (New York, 1962), pp. 98-286; Perkins, pp. 39-57; Updyke, pp. 198-234.

[36] See Stagg, pp. 294-97.

[37] Gallatin and Bayard to Monroe, May 6, 1814, Monroe Papers, LOC; Gallatin to Monroe, June 30, 1814, *Gallatin Papers.*

[38] See J.C.A. Stagg, "Enlisted Men in the U.S. Army, 1812-1815: A Preliminary Survey", *William & Mary Quarterly,* 3rd Ser., 43 (1986), 615-45.

[39] See Stagg, pp. 371-73, 397-418 and C. Edward Skeen, *John Armstrong, Jr., 1758-1843: A Biography* (Syracuse, 1981), pp. 173-204.

[40] C.P. Stacey, "An American Plan for a Canadian Campaign", *American Historical Review,* 46 (1941), 348-56. See also Stagg, pp. 455, 467-68.

[41] Charles K. Webster (ed.), *British Diplomacy, 1813-1815: Select Documents Dealing With the Reconstruction of Europe* (London, 1921), p. 126.

[42] See Perkins, pp. 65-66.

[43] *Ibid.,* pp. 62-64, 82-84, 103-04. See also J. Leitch Wright, Jr., *Britain and the American Frontier, 1783-1815* (Athens, 1975), pp. 151-85.

[44] See Perkins, p. 106. For a stimulating essay that makes the same point in the context of the British strategy of the New Orleans campaign, see James A. Carr, "The Battle of New Orleans and the Treaty of Ghent", *Diplomatic History,* 3 (1979), 273-82.

[45] See Perkins, pp. 81-101; Updyke, pp. 277-319.

[46] Harry L. Coles, *The War of 1812* (Chicago, 1965), p. 171. See also Pillar, p. 202.

[47] For a recent discussion of the changes in U.S.-Canadian relations after 1815, see Reginald C. Stuart, *United States Expansionism and British North America, 1775-1871* (Chapel Hill, 1988), pp. 79-261.

THE WAR OF 1812 IN POPULAR HISTORY

by
S.F. Wise

A comparison of the popular history written about the War of 1812 in the United States and Canada in the nineteenth century presents some remarkable contrasts.[1] There are also similarities, given the nature of the subject. Almost all of this literature is patriotic in character; that is, it treats history as a means of glorifying the national past, and seeks to maintain or enhance pride of country. Americans produced much more of it in the nineteenth century than did Canadians and on the whole were better at it, especially those who, like Benson J. Lossing, aimed at a mass market. What the Canadians lacked in literary skills and flamboyance, however, they made up in terms of patriotic vehemence.

The two societies, of course, were at significantly different stages of development. The United States was the product of two centuries of colonial experience, capped by a revolution; much of British North America was much younger, being in part a product of that revolution. The Americans, whatever the importance of state and region, thought of themselves as a people, indeed, as a new nation; British North America, at the time of the war and for two generations thereafter, was a set of separate, small societies, divided by geography, language and the compartmentalization incident upon colonial dependency. The Americans had made an important start upon the development of common cultural institutions, had a political process which periodically focussed attention upon the national stage and had a thriving press and a publishing industry. For most of the first half of the nineteenth century, British North America had few institutions in common, except those having to do with the appurtenances of empire and of religion, had no common politics, and lacked anything more than local presses. Until well after Confederation, popular historical literature tended to be regional and local in character.

The two historical literatures, therefore, make for an awkward comparison, since they represent very different stages in cultural evolution. There is, for example, an immense nineteenth century American bibliography on the war; that having to do with Andrew Jackson alone bulks as large as the whole British North American output on the war before 1914.[2] In another way as well these works are awkwardly juxtaposed. American historical publication on the war began even while hostilities were going on, in such documentary records as Hezekiah Niles' *Weekly Register*. The first Upper Canadian monograph on the war was David Thompson's *A History of the Late War*

Andrew Jackson, victor of the Battle of New Orleans.

Benson J. Lossing's rendering of the captive *Chesapeake* being led into Halifax harbor by the British frigate *Shannon*.

Between Great Britain and the United States, published in Niagara in 1832.[3] By that date many American accounts of the war had already appeared. The spate of U.S. popular history about the war peaked by the time of the American Civil War (although publications on the war, both popular and academic, have never ceased); Ontario and Canadian publication is infrequent prior to Confederation, and reaches a peak in the decade prior to the outbreak of the First World War. This temporal disjunction in the two literatures must be borne in mind, since perceptions of the war, south and north, were affected by the generational context within which they were written. Obviously to deal with two historical literatures over a century (roughly from the generation following 1815 to the first decade of the twentieth century) renders it impossible, in the compass of this paper, to mention more than a few broad themes and to refer only briefly to some of the particular interpretations different generations of Americans and Canadians put upon the war, according to the exigencies of the time. What is suggested here is simply that such broad themes do exist; that they have much to tell about the divergent values of the two societies; and that comparative analysis of historical memories of the same events in two different countries may be a useful historical exercise.[4]

I

It is an historical commonplace that all participants won the War of 1812. For Britain, the *Shannon* had avenged an embarrassing string of single-ship victories by American vessels over the Royal Navy, and the peace treaty was silent on American claims to "maritime rights." The United States had challenged proud Britannia on her own element and had done exceedingly well; and had not the "Second American Revolution" concluded with the triumph of New Orleans, when American militia defeated Wellington's Peninsular veterans? As for the British North American colonies, they had survived, and that was victory enough.

In the American states and in the British North American colonies, remembrance of the war proved enduring. For Britain, however, the war virtually disappeared from the national record. "The events of the War of 1812 have not been forgotten in England," wrote William Kingsford with some asperity, "for they have never been known there. There is a dim recollection that the public buildings were burned at Washington, and that we were defeated before New Orleans ... But the great features of the war in which the men and women of the provinces risked all they had to remain British ... have obtained little recognition 'at home'."[5] For Britain the war was a relatively unimportant sideshow. For the United States certain features of the war were rapidly assimilated into the central myths of national identity and national purpose. For Upper Canada, the manner in which the war was remembered was fundamental to the formation of the Ontario political culture and hence an intrinsic element in later Canadian nationalism.

In these developments, popular histories of the war, as well as platform oratory, played an important part. The stories they told, and especially the values they upheld, passed into the general culture of the two societies and were incorporated in children's schoolbooks.[6] Whether American or Canadian, naive or sophisticated, they had certain characteristics in common. All sought to give meaning to the war in terms of national character, national traditions and national institutions. Popular history on both sides of the border was therefore explicitly concerned with patriotic values and set out to provide lessons for a broad audience. For this reason, the popular histories of the war repay examination in terms of the evolution of nationalism in the two countries, in a unique comparative frame.

In large part the popular histories, and the stump speakers on commemorative occasions, were fostering the mythic content of nationalism, out of the wealth of incident provided by the war. There is little connection, therefore, between American and Canadian versions of the war found in the nineteenth century histories. This does not mean that the writers of either nationality sought deliberately to falsify the record; it is likely that most did not. But they saw the war with their ideological blinkers on. Many protest the veracity of their narratives. Charles Jared Ingersoll, a congressman during the War of 1812, published the first volume of his history in 1845. His aim was "to exhibit plainly the causes and course of the war;" he intended to do so truthfully, "without acrimonious condemnation of the great people the war was waged against, whose wrongs and misconduct, however, being the burthen of the story, must be told as they merit, or the truth would not be told at all."[7] Similarly, David Thompson, whose history has already been mentioned, told his readers that an "authentic" history was his chief concern.

> *A faithful and impartial account of the late war must be hailed with the most exalted enthusiasm by all who can boast the name of a Briton ... In such a work, generations yet unborn will trace the footsteps of their ancesters for the salvation of their country ... Our British youths, too, whose minds have been endangered by the poisoned shafts of designing malevolence which have been every where discharged through the country, by the many erroneous accounts ... that have hitherto been published ... will catch that patriotic flame which glowed with an unequalled resplendence in the bosoms of their fathers ...*[8]

James Hannay, who published his history of the war in Toronto in 1905, defended his impartiality against those who might accuse him of being too hard on the Americans. "No doubt," he wrote, "it will be said by some critics that in this book I have been too severe on the Americans, who invaded our country, burnt our towns, ravaged our fields, slaughtered our people and tried to place us under a foreign flag ... I see no reason why any American of the present day should feel offended [by] an absolutely truthful narrative."[9]

Because Canadian historical writing about the war was far less prolific than the American, and also because many American publications circulated freely in Canada, Canadian authors tended to see themselves as beleaguered witnesses for a special truth, almost overwhelmed by the volume of writing from the United States. Writing in 1864, William Coffin bemoaned the fact that "faithful and reliable" Canadian works were out of print, "their places having been usurped at our firesides by a flood of American publications, sensational as they are termed, written for show, designed for sale, and to this end pandering to the worst passions of a morbid nationality." Stemming the tide of American materialistic nationalism, his book would "impart ... a Canadian individuality to this Canadian chronicle of the war."[10]

Popular historians, north and south of the border, in fact toyed with the truth in a variety of ways to the national advantage: exaggeration, suppression, horrific detail for lurid effect, and the occasional use of whole cloth were their stock in trade. Most had an unquenchable thirst for rumor, unsupported allegation and local tradition favorable to their own side; for all, not impartial history but memorable testimony to the national virtues was their purpose.

The War of 1812 may have been a sideshow to the struggle in Europe, and the forces involved in it never large. But its scope was vast; it was fought on the the high seas as well as the Great Lakes; along many points on the border between the United States and British North America; throughout the Indian territories beyond the settled American frontier in the northwest; on the waters of Chesapeake Bay and in the environs of Washington; and on the banks of the Mississippi in front of New Orleans. This huge theater, or rather set of theaters, offered unlimited scope

Oliver Hazard Perry demonstrated an aptitude for heroic gestures and phrases.

to nineteenth century American popular historians. Most of them settled for their state or locale; others were much more ambitious.

The Canadians, in contrast, wrote of their own provincial experiences. There is little connection between Upper Canadian accounts of the war, and those written in Lower Canada and the Maritime colonies. It is true, of course, that American histories written on a scale beyond the local, betray nonetheless regional biases; but there is nothing in American historiography to match the barriers Canadian historians seem to have established for themselves. Though the ambivalence - indeed, hostility - of much of New England to the war somewhat cramped the patriotic flights of American historians, nevertheless, unlike the Canadians (whether pre- or post-1867) the general American histories have as their central matter the grand evolution of the country and its people; the Canadian historians, though certainly conscious of their place in the larger imperial scheme, remain local in outlook.

II

Patriotic history is inevitably about heroes, and this was a subject that the Americans handled with great flair. "Between a people and its heroes there is an intimate sympathy," according to a Rhode Island orator in a commemorative address on the fortieth anniversary of the Battle of Lake Erie. Heroes, he remarked, were "the richest product of a people;" "in the affluence of their creative force they throw back upon the soil whence they have sprung the seeds of new forces."[11] American society craved heroes; and exhibited an astonishing fecundity in throwing them up. Though the preeminent military hero of the war was Andrew Jackson, at least in terms of the volume of literature devoted to him, the American pantheon was thronged with naval officers. The frigate captains who won single-ship victories over British ships - William Bainbridge, Stephen Decatur, Isaac Hull, and James Lawrence - became instant heroes. Lawrence, killed aboard *Chesapeake* in a celebrated action against *Shannon* in June 1813, gave the U.S. Navy its popular motto, "Don't give up the ship."

Indeed, in this war as in most of its wars, American military men proved singularly adept at producing, under the most trying circumstances, the apt and memorable phrase, thenceforward to be quoted by every popular historian. Was there some consciousness that they were acting upon the stage of the nation; that their words and their behavior would be scrutinized by a large democratic audience through the press? Or were they conforming to a set of heroic attitudes already established by the culture? Certainly if one examines the exploits of Oliver Hazard Perry, victor of the Battle of Lake Erie in September 1813, one sees a hero to the manner born, and a godsend to the popular historians.

Perry named his flagship *Lawrence* in honor of the commander of the *Chesapeake*; as he sailed against the British fleet, the *Lawrence* was adorned with a banner inscribed "Don't give up the ship." In the course of the battle, the *Lawrence* being disabled, he transferred his pennant and banner to the *Niagara*. Perry, standing erect in a small boat, "the pennant and the banner half folded around him," became the subject of innumerable sketches, prints, paintings, and word pictures. The British ordered "great and little guns to be brought to bear upon the frail but richly laden vessel - laden with a hero of purest mold - but Perry stood erect, unmindful of danger." Having escaped the furious enemy fire, and leading his fleet to victory, Perry capped his triumph with the consummate dispatch, written on the back of the mandatory old envelope: "We have met the enemy and they are ours."[12] Reflecting on the Rhode Islander's gallant conduct, Josiah Headley remarked that "Such unshaken composure - such gallant bearing, stern resolution and steadiness and tenacity of purpose in a young man of twenty-seven, in his first battle, exhibit a marvellous strength of character, and one wonders more at him than his success."[13]

Americans, in fact, were at no loss to explain the heroic conduct of their military men. American life and institutions had produced a new breed of men, and the events of the war repeatedly demonstrated the superiority of American character. Samuel White, a Pennsylvania militia officer who served on the Niagara frontier, reflected after the war that Americans lived much better than Europeans. "An American," he wrote, "eats three times the quantity of animal food, he sleeps more comfortably, and lives in greater plenty of fish, flesh, vegetables and spirituous liquors. Add to this, his freedom is unbounded. He speaks his mind to any man."[14] It was this last point that was emphasized again and again in popular histories and platform oratory: American heroism arose directly out of the creative energies of a free people. In the words of a commemorative speaker:

> *Such a people carry into war all the requisites of victory, with a fulness of possession which no discipline of despotism can ever bring about. Their sight is keener, their aim is surer, their resistance is more steadfast, their assault is irresistible, there is more life in them, there is more manhood in them. In war as in peace, men are efficient in proportion as they are free, and the freest nation will be the only one that is invincible. ... from the bosom of a people thus inspired, there will spring up to lead them other Decaturs, other Perrys.*[15]

The war, then, was a great vindication of democratic self-government. No writer was more eloquent on this subject than Charles Jared Ingersoll who, while serving as a congressman from Pennsylvania, published a two-volume history of the war in the 1840s. His particular heroes were the Kentuckians, especially Governor Isaac Shelby, who accompanied General William Henry Harrison's invasion of Upper Canada in 1813 as a volunteer. Shelby's career connected the American Revolution and the War of 1812; he had commanded a regiment at King's Mountain in 1780 when a Loyalist force had been defeated. "On the top of King's Mountain," Ingersoll wrote, "Shelby helped to plant the seeds of a republic, since spread from the frozen St. John to the fervid plains of San Jacinto, and destined, by similar spontaneous accomplishment, to much further extension."[16] He and his frontiersmen were "a pure and perfect military democracy;" such soldiers were more than a match for the troops of aristocratic Europe and its colonial minions. Democracies at the outset of war always pay in defeats for the freedom they enjoy; ultimately, however, "disciplined freedom is eventually an overmatch for despotic discipline."

> *Voluntary government, voluntary religion, voluntary hostilities are American experiments, which ... have withstood foreign aggression, maintained domestic peace, escaped civil war, and advanced the arts of civilization. By happy mixture of constraint with independence, law and liberty, the United States stand now among the primary powers of the world, to which elevation the war of 1812, with its preliminary reverses and post-liminous successes, largely contributed.*[17]

Perry's battle flag bore the dying words of another American hero, James Lawrence of the *Chesapeake*.

Whereas the American public, and particularly American schoolchildren, were given a large gallery of heroes of 1812, the Upper Canadians had no such bounty. During the war the provincial press was almost non-existent, and there was no local publishing industry. It was almost a generation after the war before the first Upper Canadian account of it was printed. Yet the province had its hero: Isaac Brock. There were others; Laura Secord's feat in walking some miles to warn the British of an American force gained currency as the nineteenth century wore on, while Tecumseh was idealized by Major John Richardson both in his history of the war and in verse and novels as well.[18]

For Upper Canadians, it was Isaac Brock who had, through his leadership and example, brought about the miracle of the province's survival. In the face of overwhelming odds, Brock had won at Detroit and Queenston Heights, and given hope to a society that had all but abandoned it. William Coffin caught the impact of Brock's victories:

> *It is impossible to ignore the alarm and confusion and despondency which settled down like a black cloud upon the country, until suddenly day broke*

Governor Isaac Shelby's medal for service at the Battle of the Thames.

through the gloom and the stalwart form and sterling character of Brock strode into light. Like the white horse in a battle piece by Wouvermans, in every delineation of this war, Isaac Brock stands forth from the canvas the central figure.[19]

Upper Canadian heroine Laura Secord.

Brock's death at Queenston Heights invested his heroism with the character of sacrifice; from the first he was called "the saviour of Upper Canada." As early as March 1814, the Upper Canadian Assembly resolved to set aside money to erect a memorial to Brock on the Heights; it was constructed in 1824. That monument was blown up - "a demon's deed" - in 1840 by an Irishman who had fled Upper Canada during the Rebellion of 1837.[20]

The sequel to this outrage was one of the most remarkable manifestations of public sentiment in the short history of the province. On July 30, 1840, a day declared a provincial holiday by Lieutenant Governor Arthur, eight thousand people gathered on Queenston Heights "to determine in the most public manner, upon the best mode of reconstructing the monument." The day was "beautifully fine," reported the Cobourg *Star,* and steamers brought throngs from Cobourg, Toronto, Hamilton, Kingston, and other points. Eight of them steamed in line up the Niagara River, saluted from Fort Mississauga, "in splendid order, sweeping rapidly up to Queenston, the bands playing, colors flying, and cheered by the shouts of thousands."[21] A number of speakers addressed the assemblage; most notable was Chief Justice John Beverley Robinson, who had fought at Detroit and Queenston Heights. "No man," he said of Brock, "ever established a better claim to the affections of a country." Had he not engaged in his most risky campaign, and convinced the Americans how formidable were "a few gallant soldiers of the line, and the brave defenders of the soil," the province would have been lost. "If he had begun to compare numbers, and had reserved his small force to make a safer effort on a future day, then would thousands upon thousands of the people of the neighbouring States have been found pouring into the western portions of this province."[22]

As it turned out, the new monument was not started until 1853. When it was completed later in the decade, it was claimed to be the second highest column in the world, exceeded only by Wren's monument to the Great Fire in London. It testified, in a most visible way (especially to Americans on the other side of the river) the veneration of Upper Canadians for the man deemed responsible for their survival; as James Hannay later wrote, "the lofty column erected to his memory informs the whole world that patriotism still lives in Canada."[23]

The fact of Brock's death at the climactic moment of battle was central to the power his name exerted upon Upper Canadians. Not only was there the element of sacrifice, of Brock having laid down his life to save the province, but also death had removed the hero to another and superior level of veneration. This transfiguration was faithfully recorded in 1859 by John Symons in his *Battle of Queenston Heights.* Brock and his provincial aide-de-camp, Lieutenant Colonel John Macdonnell, who was also killed in the battle, were originally buried in one of the bastions of Fort George. Both were disinterred for reburial in 1824, at the new monument; Symons states that "Although twelve years had elapsed since the interment, the body of the general had undergone little change, his features being nearly perfect and easily recognized, while that of Lieutenant Colonel McDonell was a complete mass of decomposition."[24]

American heroes sprang from the creative forces of the people, and partook of their collective character; Brock, an upper-class English general, was an example to the people, whose task it was to emulate his virtues. "Honesty of purpose, faithful discharge of duty, encouragement of the young, support of the old and pure patriotism were all combined in him," wrote his biographer David Breakenridge Read; his "example stands out as a beacon to all generations of Canadians."[25] To William Kingsford, Brock was a leader far beyond the capacity of ordinary men; "there are men of this calibre, of whose power we cannot explain the cause, even when we feel we are subjected to it."[26] Kingsford, by no means an uncritical historian, had no flaws to find in Brock; his delineation of the hero as exemplar was of considerable eloquence:

> *No name is better preserved in Canadian history. In priority to all others, his has become a household word to each succeeding generation, as the type of chivalrous honour and unfaltering gallantry, as of one who remained undismayed in the most threatening circumstances. In the hour of danger he exposed himself like the humblest soldier in the ranks; he was foremost when toil was to be exacted, and was to be seen the most prominent wherever the call of duty pointed. He brought the mind of a statesman to every enterprise in which he was engaged ... By his own conduct he set the bright example for others to follow. If he did not spare others, he never spared himself. Gentle, considerate, kind and sympathetic with men of all ranks and in all circumstances, no commander ever shewed more firmness in the maintenance of discipline and order. It is not an exaggeration to say that even to this day in Canada, many cannot pronounce his name without the tremor of suppressed emotion.*[27]

Queenston Heights and the second monument to Sir Isaac Brock, sketched by Lossing in 1860.

Brock's insistence upon "discipline and order," said Read, should encourage the military drilling of schoolboys, since that "incites in them a spirit of patriotism, a love of country, obedience and discipline and respect for authority - all essentials for the formation of a good

The patriotic emphasis of Benson J. Lossing's *Pictorial Field Book of the War of 1812* was made evident by the frontispiece illustration.

Lossing's drawing of the ruined stone barracks and walls of Fort Erie as they appeared in the summer of 1860.

citizen and loyal subject."[28] American heroes, then, exemplified the values of the free democracy which had produced them; the Upper Canadian hero stood preeminently for order, loyalty and discipline.

III

What, according to the popular historians, was the place of the War of 1812 in the national epic? For the Americans, there could be no doubt: the war was a miraculous rounding-out of the verdict of the American Revolution. Many nineteenth century histories were subtitled "The Second War of Independence against Great Britain," or some approximation of this idea. Benson J. Lossing captured the theme vividly. Just after the end of the American Civil War he published his *Pictorial Field Book of the War of 1812,* certainly the most colorful of all the nineteenth century popular histories. Full of telling anecdote, sketches of battlefields (he visited them all), and the first-hand testimony of survivors, it was immensely popular in its day and is still a remarkably good read.

The Pictorial Field Book begins with a vignette. According to Lossing, when the British, at the end of the Revolution, abandoned Fort George at the foot of Broadway in New York, they nailed the Union flag to the top of the flagstaff, knocked off the cleats and greased the pole. John van Arsdale, "a sprightly sailor boy of 16 years," climbed the staff, pulled down the British ensign, "and unfurled in its place the banner of the United States." With that act,

> *... the work of the Revolution was finished. As the white sails of the British squadron that bore away from our shores the last armed enemy to freedom in America became mere specks upon the horizon in the evening sun to the straining eyes of eager thousands gazing seaward beyond the Narrows, the idea of absolute independence took possession of the mind and heart of every true American. He saw the visible bonds of British thraldom fall at his feet, and his pulse beat high with the inspiration of conscious freedom, and the full assurance that the power and influence of British sovereignty had departed from his country forever.*[29]

But as Lossing saw it, independence was a cruel illusion. Though Americans were free, they were still under British domination. Great Britain controlled "their trade and commerce, their manufacture and arts, their literature, science, religion and laws ... To

The Shawnee warrior Tecumseh.

this domination was added a traditional contempt of the English for their transatlantic brethren as an inferior people."[30]

For Lossing, as for other patriotic historians, New England was a special case, retaining a submissive and colonial attitude towards England. As Ingersoll put it, "among the many benefits of the War of 1812, there was none greater than breaking down the idolatry of England." The war, therefore, was both just and necessary: just because of the flagrant abuse by the British of American sovereignty, especially on the high seas, and necessary in order to create a genuine sense of nationhood.[31] For the United States, according to Lossing, the war "was an exhibition of its powers in vindication of its rights;" as a result of it, the country became "a powerful consolidated nation," when heretofore it had been a set of "weak, isolated commonwealths:" "this is the whole drama of the contest known in history as the War of 1812, or the Second Struggle for Independence."[32]

It became the object of many of the American popular historians to show the British in the worst possible light, in all their arrogance, perfidity, and old-world depravity. Among many subjects, two were particularly favored - the British use of Indians as auxiliaries, especially in the West, and the perpetration of atrocities by regular British forces, especially in the burning of Washington.

Few American historians recognized that the Indian part in the war in the West was simply a continuation of the long war on the frontier virtually coincident with settlement. Indian resistance prior to the war had been organized by Tecumseh, the Shawnee war chief, and the operations of the Indians merged into the war between Britain and the United States. Indian support was vital to British arms, but the army was not always in full control of its allies. The most notorious incident occurred at the settlement of Frenchtown (now Monroe) in the Michigan territory in January 1813. After an American force under General James Winchester had surrendered to British regulars, Upper Canadian militia and Indians, all under Colonel Henry Procter, an unknown number of prisoners, chiefly the wounded and almost exclusively Kentuckians, were slaughtered and scalped. It would be impossible to exaggerate the bitterness of the language of American writers on this and similar incidents. Henry Brackenridge, one of the earliest historians of the war, referred to Procter's "cold, deliberate, fiendlike depravity, which assimilates men to the most odious and ferocious of the brute creation."[33] Ingersoll attributed to Captain Matthew Elliott, an Upper Canadian officer in the Indian Department, a cold-blooded remark which entered many histories; when appealed to by the prisoners for medical help, he is supposed to have replied, "The Indians are excellent doctors."[34] Headley depicted Procter as "a perfect monster," filled with "deceit, treachery, falsehood, murder, and that refinement of cruelty which looks with derision on slow torture ... His memory shall be kept fresh while the western hemisphere endures, and the transaction hold a prominent place in the list of dark deeds that stand recorded against the English name."[35] Lossing, filled with indignation over the equivocal role Britain had taken during the Civil War, moved from the case of Procter to a general indictment of British barbarism:

> *When the British government, in its pride or blindness, lectures that of the United States on lust for power, barbarity in warfare and kindred subjects ... it is sometimes a wholesome service to prick the bubble of its pride. ... That conduct, the manifestation of the intense selfishness of the aristocracy of rank and wealth which have ever ruled England - will always appear darkly in the history of nations as a crime against humanity ... The employment of bloody savages to butcher their relatives in America, the demoniac treatment of captive sepoys in India, the encouragement of frightful atrocities in China ... should for-*

ever close the lips of English government when it attempts to lecture others on humanity, or claims to be, par excellence, the guardian of civilization.[36]

The place of the Canadians in this American picture of British imperial criminality was to figure as the brutal minions of the English upper class. A favorite tale of the popular historians was the finding of a scalp near the mace in the Upper Canadian legislature at the time of the capture of York in 1813. "This atrocious ornament" (the Speaker's wig, one surmises?) was borne off, with the mace, by Commodore Isaac Chauncey's squadron on leaving York, having burnt the parliament building. "The sight of an American scalp, hanging as a trophy in a public building, would naturally exasperate soldiers;" incendiarism was a natural and just retribution. Lossing found the juxtaposition of mace and scalp precisely indicative of the barbarism of empire; "the mace is the emblem of authority, and the scalp's position near it is truly symbolical of the British power in Canada."[37]

The Canadians, then, were seen as willing participants in British brutality. Lossing reserved his ugliest anecdote for the Loyalists ("Tories" were not looked upon favorably by any of the American writers). Noting that many of Butler's Rangers, "those bitter Tory marauders ... during the Revolution, who in cruelty often shamed Brant and his braves," had settled in Upper Canada, he observed that they were "mostly men of savage character, who met death by violence." An unnamed Toronto informant told him "that one of these Rangers, when intoxicated, once told him that 'the sweetest steak he ever ate was the breast of a woman, which he cut off and broiled.'" It was these violent, savage men who gave the mass of the Upper Canadian population its true character.[38]

The execration of the British for their use of the Indians was coupled with the universal condemnation of the burning of Washington in 1814. The destruction of the capital had been preceded, during 1813, by a series of British amphibious operations along Chesapeake Bay, when Virginians and Marylanders were for the first time exposed to the war. These raids were condemned as piratical maraudings; they gave to the American public an anti-hero, Rear Admiral Sir George Cockburn, "a titled incendiary." Cockburn did appear to have engaged in this form of warfare with some enthusiasm, and was certainly prominent in the burning of Washington.

The capture of the city, by a small force of British soldiers and marines, was a national disgrace for which every history has a different explanation. That of Theodore Roosevelt was inimitable; he put it down "to the ludicrous and painful folly and stupidity of a Democratic administration," to the "Doctrinaire Democracy," and to the visionary and incapable Jefferson and Madison, who "thought the war could be fought by the nation in arms; the exponents of this particular idea, the militiamen, a partially armed mob, ran like sheep."[39]

Dolly Madison.

All united, however, in condemnation of the burning of the Capitol, the archives, the President's mansion, and every other public building except the post office. Headley depicts Cockburn as literally revelling amid destruction "To bring the day's work to a fitting close, Cockburn, while the heavens and surrounding country were still ruddy with the flames, entered a brothel and spent in lust and riot a night begun in incendiarism and pillage," a vile performance Headley contrasts with the behavior of steadfast Dolly Madison, who fled the capital bearing a full-length Gilbert Stuart portrait of Washington and "the precious parchment on which was written the Declaration of Independence." Napoleon, wrote Charles Ingersoll, had destroyed not a single European capital; this culminating British atrocity finally "alienated Americans from a nation with which they said we were more naturally connected by the ties of common origin ... than any other." Its effect "was gradually to disenchant this country of colonial reverence and party disaffection ... It required inhuman English misconduct to eradicate the deep seated feeling of national attachment which prevailed on the Atlantic seaboard to a mother country."[40]

IV

Canadians had much more difficulty than Americans in formulating the meaning of the war. There was, of course, the miracle of survival, but survival of what? From the beginning, there was a consciousness that they lived in a world where external threat was permanent, a world in which there was little room for optimism. William Coffin labored, somewhat clumsily perhaps, to express this timeless Canadian viewpoint:

> *1812 ... is a sign of solemn portent to the people of Canada. It carries with it the virtue of an incantation. ... These words ... quicken the pulse and vibrate through the frame, summoning from the pregnant past memories of suffering and endurance and honourable exertion. They are inscribed on the banner and stamped on the hearts of the Canadian people - a watchword, rather than a war cry. With these words on his lips, the loyal Canadian, as a vigilant sentinel, looks forth into the gloom, ready with his challenge, hopeful for a friendly response, but prepared for any other.*[41]

At the time Coffin wrote, the United States was locked in the bitter struggle of the Civil War; to Coffin, it was natural that Canadians should feel once more "within the edge of the fatal circle," and natural, too, for them to turn back to their experience in the War of 1812 "as an example and a warning."[42]

For Americans, the war was the completion of the work of the Revolution; for Canadians, from David Thompson onward, it was simply an extension of the Revolution itself. The United States was a revolutionary power, involved in a collusive relationship with the French despotism, and timing its resort to war to correspond with the point of greatest peril to Britain. Conversely, Britain was fighting a lonely struggle against a tyrant for the liberties of humanity and the independence of nations. The Americans, therefore, were essentially hypocritical in promising "liberation;" in fact, Napoleonic France and Republican America had both been spawned by revolution and, despite differences in governmental forms, were both actuated by the same secular imperialism.[43]

These ideas stemmed from the earliest period of the war in Upper Canada, and were first articulated by John Strachan. They were given most cogent expression, however, by his old rival Egerton Ryerson, writing in 1880. In his *The Loyalists of America and Their Times,* Ryerson delivered the following indictment:

> *At the darkest hour of that eventful contest, when the continent of Europe was drenched with the blood of nations, the Tyrant had his feet upon their neck, and England alone stood erect, taxing her resources to the utmost and shedding her best blood for human freedom, the Democratic party in the United States - the ever-anti- British party - the pro-slavery party - the party in the United States least subordinate to law and most inimical to liberty ... declared war against Britain and forthwith invaded Canada.*[44]

Canadians, therefore, were essentially victims, caught up by their colonial status in the titanic struggle being waged in Europe and by their proximity to a revolutionary state now waxing in power and rapaciousness.

How, then, did they manage to survive despite the odds against them? We have already seen the importance they attached to Brock, but the nineteenth century Canadian histories of the war also concluded that survival was won because of certain qualities possessed by the people, certain strengths attaching to their institutions, and to fundamental weaknesses in the American society and polity.

A theme common to all these historians was the utterly peaceful and unoffending character of the Canadians themselves. Far from harboring any designs upon their great neighbor, they were preoccupied with the hard labor of carving a living from the wilderness. War was forced upon them; it was none of their choosing. Out of this peaceful people came the militia, and most Canadian popular historians gave scant credit to the British Army in accounting for the successful defense of the province. The militia myth had its origins in 1812, in a November sermon preached at York by the Reverend John Strachan. Referring to the victories of Detroit and Queenston Heights, he said:

> *It will be told by the future Historian, that the Province of Upper Canada, without the assistance of men or arms, except a handful of regular troops, repelled its invaders, slew or took them all prisoners, and captured from its enemies the greater part of the arms by which it was defended ... And never, surely, was greater activity shewn in any country than our militia have exhibited, never greater valour, cooler resolution, and more approved conduct; they have emulated the choicest veterans, and they have twice saved the country.*[45]

Strachan's encomium was certainly a gross exaggeration of the part played by the militia, significant though it was in 1812, but he was right in suggesting

The charred shell of the United States Capitol following the British capture of Washington in 1814.

that future historians would seize upon its role. William Withrow, for example, asserted that "It was Canadian militia, with little help from British regulars, who won the brilliant victories ... and throughout the entire conflict ... were the principal defence of their country."[46]

The militia myth was propagated so assiduously that it was widely held to be true. Placing the militia in the forefront helped to make even more dramatic a contrast which all patriotic writers wished to make: the peaceful, orderly handful of Upper Canadians against a nation of eight millions. Ryerson wrote of "the Spartan bands of Canadian Loyalist volunteers, aided by a few hundred English soldiers ... repelled the Persian thousands of democratic American invaders, and maintained the virgin soil of Canada unpolluted by the foot of the plundering invader."[47] The ordered liberty of Upper Canada instilled a discipline in the militia that compensated for their lack of numbers; the Americans, on the other hand, were a democratic "rabble that called itself an army," as Hannay put it.[48] No one drew the contrast between the steady, disciplined Upper Canadians and the disorderly troops of frontier America more graphically than Richardson. He wrote of the Kentuckians captured at Frenchtown in 1813:

> *Their appearance ... was miserable to the last degree. They had the air of men to whom cleanliness was a virtue unknown, and their squalid bodies were covered by habilments that had evidently undergone every change of season. ... They were covered with slouched hats, worn bare by constant use, beneath which their long hair fell matted and uncombed over their cheeks, and these, together with the dirty blankets wrapped around their loins to protect them against the inclemency of the season, and fastened by broad leathern belts, into which were thrust axes and knives of an enormous length, gave them an air of wildness and savageness.*[49]

"This description," said Richardson, "may be considered as applicable to the various hordes of irregular troops sent forth throughout the war from the States of Ohio and Kentucky."

Just as American historians lavished detail upon atrocities committed by their enemies, so the Canadians, for their own purposes, related the looting and inhumanity of the Americans. Although the burning of the parliament building at York was a favorite topic, most condemnation was reserved for the burning of Newark (Niagara-on-the-Lake) in December 1813, when only one house of 150 in the village was left standing, and the inhabitants were left huddled in the snow. General George McClure, the American officer responsible, was Upper Canada's Admiral Cockburn. David Thompson set the tone when he wrote of him, "The historian laments that it is not in his power to record one magnanimous act of that recreant general, to rescue his name from that gulf of infamy to which his nefarious conduct has ever doomed it."[50]

Nor was there any Canadian sympathy for the burning of Washington. Even in 1905, by which time one might have expected a less vindictive outlook, Hannay could write:

> *The burning of the public buildings was a severe measure but a just one. It was but a proper return for the burning of the public buildings of York in the spring of 1813. It was in these halls of Congress that the Acts had been passed which led to the war. It was in these now ruined buildings that the invasion of Canada had been*

sanctioned and her fields, farmhouses and villages given up to destruction. It was there the proud boast had been made that Canada could be taken without soldiers; it was there that hypocritical prayers had been addressed to an all wise and all powerful God for His aid in the murder and enslavement of the people of Canada. And now the prayers had been answered to the confusion of those who made them.[51]

James Hannay was not an Ontarian but a New Brunswicker; he was also an ardent member of the Imperial Federation movement. As Carl Berger has shown in *The Sense of Power,* this movement coincided with the rise of Canadian nationalism, and also, as it happened, the efflorescence of books, poetry and other publications about the War of 1812, culminating in the centenary observations in 1912. Hannay sought to tap the Upper Canadian experience for the benefit of all Canadians.

The reason that the Ontario memory of the War of 1812 fitted in so well with the outlook of the Imperial Federationist was because of its emphasis upon the central value of loyalty. More than any other writer of the period, Egerton Ryerson gave voice to this interpretation of the war, and he seems to have spoken for a generation. For him, as for the American historians, the War of 1812 was nothing but the continuation of the American Revolution, but his reasons for believing so were very different. In his uncompromising opinion, the war had been precipitated by the American war party, consisting "largely of the mob or refuse of the nation;" the same party that had persecuted the Loyalists during the Revolution and driven them into the Canadian wilderness; "the same party that in subsequent years aided the rebel Mackenzie and the rabble Fenians to invade Canada."[52] Canadians posed loyalism against anarchic American democratic republicanism, and it was loyalism that brought victory:

... there is this essential difference between the two armies: the little Canadian army had homes, families and liberties to defend, connection with the mother country to maintain, and the consciousness of right; the great American army ... had the consciousness of long-continued and widespread wrong in depredations against their western Indian neighbours, bloated avarice for conquest, and inveterate hatred of Great Britain.[53]

What was at the heart of Upper Canadian survival, and what precisely had been preserved? In an extraordinary paean to loyalty and the values surrounding it, Ryerson defined the Ontario legacy from the war as "the sacred love of hearth and home, the patriotic love of liberty, and that hallowed principle of loyalty to truth, and law, and liberty combined, which have constituted the life and development and traditions and strength and unity and glory of British institutions and of the British nation from the resurrection morn of the Protestant Reformation to the present day."[54]

Such views were obviously not exportable to Quebec, which in any event had its own special view of the war, and would have been incomprehensible in the Maritimes where the war was remembered, on the whole, as a prosperous opportunity. Only in Upper Canada did the war generate such intensity of feeling. Ontario's expansionism, and the distinctive form of nationalism expressed by Ontarians, derived in significant part from the collective memory of the experience of the War of 1812.

By the time of the centenary of the war, there were some signs that the old fires were diminishing. The United States no longer seemed so menacing (even though the American embrace had once more been rejected in the federal election of 1911), and at the same time there was a good deal of recognition, especially along the Niagara frontier, that the two countries had shared interests as well as a history that divided them. Imperial Federationists like Sir George Parkin and Principal G.M. Grant, among others, pointed out that the Anglo-Saxon peoples, including the Americans, shared a common mission towards the lesser peoples of the world, and urged closer relations with the United States.[55] In his *Naval War of 1812,* published two years after his graduation from Harvard, Theodore Roosevelt asked his readers to keep in mind "that the Americans and the British are two substantially similar branches of the great English race, which before and after their separation have assimilated and made Englishmen of many other peoples."[56] The British failed to realize how misguided was war with the United States; had they won, it would have given "a new lease of life to the Indian nationalities, the hemming in, for a time, of the United States, and the stoppage, perhaps for many years, of the march of English civilization across the continent. The English of Britain were doing all they could to put off the day when their race would reach to a world-wide supremacy."[57] As for the Canadian militia of the War of 1812, they were virtually honorary Americans:

A New Englander and an Old Englander differed little enough, but they differed more than a frontiersman born north of the line did from one born south of it. ... The only un-English element in the contest was the presence among the Canadian English of some of the descendants of the Latin race from which they had conquered the country. Otherwise the men were equally matched.[58]

This message of Anglo-Saxondom, and others like it, found some response from speakers at the centenary of the Battle of Queenston Heights. Dr. James Hughes, chief inspector of Toronto schools, reflected the new spirit:

> *We have no wish to fill the hearts of the pupils in our schools with animosity towards the great nation whose fertile fields and happy homes we see beyond the great river that separates it from our own fair land. We wish to develop in our children a spirit that will lead them to say to the people across our borderland not "Hands off Canada," but "Hands together to achieve for God and for humanity the highest and broadest and truest ideals that have been revealed to the Anglo-Saxon race."*[59]

Despite many polite affirmations of amity, recognition of common interests and problems, and such doubtful compliments as one speaker's tribute to "our brave but defeated enemy," the old memories remained powerful. The address of Dr. Alexander Fraser, the Provincial Archivist, at the celebration of the anniversary of the Battle of Lundy's Lane, was characteristic of the content of the speeches of most speakers on these occasions. "Heaven," he said, "is not always on the side of the big battalions." The war was one of aggression by the United States against a weak and peaceful people, but "iron was in their blood:"

> *... we were strong in our faith, strong in our loyalty, and invincible in the defence of our home and country. ... That war gave Canada a saga of glowing tradition, an epic of patriotism, an historic pageant of men and women whose deeds will be our national inspiration and whose names will be our everlasting glory.*[60]

The Upper Canadian memory of the war, as transmitted through the popular historians, failed to become "our national inspiration." Why American popular historians were much more successful is a question that does not concern us here. As for the Upper Canadian epic, it was too narrowly and exclusively cast to be incorporated in the culture of either Quebec or the Maritimes, and in any event bore little relation to the wartime experience of those provinces. Though the resonance of the War of 1812 lingers still in Ontario, never again was its patriotic meaning to be proclaimed with the same vigor and conviction as it was during the centennial observances of 1912-14. The War of 1812 was shortly to be overshadowed by another and much greater conflict, and memories of that war (and others that followed) stand between us and the tradition the popular historians sought to transmit.

Notes

[1] By "popular history" I mean all historical writing addressed to the general public rather than to an audience primarily academic.

[2] Since this conference is concerned with the Niagara frontier, material for this paper has been drawn from American and Canadian sources dealing only with the Upper Canadian theater of operations or from histories which address events in the theater as part of the general context of the war.

[3] David Thompson was a former soldier in the Royal Scots who had turned to school teaching in Upper Canada. When he could not meet the costs of printing his book, he was imprisoned for debt.

[4] A further qualification is necessary at this point. As already mentioned, the Canadian material examined in this paper relates exclusively to Upper Canada. The Lower Canadian, New Brunswick and Nova Scotian experiences were all very different, and I intend to deal with them in another place.

[5] William Kingsford, *History of Canada* (10 vols.; Toronto, 1887-98), VIII, pp. 579-80.

[6] An examination of school textbooks held in the Glenbow Archives in Calgary reveals the degree to which the Upper Canadian version of the war entered into the schoolbooks of the Prairie West until at least the Second World War.

[7] Charles Jared Ingersoll, *Historical Sketch of the Second War Between the United States and Great Britain,* Vol. I (Philadelphia, 1845), p. 16.

[8] David Thompson, *History of the Late War Between Great Britain and the United States of America with a Retrospective View of the Causes from Whence it Originated* (Niagara, 1832), pp. v-vi.

[9] James Hannay, *History of the War of 1812* (Toronto, 1905), p. vii.

[10] William F. Coffin, *1812: The War and its Moral: A Canadian Chronicle* (Montreal, 1864), p. 19.

[11] George H. Calvert, *Oration on the Occasion of Celebrating the Fortieth Anniversary of the Battle of Lake Erie, 10 September, 1853,* 2nd edition (Providence, RI, 1854), p. 28.

[12] Benson J. Lossing, *The Pictorial Field Book of the War of 1812, or Illustrations by Pen and Pencil, of the History, Biography, Scenery, Relics, and Traditions of the last War for American Independence* (New York, 1868), p. 286.

[13] Josiah T. Headley, *The Second War with England* (2 vols.; New York, 1853), I, p. 286.

[14] Samuel White, *History of the American Troops During the Late War Under the Command of Colonels Fenton and Campbell* (Baltimore, 1830, reprinted Rochester, 1896), p. 70.

[15] Calvert, pp. 20-21.

[16] Ingersoll, I, pp. 179-80.

[17] *Ibid.,* I, p. 104.

[18] Richardson's poem, *Tecumseh, or the Warrior of the West,* was published in London in 1828. He returned to Tecumseh in several later publications.

[19] Coffin, p. 34.

[20] John Symons, *The Battle of Queenston Heights, Being a Narrative of the Opening of the War of 1812, with Notices of the Life of Major General Sir Isaac Brock, K.B. and Description of the Monument Erected to his Memory* (Toronto, 1859), p. 25.

[21] Cobourg *Star,* Aug. 5, 1840.

[22] Quoted in D.B. Read, *Life and Times of Major General Sir Isaac Brock, K.B.* (Toronto, 1894), p. 259.

[23] Hannay, p. 84.

[24] Symons, pp. 22-23.

[25] Read, p. 263.

[26] Kingsford, V, p. 234.

[27] *Ibid.,* pp. 237-38.

[28] Read, p. 263.

[29] Lossing, pp. 23-24.

[30] *Ibid.,* p. 19.

[31] Ingersoll, I, p. 389.

[32] Lossing, p. 35.

[33] Henry M. Brackenridge, *History of the Late War Between the United States and Great Britain, Containing a Minute Account of the Various Military and Naval Operations,* 5th edition (Philadelphia, 1844), p. 91.

[34] Ingersoll, I, p. 137. He reprinted, in its entirety, Benjamin Franklin's forged Inventory of Scalps purportedly delivered to General Frederick Haldimand by the faithful Seneca in 1782, *Ibid.,* pp. 276-78.

[35] Headley, I, pp. 185, 187.

[36] Lossing, p. 360n.

[37] Ingersoll, I, p. 273; Headley, I, p. 212; Lossing, p. 591. Lossing was quoting *Niles' Weekly Register.*

[38] Lossing, p. 532.

[39] Theodore Roosevelt, *The Naval War of 1812, or the History of the United States Navy During the Last War with Great Britain, to which is Appended an Account of the Battle of New Orleans,* 3rd edition (New York, 1883), pp. xxiii, 455, 456.

[40] Headley, II, p. 128; Ingersoll, I, p. 203.

[41] Coffin, p. 17.

[42] *Ibid.,* p. 18.

[43] David Thompson's history was the first Upper Canadian book to put this thesis, but it was an argument already familiar among provincial politicians and in the press. See Thompson, pp. 260-62.

[44] Egerton Ryerson, *The Loyalists of America and Their Times, from 1620 to 1816* (2 vols.; Toronto, 1880), II, p. 316. The degree to which this originally Tory perspective became a part of the political culture of Ontario is remarkable. As early as 1849, George Brown argued that the United States had demonstrated "the most selfish indifference to the freedom and independence of Europe" by going to war in 1812, *"because they have no love of liberty as a nation." Globe,* Dec. 6, 1849.

[45] Quoted in J.M. Hitsman, *The Incredible War of 1812: A Military History* (Toronto, 1965), p. 93.

[46] William A. Withrow, *A Popular History of the Dominion of Canada, from the Discovering of America to the Present Time* (Toronto, 1878), p. 340.

[47] Ryerson, p. 379. Egerton Ryerson was by no means the first to use such imagery. Upper Canadians habitually put themselves in the situation of the Spartans at Thermopylae, or referred to the "Persian hordes" of Americans. This historical frame of reference, a commonplace in the society, appears to have strongly influenced the iconography of the second Brock monument, which is classical Greek in character.

[48] Hannay, p. 55.

[49] John Richardson, *The War of 1812 ... Containing a Full and Detailed Narrative of the Operations of the Right Division of the Canadian Army* (originally published in 1842; A.C. Casselman, ed., Toronto, 1902), p. 140.

[50] Thompson, p. 216.

[51] Hannay, p. 351.

[52] Ryerson, II, pp. 318, 333.

[53] *Ibid.,* p. 353.

[54] *Ibid.,* p. 457.

[55] See Carl Berger, *The Sense of Power: Studies in the Ideas of Canadian Imperialism* (Toronto, 1970), pp. 228-30.

[56] Roosevelt, pp. 26-27. Roosevelt compares British and American seamen, whom he found to be "bold and hardy, cool and intelligent, quick with their hands and showing at their best in an emergency," with Portuguese and Italian sailors, often good seamen, but "treacherous, fond of the knife, less ready with their hands, and likely to lose either their wits or their courage when in a tight place." *Ibid.,* p. 35.

[57] *Ibid.,* p. 457.

[58] *Ibid.,* pp. 278-80.

[59] Alexander Fraser (ed.), *Brock Centenary, 1812-1912: Account of the Celebrations at Queenston Heights, Ontario, on the 12th of October 1912* (Toronto, 1913), p. 68.

[60] Lundy's Lane Historical Society, *The Centenary Celebration of the Battle of Lundy's Lane, July the Twenty-fifth, Nineteen Hundred and Fourteen* (Niagara Falls, Ont., 1919), p. 40.